THE SIGNET ENCYCLOPEDIA OF WHISKEY, BRANDY, AND ALL OTHER SPIRITS

by

E. Frank Henriques

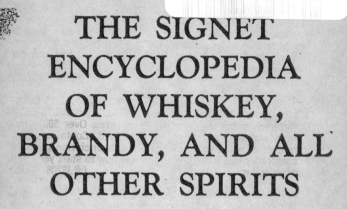

Ⓞ

A SIGNET BOOK

NEW AMERICAN LIBRARY

TIMES MIRROR

Ⓢ   SIGNET TRADEMARK REG. U.S. PAT. OFF. AND FOREIGN COUNTRIES
     REGISTERED TRADEMARK—MARCA REGISTRADA
     HECHO EN CHICAGO, U.S.A.

SIGNET, SIGNET CLASSICS, MENTOR, PLUME AND MERIDIAN BOOKS
are published by The New American Library, Inc.,
1301 Avenue of the Americas, New York, New York 10019.

First Signet Printing, April, 1979

1 2 3 4 5 6 7 8 9

PRINTED IN THE UNITED STATES OF AMERICA

QUESTIONS YOU NOW CAN ANSWER BEFORE YOU OPEN A BOTTLE

What are the distinctive qualities of Tennessee bourbon—and how far is Jack Daniels really ahead of its neighbors?

What is America's most popular expensive English gin—and can you really taste the difference?

What is your best value in a moderately priced French cognac? And what would be your best choice if you want to spend a bundle?

How do you drink tequila the way the Mexicans do?

What is the difference between Russian vodka and American?

How can you enjoy the after-dinner pleasure of *B&B* while saving dollars a bottle?

What is the best California brandy now available?

This is just a tiny sampling of the hundreds upon hundreds of common and uncommon questions answered with substance and style in the book that can justly call itself the thinking man's (and of course, woman's) guide to one of nature's most glowing gifts.

THE SIGNET ENCYCLOPEDIA OF WHISKEY, BRANDY, AND ALL OTHER SPIRITS

Prices quoted in this book were applicable at the time of printing but may be subject to change.

SIGNET Books of Special Interest

Introduction

I am a priest—of the Episcopal Church, as it so happens—and I have a confession to make. I once wrote, in a previous book, *The Signet Encyclopedia of Wine*, that spirits are often of the devil. Now it is not for that statement that I am apologizing, for it's true. But I implied that only distilled spirits could be instruments of Satan, not wine. That is patently absurd. The simple truth is that any alcoholic beverage—wine, spirits, beer, Hadacol (of notorious memory), *Zwetschgengeist* (German plum brandy) —can be abused. What I should have said is that distilled spirits, because of their potency, are more readily abused than other types of alcoholic drink. That is as true as rain and God.

This book is an attempt—perhaps minor, but certainly fervent—to steer a sober and frugal course through the kaleidoscopic and bewildering maze of spirits and liqueurs: to measure quality, to state values, to name names, and to brand brands, and, most important of all, to inculcate a sane, godly, and sober use of spirituous drink.

God in His bounty gives mankind alcohol. For relaxation, joyousness, conviviality, gaiety, hilarity, silliness, and buffoonery— but not for intoxication and unrealistic escape.

Properly used, alcohol can work beneficent magic. It can give courage to the timid, buoyancy to the depressed. It can render the mute eloquent, can bestow a sense of humor upon the humorless. It can transform an awkward, self-conscious group of strangers into a happy, loving family. It can make a happy occasion a glorious and unforgettable one. But always with one huge proviso: *cautiously ingested!*

This is a big, brave book—I say it with all modesty. A big book: It encompasses all the great spirits and liqueurs of the world. A brave book: It treads a most dangerous terrain, the evaluation of alcoholic beverages. There is surely no cranny of this universe more fraught with danger than this. Here everybody is an expert. There are no nonprofessionals here, for everybody knows what *he* likes. And what *he* likes is best—else *he* wouldn't like it, would he? The Romans said it all: There is no arguing about tastes.

Finally, this book is not simply one man's lofty opinions—or prejudices, as you will. This book represents the consensus of expert opinion regarding spirituous beverages.

—E. Frank Henriques

Sutter Creek California

A note to the reader

Prices listed in this book are, of necessity, approximate. They are usually an average between prevailing prices on the U.S. East Coast and West Coast. Likewise, prices will often vary locally, depending on local taxes, your source of supply, special sales, and even the season of the year.

A

ABISANTE The name looks something like "absinthe," and this modern American liqueur even tastes like old-time banished absinthe. Of course it's not a stupefying 153° like its late-19th-century forebear, but it has the same color (pale green), it has the same anise flavoring, it smells the same, and it even turns milky when mixed with water, just as the original stuff did.

Some American firms make several anise-flavored drinks. When they do so, the anisette will always be the sweetest and lowest in proof (around 60°). The anesone will be drier and higher-proof (80° or 90°). The abisante will be the highest proof (often 100°).

Leroux makes a fine abisante, a stout 100°, at around $7. There is also a walloping, rollicking 120° version at about $1 more, which probably makes it the highest-proof liqueur in the U.S. It is the better buy of the two versions: 51¢ per ounce of alcohol, vs. 54¢ for the 100°.

Most abisante sells for around $7. It's appreciated when taken straight—and carefully.

ABSINTHE Technically it's akin to gin—essentially, unsweetened neutral spirits—but on a popular level, it's that mysterious, powerful, outlawed potion connoting bohemian Paris at the turn of the century. Today absinthe is illegal in most of Europe and the U.S. It is the wormwood, said to be harmful and to drive men mad, contained in the absinthe that brought about its proscription.

Clandestine absinthe can still be found on this earth, but why bother? Today there are legal versions of absinthe available, minus the wormwood, under such names as **Pernod, Ricard, herbsaint, pastis,** and **abisante,** not to mention a vast array of simple anise-flavored liqueurs made around the world. (For a complete listing, see **anis(e) and anisette liqueurs.**)

Until a few decades ago, the real thing, classic absinthe, wormwood and all, could still be lawfully obtained in at least one place, Spain. It was made by the French firm of Pernod in Tarragona, Spain, and was called Liqueur Veritas—"Truth Liqueur." But in 1937 it too was outlawed.

But if you're really absinthe-minded, you can simply make your own with real wormwood —it's available in any health-food store. There is nothing whatever illegal about it—and that fact, that it is *not* illegal, will drastically reduce the number of homemade absinthe enthusiasts.

One book—*Making Cordials and Liqueurs at Home,* by John

1

P. Farrell (New York: Barnes & Noble, 1974), pp. 65–69—lists three different absinthe recipes: one anise-flavored, one peppermint-flavored, and the third simply wormwood-flavored. The last formula requires only three ingredients: brandy, honey, and wormwood.

Old-time absinthe (and today's bootleg variety) was flavored mainly with wormwood and aniseed, plus a number of other flavorings such as cinnamon, lemon, and cloves. It is the anise flavor that predominates, however, in both the legal and illegal versions, giving it a distinctly licorice flavor, quite similar to that of the Greek liqueur **ouzo.** Absinthe turns milky when mixed with water.

Turn-of-the-century absinthe was fiercely potent stuff, around 150°. Today's versions are much more civilized, usually 90°.

The classic method to drink absinthe or any of its legal or illegal descendants is by the "absinthe drip" method: Pour icewater slowly over a sugar cube held in a slotted spoon into a cocktail glass containing a jigger or two of absinthe or absinthe substitute. That was the "in" ritual of the flapping '20s.

ADVOCAAT (ADVOKAAT)

It's almost as much a food as it is an alcoholic beverage, for advocaat is a very rich, very sweet Dutch-invented eggnog of low alcoholic content (usually around 30°), more egg than nog. It's made from egg yolks flavored with coffee and various spices, including vanilla and fennel, and "baptized" with sweetened brandy (usually).

The Dutch recommend advocaat as a tonic, and it is obviously very nutritious—and fattening.

Advocaat is Dutch for "attorney," and the derivation seems to be that the old-fashioned home-brewed variety was rarely the innocent, innocuous kind of advocaat commercially available today. It was so liberally laced with brandy that the tongues of ardent consumers were thoroughly loosened, and they talked as well—or at least as much—as lawyers.

Bols Advocaat (30°) is well known and sells for around $4.50 (24 oz.). **Old Mr. Boston** calls its advocaat "Egg Nog Liqueur" (30°), and it costs about the same. And is about as good—or bad, depending on your point of view.

The Mexican people also cherish their bottled eggnog. They call theirs Rompope—no reference whatever to the Pope of Rome; it's three syllables, *rohm-PAW-pay*. It's available only south of the border—perhaps mercifully so.

ALMADÉN CENTENNIAL BRANDY

Almadén has been in the wine business for more than a century (since 1852) but has been making brandy only since 1952. The winery boasts that its brandy is aged in small oak barrels, more than 30,000 of them. This is laudable, as small cooperage makes for better aging of alcoholic beverages, whether brandy or wine, since the liquid has more "breathing" area. Almadén's Centennial Brandy is wholly satisfactory, pleasant, smooth, with slight sweetness. A solid and upstanding California brandy, neither better nor worse than its similarly priced competitors. For a listing of California's best brandies, see under **United States—brandy.**

AMARETTO This is probably today's most "in" liqueur, though the name meant absolutely nothing in the U.S. a scant ten years ago. Today you're a rube, some say, if amaretto does not grace your bar.

Few Americans realize that amaretto is actually a very old liqueur—perhaps dating back to the 16th century. It clearly goes back at least to 1807.

Amaretto is an almond-flavored liqueur, originally from the town of Saronno, near Milan, Italy. The original, now made in a modern plant near Lake Como, is still called "Amaretto di Saronno," and the simple name "amaretto" has now become a generic term meaning any kind of almond-flavored liqueur. So today you have Amaretto di Torino (from Turin, or Torino, Italy, under the **Leroux** label), Amaretto di Galliano (made by the same people who bring you **Galliano**—Vaccari—but not recommended because of too many off flavors; Vaccari had best stick to its Galliano, and even Amaretto di Cupera (by **DeKuyper,** the name being the Italianization of the Dutch name).

The delightful almond flavor of amaretto (di Wherever or Whomever) is due, ironically, not to almonds at all, but to crushed apricot pits. (Laetrile, that highly controversial cancer "cure," is also made from apricot pits. Folks may argue endlessly about the efficacy of Laetrile, but nobody who's ever tasted amaretto is ever going to argue about its efficacy—for whatever ails you, cancer included.) Other herbs and fruits are also used, including apricots, and even perhaps some real almonds—on occasion!

The only things that multiply faster these days than new liqueurs are new cocktails from new liqueurs. The principal source of these recipes, of course, is the people who produce the liqueurs; their copywriters stay up nights inventing new drinks with new names. Here are a few brand-new ones employing amaretto: French Connection (brandy and amaretto, 2:1), Boccie Ball (amaretto and orange juice), Godfather (Scotch or bourbon with amaretto, 3:1), Saronno (brandy and amaretto, 1:1), Godmother (vodka and amaretto, 1:1), Zorba (Metaxa and amaretto, 2:1).

Besides the original Amaretto di Saronno, a passel of imitation amarettos (if the Americanized plural offends your ear, try *amaretti*) from Italy are being imported to the U.S. these days. Besides those mentioned above we have Amaretto Porto Fino (23 oz.), Amaretto Landy Frères (who also have a Landy Amaretto with Orange) (fifth), Amaretto di Capri (fifth), Amaretto del Vesuvio (fifth), Amaretto di Loreto (fifth). They're priced between $10 and $12.

American amarettos also abound. They're clearly not the quality of the imports, but neither are they $12 for 23 oz. In fact, they average out to less than half the price of the Italian versions. Here are some of the more widely distributed brands:

Amaretto Crema Liquore (Hiram Walker), 50°	$7 (24 oz.)
Amaretto di Amore (Fleischmann), 56°	7 (fifth)
Amaretto di Angelo, 56°	5 (fifth)
Amaretto di Cupera (DeKuyper), 56°	7 (24 oz.)
Amaretto di Gaetano, 56°	5.50 (fifth)
Amaretto Lolita, 53°	6.50 (750ml)
Amorita Amaretto, 56°	7 (fifth)
Arrow Amaretto, 56°	6 (24 oz.)
Dubouchette Amaretto, 56°	5.50 (28 oz.)
Garnier Amaretto di Amore, 56°	5.50 (fifth)
Mohawk Liquore Amaretto, 48°	6 (quart)
Regnier Amaretto, 54°	7 (24 oz.)
And variations:	
Amaretto and Brandy di Amore, 65°	$8 (fifth)
Amaretto and Brandy di Gaetano, 65°	6 (24 oz.)
Gaetano Chocolate Amaretto, 52°	5.50 (24 oz.)
Leroux Chocolate Amaretto, 54°	6 (24 oz.)
Regnier Chocolate Amaretto, 54°	7 (24 oz.)

AMBASSADOR SCOTCH WHISKY Ambassador Scotch Whisky is made by Taylor & Ferguson Ltd., of Dumbarton, Scotland, which is part of Hiram Walker & Sons, Ltd., which in turn is part of **Hiram Walker–Gooderham & Worts Ltd.** of Canada. Nothing is simple anymore. Other Scotch whiskies produced by Hiram Walker at Dumbarton and roundabout include **Lauder's** and **Ballantine's.**

Ambassador Scotch comes to the U.S. in three "flavors," all of premium quality: De Luxe, 8-year-old, 86°, around $8.50 (25.4 oz.); Royal, 12-year-old, 86.8°, around $11.50 (fifth); and 25-year-old, 86°, around $40 (fifth). All are excellent whiskies, though not necessarily worth the price. Ambassador Scotches are medium-bodied, with distinct "peatiness." The most highly acclaimed—and the tribute is quite universal—is the 12-year-old Royal. Some Scotch snobs who do not deign to drink any Scotch less than 20 years old are quite impressed with Ambassador 25-year-old. Indeed, at $40 per fifth, it impresses mightily.

The company prides itself on the lightness of its Ambassador Scotches. They are made, says the firm, by blending forty-five of the lightest and smoothest Scotches to be found.

AMERICAN DISTILLING COMPANY This is a very large spirits-and-wine firm, dating back to 1892, founded and still headquartered in Pekin, Ill. (The principal distillery is in Pekin; executive offices are in New York City.) Total sales in 1977 were over $100 million. American started out by distilling whiskey, but today the firm produces and distributes not only whiskeys, but gins, vodkas, rums, and other spirits, including liqueurs, as well as wines. The import arm of the company is L'Aiglon Wine & Spirits Import Company.

Here are American's most important whiskeys: **Bourbon Supreme Rare Straight Bourbon,** Canadian Host (Canadian), Canadian Supreme (Canadian), Dunphy's (Irish), Guck-enheimer (blend), **King James Scotch**, Meadwood (bourbon, and blend), and Town Club (blend).

In other spirits, American dispenses: American Five Star Brandy, Burton's Gin, **El Toro Tequila**, Mi Amigo Tequila, Ron Querida Rum, Semkov Vodka, and **Tvarscki Vodka.**

American also has Piping Rock liqueurs, Bisquit cognacs, and a sprinkling of import-ed wines and liqueurs, includ-ing Gonzalez Byass Sherry (re-cently acquired), Graham ports, Ricard Pastis, and Charles Heidsieck Champagne.

As odd as it may sound, American sells a huge amount of bourbon whiskey in West Germany. Incredibly, West Germany is the second-largest bourbon market in the world. (The U.S., of course, is number one.) American produces a special bourbon for German export: Pennypacker Bourbon, 86.8°, selling for about 14.50 DM per 70 centiliters, which translates to somewhat less than $7 for 23.7 oz., about 2 oz. less than a standard fifth. In 1977 the West Germans drank more than 2 million bottles of Pennypacker Bour-bon. Gesundheit! Pennypacker is not available in the U.S.

AMER PICON With that name, it ought to be from America, but it's as French as Brigitte Bardot. And it's not pronounced the way it looks either — say *ah-mir pea-coh*. *Amer* means "bitter" in French.

Amer Picon is a **bitters,** in-vented in Algeria by a French distiller in 1835. It is said that the French Foreign Legion marched on Amer—they "im-pregnated" their canteen water with it.

Amer—if we may call it familiarly by its first name—is made with a base of wine and brandy and is liberally laced with quinine and a multitude of herbs, spices, and peelings. It's strictly an apéritif, but not to be taken straight—not unless you want your hair to turn greenish purple. Dilute your Amer Picon with water and ice, and you may sweeten it with **grenadine** or **cassis,** but it's really more authentic with-out the sweetener. It's 78° and sells for around $9 (fifth).

AMORITA AMARETTO This is an American-made **amaretto** and an excellent one. It does not have the depth and full-ness of the original Amaret-to di Saronno, but it's a pretty good replica, at about half the price. It is better than many Italian amarettos. It has just a whisper of chocolate in it, and this is well balanced with good almond flavor. Amorita Am-aretto sells for around $7 per fifth, an excellent value.

ANCESTOR, DEWAR'S SCOTCH WHISKY This fine Scotch whisky, a full 12 years old, is made by John Dewar & Sons Ltd., of Perth, Scotland, the same folks who make "White Label." This is their "top of the line." Dewar's orig-inally made two deluxe Scotches, Ne Plus Ultra, and Victoria Vat. The Ne Plus Ul-tra is still marketed in a few countries, but Victoria Vat was dropped just before World War II, because of confusion with **Vat 69 Scotch.** It became An-cestor. The name derived from a picture which hangs in Dewar House, Perth, entitled "The Whisky of His Forefathers"; it depicts the laird having a dram of Dewar's Whisky, and his ancestors, recognizing what he is drinking, stepping out of their portraits to join in. The painting dates from the 1890s. Ancestor is 86.8° and sells for about $12 (fifth).

ANCIENT AGE KENTUCKY STRAIGHT BOURBON WHISKEY

It's popular and it's good. Ancient Age is a **Schenley** product, and it comes in both a 5-year-old version and a 10-year-old, the latter selling for only about 50c more per fifth, making it the better buy of the two.

Ancient Age is comparatively light-bodied for a straight. Schenley points with pride to the Kentucy limestone water in its lineage. (Fifty other Kentucky bourbon producers do the same.) Ancient Age, or AA, as the label touts it, is medium-priced for an 86° straight—no great bargain, but no rip-off either. (For a listing of comparative prices of straight bourbons, see under **bourbon**.)

ANGOSTURA BITTERS

This is one of the most famous **bitters** in the world, and it has a long history. It was first made by a German-born medical doctor, Johann Gotlieb Benjamin Siegert, in the city of Angostura, Venezuela, in 1830—his signature is still on the bottle. The good doctor concocted Angostura while searching for a cure for equatorial diseases.

The Angostura people take pains to point out that their bitters is not named after Angostura bark—and, in fact, contains none—but from the city of Angostura, now Ciudad Bolívar. The bark, in fact, was named after the city. Angostura is still produced today by the Siegert family, but in Trinidad (West Indies) not Venezuela.

The Siegert firm still recommends Angostura as a "stomachic" and stimulant to appetite: "1 to 4 teaspoonfuls before meals." They also recommend it for flatulence, taken in the same quantity, only after one's meal, not before. But the cure may be worse than the disease, for all bitters are absolutely vile when taken straight. They have a marvelous inviting aroma, but they're guaranteed to part your hair, singe your eyebrows, and curl your toenails when consumed straight!

In fact, Angostura is used today almost wholly as a flavoring ingredient—not only in alcoholic beverages (where it is absolutely essential in some mixed drinks, most notably the **Old Fashioned** and **Manhattan)** but also in cooking, especially in soups, salads, gravies, and stews. (The label lists a dozen other flavoring uses, including fish, grapefruit, and ice cream.)

Angostura Bitters is 45° by volume and sells for about $2.50 for 8 oz., which would make it about $10 per quart. It's a good thing that a little goes a long way.

ANIS(E) AND ANISETTE LIQUEURS

Americans find it hard to believe, but anise-flavored liqueurs are probably the world's most popular cordials. They're made in virtually every major country of the world, and are especially appreciated around the Mediterranean. They come in a variety of proofs, from 50° to 100° mainly, and even in various colors, although most are clear white, and under a myriad of names, labels, and brands.

Anise-flavored beverages are the natural descendants of that shadowy, bohemian drink of Paris and London around the turn of the century, absinthe. Absinthe was later outlawed in the U.S. and through most of Europe, because of its wormwood content. The wormwood was dropped, the aniseed content increased, and behold, you have anise liqueurs.

The herb anise (pronounced *ah-nees*) has a distinctly licorice flavor; it is the seed of the plant that is used in these liqueurs.

Strictly speaking, not all anise-flavored beverages are liqueurs, although they're often referred to as such. Some of them are actually anise-flavored brandies, for their base is not a neutral spirit, but a true brandy, distilled spirit made from wine.

The terms "anise" (or "anis") and "anisette" are used rather interchangeably on labels, but only "anisette" is found on U.S. labels.

Here are the world's principal anise-flavored drinks according to their country of origin:

U.S.: Almost every major American maker of liqueurs makes an anise liqueur, always labeled "anisette." These are simply sweetened aniseed over a base of neutral spirits. For this reason—simplicity of manufacture, as well as low proof—they are not expensive. They range mostly from 40° to 60°, the lower-proof ones

(J.W. Dant, Du Conte, Mohawk, all 40° or 42°) being the least expensive, less than $4 per fifth. The 60° varieties—Dubochett (¾ quart) and Leroux (24 oz.)—are around $5.50. At least one American anisette turns cloudy when mixed with water: Arrow, 60°, around $5.

France: Produces the finest and the most popular of the world's anise-flavored liqueurs, including **Ricard, Pastis, Pernod,** and **Marie Brizard** Anisette. The last is undoubtedly one of the best-known of all the world's anise-flavored drinks. In fact, it is the *grandmère* of all anise drinks, having been first produced by Madame Brizard in the 18th century, from a secret formula which she inherited. It is still one of the finest anise beverages made. It sells in the U.S. for around $9.50 (23.6 oz).

Another French anisette is La Tintaine. It comes with a stick of fennel in the bottle; it's not commonly available in the U.S. Both Cusenier and Garnier, French producers, make fine anisette, 50° and 54° respectively, about $6.50 (both 24 oz.).

Spain: Makes **ojen** and Anis del Mono. The former's not generally available in the U.S.; the latter is made in Barcelona, comes in both sweet and dry versions, is higher proof than most "aniseed" drinks (78°), and sells in the U.S. for around $8 (23.7 oz.).

Italy: Anisetta Stellata, made in Pescara, is not commonly seen in the U.S. Anesone is less sweet than most anise drinks. Italians like to take their anesone straight or in their coffee. Stock makes a fine one, 90°, available in the U.S. at around

$8.50. Elixir de China is quite sweet, a luscious after-dinner drink, but unfortunately is not commonly found in the U.S. Sambuca is an Italian licorice-flavored liqueur, but its flavor does not come from aniseed.

Portugal: Escarchado contains sugar crystals. Look for it in Portugal, as it is not imported to the U.S.

Greece: Mastika and ouzo are technically brandies.

Turkey and Middle East: Raki is aniseed-flavored: it can be made from various bases.

ANTIQUE KENTUCKY STRAIGHT BOURBON WHISKEY Along with about fifty other whiskeys, Antique is the property of that mammoth of the spirits industry, Seagram. It's good whiskey, at a good price. It even seems to have improved slightly in recent years. In comparison with other straight bourbons, Antique is light in flavor. It is 80° and sells for around $5 (25.4 oz.).

APPLEJACK This is a true fruit brandy, not simply a fruit-flavored brandy, and an American-made one at that. And a good one besides. Applejack may still suggest secret mountain stills and high-explosive potency, but in these latter times it has become a wholly respectable, totally delectable potion. It's the American equivalent of the French Calvados. Perhaps applejack doesn't quite reach the spirituous heights that Calvados so frequently attains, but it is a wholesome, healthful, tasteful beverage, and indubitably America's finest fruit brandy—especially since it is her only one!

Unlike Calvados, American applejack often contains some neutral grain spirits, at times up to 65%. This accounts for applejack's lightness when compared with Calvados.

Half of the fun of drinking fruit brandies is in not drinking them—that is to say, in sniffing them, enjoying and celebrating their bouquet. Use a medium-size balloon-shaped glass, and swirl and sniff and inhale.

The principal brands of American applejack are Laird's (a dependable name—comes in both a blend, with neutral grain spirits, 80°, and a straight, 100°), Hildick (80°—blended only), and Spea's (comes in an 80° and a 6-year-old 86.5°).

APPLETON RUM Appleton Rum is made by a firm with the wonderful name of the House of J. Wray and Nephew Limited. The company was established in 1825 in Kingston, Jamaica, making it (as far as is known) the oldest extant rum company in the world. It was founded by John Wray, who later took his nephew, Col. Charles J. Ward, into the business. Through 150 years the company has changed hands several times, but has always remained in the hands of local people.

The name "Appleton" comes from the lush and beautiful Appleton Valley on the island, where the firm has its principal distillery.

Appleton Rum commonly comes to the U.S. in four versions: Appleton White, Appleton Special (Gold), and Appleton Punch (Dark), all 80° and about $6.75 (fifth); and Appleton Punch (Dark), 97° and about $7.50 (fifth). Appleton rums are universally accepted as fine, tasty, consistent Jamaican rums. Probably only a true connoisseur would be able to distinguish them from other similarly priced Jamaican rums—and, in fact, they are a mite cheaper than most—but this does not make them less good, only equally good.

APRICOT LIQUEURS AND BRANDIES
Apricots are good eating and equally good drinking. Apricot liqueurs and brandies are among the most popular of all liqueurs. Apricot liqueur is sweeter and of a lower proof than apricot brandy, and also cheaper. The brandy is nevertheless by far the more popular.

Most American liqueur firms make both an apricot liqueur and an apricot brandy, and these are wholly adequate, full-flavored beverages, totally satisfactory for virtually every purpose—cooking, mixing in cocktails, flaming—except perhaps for discriminating sipping. For this latter noble and leisurely purpose one would suggest ascending to one of the more elegant and distinguished—and more expensive—apricot liqueurs from Europe.

The most famous and probably still the best is **MARIE BRIZARD** Apry, 50°, around $10 (23.6 oz.). Like all truly fine liqueurs, Apry (pronounced *ah-pree*) is not made from a single fruit—apricots—but is a judicious and happy blend of many subsidiary flavoring agents. Apry even includes some Cognac in its base.

Another well-known and well-loved apricot liqueur is Garnier's Abricotine—*abricot* means "apricot" in French.

Garnier now makes its liqueurs in the U.S. as well as in France, from French-made essences. Abricotine is an elegant, deliciously complex beverage, with almond undertones—the hint of almond comes from the apricot pits. It is 60° and sells for $9.25 (24 oz.).

None of these apricot beverages is a true apricot brandy, however—by definition and law such a beverage must be made wholly from fermented apricots, and would be colorless. One such is made: Barak Palinka, from Hungary, where it is acclaimed as the national liqueur.

All else failing, you can always make your own apricot liqueur from either fresh or dried apricots. You simply macerate the fruit, along with some crushed almonds and a piece of cinnamon stick, in some neutral spirit (vodka will do) for a few weeks. For details and precise quantities, see Emilio Cocconi, *Liqueurs for All Seasons* (Wilton, Conn.: Lyceum Books, 1975), page 21.

AQUAVIT Akuavit, akavitt, aqua vitae, akvavit, akavit, aquavita, or any reasonable approximation to any of the above—spell it almost any way you want to, but see that you pronounce it *AHK-vah-veet*. It means "water of life," which is exactly the same name given to a number of other spirits, notably brandy and whiskey.

Aquavit is a potent, colorless—in pigmentation only, not in character—spirit beloved by Scandinavians. It's made from potatoes, mostly, but also grain, and it's usually flavored with caraway. You can even make your own aquavit (or a reasonable facsimile) by simply adding 2 oz. of caraway seed to a fifth of vodka, and sticking it in the freezer for a couple of days. Even Swedes swear it's the real thing!

The best-known and best aquavit comes from Denmark. The original is made in Aalborg, Denmark, from whole potatoes and crushed malt (made from grain mash). Aalborg Akvavit comes to the U.S. in two styles: the clear Aalborg Taffel Akvavit, 86°, with a predominantly caraway flavor; and the golden Aalborg Jubilaeums, 90°, with a predominantly dill flavor. They sell for around $8 (750 ml.) and $9 (fifth), respectively (western U.S.).

Aquavit is not ordinarily aged, but when it is, it improves. If the aging is done in oak casks, the spirit takes on a touch of brownish coloring and even acquires a slightly "bourbonish" flavor.

"Linie Aquavit" means "Equator Aquavit." It comes from Norway and it's just about the only spirit left in the world today that still enjoys travel—Madeira wine, for one, used to be, but no longer. Linie Aquavit is put aboard ship in casks in Norway, crosses the Equator at least twice (to and from Australia, usually), and then returns to Norway for bottling. All the data on its peregrinations are proudly displayed on the label. Linie Aquavit is a wonderful, smooth beverage, sometimes available in the U.S., and well worth looking for.

There's a ritual for drinking aquavit. You don't just belt it down, slob-fashion. You salute your neighbor—and then belt it down! It's the ceremony of *Skoal:* Raise your glass, look your neighbor in the eye, say *Skoal* loud and clear, and down the hatch. The ritual may be repeated a second time, perhaps a third, bearing in mind that this is a 90° beverage.

Aquavit is always served icy-cold, often with a beer chaser. In Scandinavia it usually accompanies food, especially spicy and salty foods such as herring, anchovies, and kippers. It may even be served throughout the meal, though beer would seem a more civilized way of proceeding. Aquavit always accompanies the cheese course.

A kindred spirit is kümmel, which is sometimes described, with a good deal of accuracy, as aquavit with sweetening.

ARAK (ARRACK) The Arabic word *arak* originally referred to the fermented juice of the date—it means simply "juice" —but today it means any kind of native spirit, usually a rough and fiery one. The best-known is Batavia arak, a rum from Indonesia. A variation of the name is raki. There is even a made-in-America arak, Yousef; it's a 90° arak made in California.

The Bedouin's Revenge is a simple, tasty drink made with arak. Pour a jigger of arak over the rocks, add a few dashes of bitters, fill the glass with tonic water. Stir, garnish with slice of lime, and you're already revenged!

ARANDAS TEQUILA If you're a true tequila aficionado and want some fine sippin' tequila, at a good price, look for Arandas. It comes in the two standard versions, White and Gold ("Oro" on the label), both 80°. The Gold fetches about $5.75 and the White, about $5.50 (fifth).

ARISTOCRAT BRANDY This California brandy and A.R. **Morrow Brandy** are sister brandies—if that's sexist, make them brother brandies, or somewhere in between. At all events they're made by a giant cooperative, the California Wine Association. They are good examples of California brandy: light, clean, slightly sweet, fruity. Aristocrat is somewhat older than the A.R. Morrow, and sells for a little more: about $5.50 (fifth) vs. $4.75. Standard brandy, standard price.

ARMAGNAC By general consensus this is the second-best brandy in the world—the first being Cognac—and there are even brandy fanciers who say Armagnac is the world's finest, bar none. Like Cognac, it's a French brandy, made in the southwest corner of France, at the foot of the Pyrenees. Unlike Cognac, it's not widely known or appreciated. For that reason it's often a better buy than Cognac.

Armagnac is made rather differently from Cognac, though from virtually the same grapes, and it is aged differently. It is indeed a very different spirit: drier than Cognac, bigger-bodied, heavier, more pungent. If Cognac is the drink of heroes —witness Napoleon and Churchill, both Cognac lovers —Armagnac is for super-heroes.

Armagnac is encrusted with the same abracadabra of stars, initials, and Napoleonic verbiage on its labels as Cognac. All of these markings and symbols mean just as much—or rather, just as little—as they do with Cognac. For details, see under **Cognac.**

There are no big famous names in Armagnac (as there are in Cognac), so one has no alternative but to test by tasting. Know that in the past there have been some poor Armagnacs shipped to the U.S., even some fraudulent ones claiming to be 99 years old.

Here are some reliable Armagnacs to launch your research:

Samalens: Made by the House of Samalens which was founded in 1882 and has never produced anything but Bas Armagnac, the highest type. (*Bas* means "lower," but it refers to geography, not quality.)

Clé des Ducs: Made by the House of Izarra, it is the best-selling brand of Armagnac both in France and in the world.

Marquis de Montesquieu: Not just a brand name, but a real person, the Duc de Fezenac, a French parliamentary deputy. He's wholly authentic and so is his brandy, for he is a descendant of the famous French hero d'Artagnan, of *Three Musketeers* fame, who came from this area.

Marquis de Caussade: Produces a fine 10-year-old Armagnac, highly recommended.

Bellows Bas Armagnac: This is 10 years old.

Prime de Chabot: Has a Blason d'Or (3-Star) version that is smooth and good.

ASBACH URALT Asbach is the name of the company that makes it, and *uralt* simply means "old." It's Germany's best-known, and best, brandy. It is also the only German brandy commonly available in the U.S.

Asbach & Company does all the right things to produce a good brandy: starts with good grapes (almost wholly from France's great brandy regions), distills the brandy twice in pot stills, and ages it in Limousin oak. And the brandy is appreciative of all this solicitude—Asbach Uralt is a fine, smooth, flavorful beverage, eminently sippable or mixable.

But now for the bad news: It sells for around $11 (fifth).

AURUM The Latin word *aurum* means "golden," and that's the color of this orange-flavored liqueur from Italy's Abruzzi Mountains. The base is aged brandy, making it a counterpart to France's illustrious Grand Marnier, which has a Cognac base. Indeed, Aurum is quite similar to Grand Marnier in taste, though it lacks some of the latter's delicacy and finesse. But it is excellent cordial withal. Aurum comes to the U.S. at 78° and fetches about $10 (fifth).

AUSTRALIAN WHISKY Like the Japanese before them, the Australians set out to make Scotch whisky in their own land. Both countries ended up with good, Scotch-like whiskies, distinctive in their own right, but not Scotch. This lends some credence to the Scottish claim that Scotch can be made only in Scotland.

Australian whisky is a good bottle of spirits—a harmonious blend of malt whisky with lighter grain whisky. It is rarely imported to the U.S. because of the prohibitive freight and duty. But if you happen to encounter it, give it a try. It's different and it's good.

B

B&B Short for **Benedictine** and **brandy** in equal parts. You can buy it ready-made by the same folks who make Benedictine, 86°, just like Benedictine, at the same price, around $12.50 (23 oz.). It's precisely what the doctor ordered if you like the flavor of Benedictine but find it overly sweet, or if you like brandy but find it too harsh, or for almost any other reason. You can even buy it in a two-compartment bottle, an ingenious cloven receptacle, with Benedictine on one side and B&B on the other. But at $14.65 or more, know that you are paying $2 plus just for the silly bottle. Best advice of all: Buy your own favorite brandy, and mix it with straight Benedictine. However concocted and constituted, B&B is one of the best after-dinner libations known to man —or angel.

BACARDI (COCKTAIL) Like most reputable rum cocktails, the Bacardi, named after the internationally famous rum, is essentially a combination of two celestially linked ingredients, rum and lime. In fact, the Bacardi is simply a Daiquiri with a splash of grenadine. It's *muy simple:* 1 jigger of rum—try to make it Bacardi for authenticity's sake, and lest you be struck by lightning; juice of half a lime; 1 teaspoon grenadine. Shake well with ice and strain into a cocktail glass, or serve on the rocks.

BACARDI RUM Bacardi is the brand name of a rum, and a good one, originally from Cuba, but now made in a number of countries, including Venezuela, Martinique, Spain, and even Canada. It's properly pronounced with the accent on the first syllable: *BAH-car-dee.* And it is also the name of a corporation (the parent company, Bacardi Corporation, based in Puerto Rico) and an American company (Bacardi Imports of Miami, Fla.).

In recent years Bacardi has become the envy of just about the entire American spirits industry: Bacardi rums have posted impressive sales increases, while most brands of spirits have suffered consistent and sometimes heavy losses.

In 1977 Bacardi Rum sold a million more cases than it had the previous year: up an astounding 20%, to more than 5 million cases. This made it, in fact, the third-largest-selling brand of liquor in the U.S., outsold only by **Seagram's 7 Crown Blend** (6.5 million cases) and **Smirnoff Vodka** (5.8 million cases). Bacardi is the best-selling rum in America, and by a wide margin. And the end, apparently, is nowhere in sight.

13

Much of this success, of course, has been due to good management and astute advertising, but Bacardi has also benefited from America's recent penchant for lighter spirits and different spirits (tequila and vodka have also been big gainers over the past five years).

Business has been so good, in fact, that that staid old matron of the spirits industry, **Hiram Walker–Gooderham & Worts Ltd.**, of Canada, recently (1978) purchased a 12% interest in the Bacardi Corporation for a cool $45 million, and has offered to buy 13% more.

Bacardi Rum started in Cuba in 1862, when a man by the name of Don Facundo Bacardi Masó paid $3,500 for a tin-roofed shed, some fermenting tanks and barrels, and an ancient cast-iron pot still. Included in the price was a family of fruit bats living in the dilapidated quarters, and to this day a bat is the Bacardi emblem. For many years Don Facundo had been making a wonderful light, tasty rum for his own consumption and that of his friends. Most of the rum of that day was pretty gruesome stuff, and Don Facundo's distillate was an instant success.

Two classic rum drinks, both inventions of the early 20th century, gave added impetus to the sale of Bacardi Rum: the **Daiquiri** and the **Cuba Libre**.

By 1930, demand for Bacardi Rum was so great that a distillery was opened in Mexico. Today there are several Bacardi plants in Mexico, including an ultramodern executive building designed by Ludwig Mies van der Rohe, situated on the Pan American Highway, near the village of Tultitlán, just 20 miles north of Mexico City. The company's prime distillery is in the state of Puebla, amid the lush sugar-cane fields of the Atencingo Valley.

Between 1930 and the present, Bacardi opened plants in a half-dozen other lands, including the Bahamas (Nassau), Brazil (Recife), Spain, and Puerto Rico, where the "parent" plant is now located. Bacardi had begun its Puerto Rico operation as far back as the 1930s, but it wasn't until 1960, when Castro confiscated the Bacardi holdings in Cuba, that Puerto Rico became the center and heart of the Bacardi empire.

Bacardi produces four rums: Light (Silver Label), 80°; Dark (Amber Label), 80°; Bacardi 151°; and Añejo, 80°, 6 years old (*añejo*, pronounced *ahn-YEAH-ho*, means "aged"). The "Ron" Bacardi on the label is not the name of one of the Bacardi boys—ron is "rum" in Spanish. The 151° is not for straight drinking, but for cooking and flaming. Bacardi Light and Dark sell in the U.S. for about $5.75, the Añejo for $7.50, and the 151° for about $9 (fifths).

Among rums of the same type (light-bodied or heavy-bodied), one brand is usually pretty much the same as the other. In some blind tastings conducted a few years ago by the Consumers Union, however, expert tasters gave their highest marks to Bacardi Amber Label. Bacardi's Silver Label they found to be only of middling quality. See *The Consumers Union Report on Wines and Spirits* (Mount Vernon, N.Y.: Consumers Union, 1972).

The Bacardi Rum consumed in the U.S.—and incredibly it is said that 75% of all rum consumed by Americans is Bacardi—is distilled in Puerto Rico and shipped in bulk to the U.S., where it is bottled and marketed by Bacardi Imports of Miami.

BAHIA This is a coffee-flavored liqueur made in Brazil and imported to the U.S. by the giant spirits and wine conglomerate Heublein. Brazil produces some of the finest coffee beans in the world, and it shows in this *good*, not superb, liqueur. Bahia has a good, bittersweet taste of roasted coffee beans, but it also has an ever so slightly medicinal aftertaste. It is 50° or 53° and sells for around $10 (23 oz.).

BAILEY'S ORIGINAL IRISH CREAM With its three celestial ingredients, Irish whiskey, Irish cream, and chocolate, it could hardly go wrong. And it hasn't and it won't. Bailey's Irish Cream (about 60°) is a wondrous liqueur, sinfully luscious. Unfortunately it is not yet available in the U.S., though it has already met with considerable success in European markets. Let us pray. . . .

BALLANTINE'S SCOTCH WHISKY Ballantine is an old and honored name in Scotland. There were Ballantines of note as far back as the 13th century. But it was only in the early 19th century that the family got into the spirits business. Around 1830, George Ballantine was selling wines and spirits from his grocery store in Edinburgh, Scotland. Before long he was bottling and exporting Scotch whisky. When he died, in 1892, the name of Ballantine Scotch was famous. In 1937, George Ballantine & Son was purchased by **Hiram Walker-Gooderham & Worts Ltd.**

Ballantine's Scotch is said to have reached its present eminence when it became the "in" drink at New York's celebrated "21." Today it is internationally acclaimed.

Ballantine's Scotch is made at Dumbarton, Scotland, where the River Leven empties into the Firth of Clyde, adjacent to the famous Dumbarton Rock, from which Mary Queen of Scots escaped to France in 1548. Four miles upstream is Loch Lomond, made famous in poem and song by that quintessential Scotsman Bobbie Burns.

The Ballantine operation is gigantic. The Dumbarton Distillery alone produces some 10 million gallons of whisky a year. The company also operates six distilleries in the north of Scotland. The nearby maturing warehouses at Dumbuck contain 30 million gallons of Scotch, worth $500 million. This liquid gold is guarded not by armed sentries, not by electronic devices, but by the "goose guard." A large flock of white geese patrols the warehouse grounds, the same method used by the ancient Romans to guard their camps. Should anyone venture within hailing—or stealing—distance, the geese put up an instant, infernal clangor.

Ballantine's is fine Scotch whisky. Even the lowliest grade is more expensive than most, and the highest grades are extremely expensive. But Ballantine's is worth the difference if you truly appreciate Scotch whisky and you religiously sip your Scotch "neat." One expert waxes poetic:

"Creating a famous Scotch such as Ballantine's—with its inimitable flavor, bouquet and elegant amber color—is as complex as composing a haunting melody. It requires orchestrating essences from Scotland's Lowlands, Highlands and wild offshore islands into one smooth sophisticated blend" (Jan Aaron, "Natural Enjoyment from Scotland," *Harper's Bazaar*, December 1974).

Ballantine's Scotch comes in four different grades, all 86°. The "regular" sells for $7 (California) to $8 (New York); the 12-year-old for $11 (California) to $12 (New York); The 21-year-old for about $25: and the 30-year-old for $45 (all fifths).

BANANA COW (COCKTAIL) This is neither a hamburger served with sliced bananas nor a banana with beef-jerky filling. It's another one of Trader Vic's inventions (like the Mai Tai), and he stoutly maintains that this is the best of all hangover remedies. At any rate it's nutritious and delicious, a healthful liquid breakfast. Into a blender put:

1 ripe banana, 1 tsp. powdered sugar, ½ cup milk, 1 jigger rum, 1 cup cracked ice, dash bitters, dash vanilla.

Blend at high speed until smooth. Good drinking! Or eating! And if this doesn't cure your hangover, you may die—which is probably what you've been praying for anyway.

Note that there are at least two commercial Banana Cows, Hereford and Aberdeen (see **Hereford's Cows**), but the homemade version above is far preferable—better conformation!

BANANA LIQUEUR Bananas, for some reason — perhaps because of their distinctiveness—are more easily bottled, that is to say, made into liqueurs, than are most fruits. And so banana liqueurs are made around the world, from Mexico to Turkey to Australia to America to Europe.

The French call theirs crème de banane (pronounced *bahnahn*), and American firms call theirs either *"banana liqueur"* or—in an illogical combination of English and French—'crème de banana."

Banana liqueurs are usually yellow (occasionally white), very sweet, and redolent in aroma and taste of ripe bananas. (Banana flavor is easily imitated, and if a liqueur is so flavored with an imitation flavor, this must be stated on the label.)

Domestic banana liqueurs, most of them 50° to 60°, sell in the U.S. for around $5.50 (24 oz.); the imports sell for around $10 (also 24 oz.), and they are not that much superior—some are not superior at all.

Banana liqueurs find their way into a number of mixed drinks—Stan Jones' *Complete Barguide* (Los Angeles: Barguide Enterprises, 1977) lists no less than thirty-three mixed drinks made with banana liqueurs—but their most notable contribution to the advancement of civilization is the Banana Daiquiri (see under Daiquiri).

BARBADOS (and TRINIDAD) RUMS These are "intermediate" rums in both color and taste, somewhere between the lightbodied (e.g., Puerto Rico) and the heavy-bodied (Jamaica) rums. Very few Barbados rums are found in the U.S., but if you fancy rum at all, these are worth searching for, as they have a unique flavor, called "leathery" or "smoky." An implausible array of flavoring agents is used: coconut shells, vegetable roots, Madeira wine, bitter almonds. These are wellmade rums, and the best are worthy of being sippingly appreciated—before the hearth or upon the heath.

Trinidad rums are very similar to those of Barbados, and are equally difficult to find in the U.S. The most widely distributed brand seems to be Siegert's Bouquet (86°), selling around $7 (fifth). Rum fanciers insist that these rums are the only proper ones to use in a Rum Swizzle.

BARTON BRANDS, LTD. Barton Brands, of Chicago, is a *small* American spirits conglomerate; they do a mere $100 million in sales per year. They market *only* a dozen different spirits. If this doesn't sound like a miniaturized operation to you, consider, for example, Seagram, which does more than $2.2 billion in annual sales, and markets more than a hundred different brands of spirits and wines.

Barton Brands is very American, in both history and output. Barton now has a few imports—some good, some bad—but the company grew up amid the limestone water springs of Nelson County, Kentucky, home of much of the world's best bourbon whiskey. And Barton knows how to make good bourbon at a reasonable price; see the next two entries and also **Kentucky Gentleman Kentucky Straight Bourbon Whiskey.**

Besides its American whiskeys, Barton Brands markets those imported spirits: Barton Vodka, Highland Mist Scotch, **House of Stuart Scotch,** Monte Alban Mezcal (see under **mezcal), Montezuma Tequila,** and **Sabroso** coffee liqueur.

BARTON RESERVE BLENDED WHISKEY This is one of the very few blended whiskeys that still comes in a 90° version, as well as in 80° and 86°. In all three proofs this is a good, smooth whiskey, and usually an excellent value. Barton Reserve 90° sells for about $5.50 (fifth). There is also a Very Old Barton (86°, 90°, and 100°), 8-year-old available in some markets. It is also a good value at $6.25 (fifth).

BARTON'S Q.T. PREMIUM LIGHT WHISKEY Light whiskey is for people who don't like whiskey—or more precisely, bourbon for people who don't like bourbon. In effect, light whiskey is a bourbonless bourbon. (Logically, the name "bourbon" cannot be on the label.) Light whiskeys are the Johnnies-come-lately to the bourbon scene; the type was introduced only a decade ago. Barton's Q.T. is a good example of the new breed: light, soft, easy-drinking. This is good whiskey—but then so are the other ten lights listed under **bourbon.**

Light whiskeys are very similar to Canadian whiskies, and in fact it is often impossible to distinguish between them. Barton Q.T. has an ad that says, quite truthfully, "Close your eyes and you'll swear it's Canadian."

Q.T. (80°) sells for around $5 (fifth): standard price, standard light. But good. It is America's best-selling light whiskey.

BATAVIA ARAK It's not a prehistoric scaly horned monster —it's an **arak,** a rum from Batavia, on the island of Java in Indonesia. It's a true rum (made from molasses), the best-known and the best outside of Caribbean rums. It's a pungent, extremely dry, aromatic beverage, and is especially appreciated by the Dutch and the Swedes, who usually take it neat, except when they down it in the form of **Swedish Punsch.** Arak gets its distinctiveness from several sources: wild native yeasts, the special quality of the local water, and the red Javanese rice used for flavoring. It's well aged, usually 10 or more years old when bottled.

(JAMES B.) BEAM DISTILLING COMPANY Whiskey-producers are a notoriously close-mouthed clan. And understandably so, for formulas and production procedures must be carefully guarded. But some-

times the secrecy can become obsessive—as with the Beam Distilling Company. The Beam Company will scarcely admit that it produces whiskey, which it does quite well, and has been doing for almost 200 years. Jacob Beam made whiskey, first in Virginia and Maryland, and later in Kentucky, in the late 1780s. Several generations later, Col. Jim Beam resurrected the family business after Repeal.

Beam makes a formidable array of bourbons under the Beam surname, all of them Kentucky straights:

Beam Bicentennial (100 months), 80°, $7 (fifth); **Beam's Choice** (8 years), 80°, $7 (fifth); Beam's Personalized Private Stock (4 years), 80°, $6 (750 ml.); Beam's Pin Bottle (8 years), 86.8°, $8.75 (fifth); (10 years), 86.8°, $10 (fifth); Beam's Royal Reserve (12 years), 86°, $15 to $16 (fifth); Beam's Sour Mash (101 months), 90°, $7.75 (25.4 oz.); Jim Beam (4 years), 80°, $6 (fifth and 25.4 oz.).

Then there is also Jim Beam Rye (7 years), 80°, $6.50 (fifth and 750 ml.), and the firm's less expensive brands, also Kentucky straight bourbons—Belle of Kentucky, 80° and 86° ($5 to $6 a quart); Distillers Reserve, 80° and 86° ($5 to $6 a quart).

Jim Beam (4 years old, 80°) is America's most popular bourbon, and by a comfortable margin. It leads second-place Early Times, a Brown-Forman product, by more than a half million cases a year. (Jim Beam's total annual sales are now around 2.7 million cases.)

Jim Beam is unquestionably fine bourbon whiskey—somehow the American drinking public has unerring instincts in these matters: all of America's best-selling spirits are excellent beverages. Jim Beam bourbon has millions of staunch devotees who will allow no other bourbon to cross their loyal lips. But truth to tell, Jim Beam is not all that superior: good bourbon, yea—super-superlative bourbon, nay. In fact, in one important bourbon tasting, Jim Beam had the lowliest ranking of all: merely "acceptable." (See *The Consumers Union Report on Wines and Spirits,* Consumers Union, Mount Vernon, N.Y., 1972, p. 134.)

Besides its "sippin'" bourbons, the Beam Distilling Company is also known for the decorative ceramic bottles in which it markets a lot of its whiskey. These wonderful, colorful decanters are true Americana. Current models depict everything from Martha Washington and an A. C. Spark Plug to King Kong and Bing Crosby. Beam has been making these decanters for twenty-five years, and there have been many different series through the years: centennial series, automotive series, gambling casino series, political series, and many more. To date, more than 500 different decanters have been produced. There is even a book on the subject: *Jim Beam Bottles* by Al Cembura (9th ed., 139 Arlington Avenue, Berkeley, CA. 94707, $6.95). Some of the decanters have become collectors' items.

A "Man in a Barrel" decanter, symbol of Harold's Club Casino (Reno, Nevada), issued in 1957, brings around $460. A second "Man in a Barrel" issued the following year is worth only half as much—evidently more bottles were produced. The #1 man in a barrel has a mustache and is smiling; #2 man lacks both mustache and smile—he obviously lost both at Harold's Club. A silver decanter made in limited numbers for Harrah's Club Casino (Reno) in 1963 is now valued at about $1,200. But grand prize winner is a simple blue and gold decanter made in 1964 for the hundredth anniversary of the First National Bank of Chicago. Only about 117 were made, and they were presented to the bank's directors; it's valued at an astounding $3,000.

But if one buys Beam decanters for the whiskey contained as well as the decorative container, one had best be wary, for they not only contain different grades of whiskey of varying proofs, but they also contain varying amounts of whiskey. They range in price from around $11 (fifth, 80°, election donkey or elephant) to around $40 (25.4 oz., 80°) for the Stutz Bearcat. But this is probably all rather academic, for most of the people who buy Beam decanters would never dream of drinking the whiskey! The container is more valuable than the contained. (Like some beautiful people.) Ironically it is illegal for a private individual to sell a Beam decanter containing whiskey—no one can sell whiskey in these United States without proper licensing.

BEAM'S CHOICE KENTUCKY STRAIGHT BOURBON WHISKEY Good, standard straight bourbon whiskey,

8 years old and 86°, but judged by taste alone—and what else is there to judge by other than snob appeal?—it's no better and no worse than a host of other straight bourbons. Unless you want to impress someone, this is not a very good value at about $7 (fifth). It is **charcoal-filtered.** (For a listing of the best buys in bourbon, see under **bourbon.**)

Note that there is also a plain Jim Beam, 4 years old and 80°, America's most popular straight bourbon.

BEAULIEU BRANDY It was rather nice while it lasted—somewhat sweet, beguiling—but it came and went in a few short years. Some bottles of Beaulieu Brandy are still lurking about, however, and they should be worth searching out, for this is—or was—a nice California brandy to start with, and it just might become a collector's item a few decades down the line.

BEEFEATER GIN This British dry gin is undoubtedly today's most prestigious gin. Among gins it is the ultimate status symbol—the Beefeater Martini is one of the world's most called-for mixed drinks.

Beefeater has long been a favorite. It was first made some 150 years ago, in London, by a young pharmacist by the name of James Burrough. James Burrough Limited still makes Beefeater Gin, and the company is still controlled by the Burrough family.

Beefeater has not only survived, it has thrived. In the U.S. today Beefeater outsells all other imported gins combined. But perhaps it is just as well that some of James Burrough's other concoctions have not come down to us, for his recipes have. He made some wondrous potions, including English Champagne (a near-sacrilegious thought), a medicine called Sir Henry Halford's Recipe for Nervous People (in pre-Valium days), and most intriguing of all, artificial ass's milk!

The name "Beefeater" was conferred upon James Burrough's gin for the simple and good reason that "Beefeater" connotes tradition and prestige, and it is synonymous with London.

Beefeater is quality gin, beyond doubt, and with a price to match: about $7.50 (fifth), vs. $4 to $5 for most American-made gins. It definitely receives extra care and love: It is made from juniper berries from northern Italy and coriander seed from the marshes of Essex, it uses only pure London water from a well beneath the distillery, every day's production is carefully tasted before it leaves the distillery, and every bottle is individually numbered so that it may be traced in case of a problem.

All these things are true. Yet the unarguable fact remains that the difference between Beefeater Gin and the lowliest private label on the American market is infinitesimal. Differences can be detected by a microscope, or a very, very, very talented and sensitive palate. For the vast majority of humankind, the difference is *not* worth $3 to $4 per fifth. In one blind tasting, experts were able to identify Beefeater as an import less than 15% of the time—see *The Consumers*

Union Report on Wines and Spirits (Mount Vernon, N.Y.: Consumers Union, 1972), p. 148. If Beefeater is your favorite gin, know that you're paying mostly for prestige, history, éclat.

BELLOWS WHISKEYS Bellows & Company dates back to 1830, when the firm was a purveyor of choice wines, tobacco, whiskey, and food specialties. It wasn't until after Prohibition, however, that the Bellows brand of whiskey rose to prominence, along with their Partner's Choice and Club brands.

Today Bellows is a property (along with a dozen other brands of whiskey) of the giant spirits conglomerate National Distillers Products Company. Bellows now comes in three "varieties": Bellows Rare, 80°; Kentucky Straight Bourbon; Bellows Reserve Blend, 86°; and Bellows Partner's Choice Blend, 80° and 86°. All sell between $5 and $6 (fifth) and all are good, reliable whiskeys, economically priced.

BENCHMARK, SEAGRAM'S KENTUCKY STRAIGHT BOURBON Here's an unusual bourbon, some say unique in our land. Most bourbons are indistinguishable one from another, but in one well-publicized professional tasting a few years ago—see *The Consumers Union Report on Wines and Spirits* (Mount Vernon, N.Y.: Consumers Union, 1972) —this whiskey was given a higher rating ("Very Good") than any of the other forty-odd bourbons tasted. Benchmark is 86° and is in the more expensive class of bourbons: about

$6.75 (fifth). But if you're a true bourbon lover, you may find it worth the difference.

BENEDICTINE An inspired and inspiring liqueur, of French lineage and churchly origins. It's named after the Benedictine monks who invented it around the year 1500. The name means "blessed," and so it is: a heaven-blessed culmination to any fine meal. Or, as the spirit moveth sundrily, to be tenderly and appreciatively sipped, *solus* or *sola*. Or, even better: *solus cum sola.*

And it's still heavenly even when thinned, "on the rocks." And if you find it too sweet for your sophisticated palate, try **B&B,** which is simply half Benedictine and half brandy.

Those wise old medieval monks used Benedictine to cure malaria and to restore the pooped, drooped brethren. It is no less salubrious and efficacious 450 years later.

To this very day Benedictine is made on the site of the original monastery, although it is now a commercial enterprise, not a monkish one. And it is still made according to the original and secret formula, using some twenty or thirty different herbs and spices. It is said that only three people in the world know the formula, and they are never allowed to be in the same place at the same time.

There's no worry here about brand names—there is only one Benedictine, the real thing, the one heavenly potion.

The prominent D.O.M. on the label stands for "Deo Optimo Maximo," "To God, most Good, most Great." And perish the atheistic Communist who wouldn't drink (Benedictine)

to that! Costs about $12.50 (23 oz.).

BIG FOUR These are exactly what the name says: the four biggest producers of distilled spirits in the U.S. They are, according to rank, from the largest to the smallest: **Seagram Company Limited; Hiram Walker–Gooderham & Worts Ltd.; Schenley Industries, Inc.; and National Distillers Products Company.**

Other large spirits conglomerates include: **Heublein Inc.; Brown-Forman Distillers Corporation; American Distilling Company;** Glenmore Distilleries Company; and Publicker Industries.

The big four, together with these other important conglomerates and distilleries, account for more than 80% of the spirits sold in the U.S.

BISQUIT COGNACS It has nothing to do with anything you put butter and honey on for breakfast, and it's pronounced "Boes-kwee." It's a proper name, the name of the founder of the firm of Bisquit-Dubouchie, Jarnac, France, in the very heart of the Cognac region. Only the company's Extra Vieille brand of Cognac has the full name of the company on the label—the others have simply Bisquit. The firm was founded in 1819, and was a bigger name in the 19th century than it has been through much of the 20th. But that seems to be changing, particularly over the past decade, since the company was taken over by the spirit conglomerate, the House of Ricard.

Three grades of Bisquit Cognacs are commonly available in the U.S.:

V.S. or 3 Star, 80°. The V.S., Very Special, name is used only in the U.S. This is a sweetish, grapey, light-bodied Cognac, acclaimed by many as one of the best values in Cognacs of this category, second only to Martell 3 Star. About $12 (fifth).

V.S.O.P. Fine Champagne, 80°. The company exults in the "length" of this Cognac: its ability to linger on the palate, but some experts have faulted it for its heaviness and lack of perfect balance. $15 (fifth).

Extra Vieille: Top of the line, totally elegant; it comes in a Baccarat crystal decanter at around—steady!—$75 (fifth).

There is also a Napoleon Fine Champagne, 80°, not ordinarily seen in the U.S. It is an excellent Cognac by everybody's standards: well balanced, suave, with good woodiness.

BITTERS As the name says they're bitter. They are also highly concentrated, very aromatic, and quite "spirited." We don't ordinarily think of bitters as alcoholic beverages, but they are most decidedly such, ranging from around 45° to 90°.

The forebears of today's bitters were the medicinal and magical elixirs of the Middle Ages. These were distillations made from herbs, barks, and all manner of strange materials, but presumably not including the delicacies Shakespeare had the Witches in *Macbeth* put into their cauldron:

Eye of newt, and toe of frog,
Wool of bat, and tongue of dog,
Adder's fork, and blindworm's sting,

Lizard's leg, and howlet's wing. [Act IV, Scene 1] These medieval nostrums had to be vile-tasting, of course, in order to be effective. In the same way, American bitters may be said to be the legitimate descendants of all the quack patent medicines and snake oils that were hawked in country lane and carnival side-show a century ago.

Bitters have a spirit base and are flavored with an array of fruits, peels, herbs, spices, barks, roots, seeds, and leaves. Their formulas, of course, are jealously guarded secrets, and it is said of some of them that the recipe is known to only one man, and he reveals it to his successor only on his death-bed.

Bitters are of two kinds: those used for flavoring mixed drinks and not consumed on their own (Angostura; Pey-chaud's) and those enjoyed on their own, either as aperitifs or digestifs (Compari, Fernet Branca— see the latter under Hangovers and hangover cures).

BLACK & WHITE SCOTCH WHISKY
This familiar whis-ky got its name from the fact that it originally came in a black bottle with a white label. In those days it was called Buchanan's Blend, after James Buchanan, who created it, around 1880, in London. People began asking for that "black and white" whisky, so Buchan-an made the name official. He happened to be an animal lover, so he put a black and a white Scottie on the label.

Black & White today is the property of Distillers Company Limited of London and is im-ported by Heublein. It has suf-fered serious slippage in sales in recent years because of the trend toward more economical Scotches bottled in the U.S., not in Scotland. Black & White is good whisky, but it is one of the more expensive bottled-in-Scotland Scotches. It is 86.8° and sells for around $7 (fifth) on the West Coast and a little more in the Eastern U.S.

BLACKBERRY LIQUEURS
These are the most popular of all the berry liqueurs, probably because blackberries are plenti-ful around the world. Practical-ly every American liqueur firm makes a blackberry liqueur (or cordial) or a blackberry-fla-vored brandy (often called Blackberry & Brandy)—some-times both. They are virtually the same beverage, but when one company makes both, the liqueur (sometimes called Crème de Blackberry) is almost always the sweeter and the low-er in proof of the two.

Broadly speaking, Ameri-can-made blackberry liqueurs are every bit as good as Euro-pean ones, at sometimes half the price. American brands sell generally in the $5 to $6 bracket, while European im-ports are often $10 and more.

Blackberry liqueurs are not flavored solely with blackber-ries—no liqueurs, in fact, are so simply made from the one named principal flavoring agent. These liqueurs are made from a number of different ber-ries, with blackberries being the principal source of flavor. They also frequently contain a small percentage of red wine.

A few true blackberry bran-dies—distilled from blackber-ries, not simply flavored with blackberries—are made in Europe, but none of them is imported to this country. Brombeergeist (or Brombeerlikor) is one.

Jezynowka is a Polish blackberry liqueur. (Leroux puts the name on its domestic blackberry-flavored brandy.) Dolfi's blackberry liqueur is labeled Liqueur de Mure.

Blackberry cordials are usually quite sweet; they are full-bodied and deep-purple in color. They are best enjoyed chilled or on the rocks. And, of course, you can always pour them over vanilla ice cream.

BLACK RUSSIAN (COCKTAIL) This is the drink that made Kahlúa Coffee Liqueur famous. And it has probably been responsible for more unspeakable hangovers than any other mixed drinks of recent invention. Black Russians are a sinister breed, deceptively potent, engagingly soft and alluring. They taste like chocolate malt milkshakes, but don't behave like them. The Black Russian is simply one part of a **coffee liqueur** (Kahlúa is just one of the many) to two parts of vodka. Serve it on the rocks, or shake well with ice, then strain.

BLACK VELVET There are two Black Velvets—one's a mixed drink and the other is a brand name for a Canadian whisky. The mixed drink is of Irish origin, a half-and-half mixture of Guinness stout and champagne. You're cautioned to pour them simultaneously into a chilled tall glass—no ice, please—slowly, lest the velvet runneth over. Some are convinced this is the best beverage on either side of the At-

lantic, some hold it in abomination. One British author calls it "a crackpot beverage . . . a barbarity." It does indeed seem an adulteration of two wholesome beverages, neither of which really needs mixing with anything. The Germans call it a *Bismarck*.

Black Velvet Canadian Whisky, 80°, is a good standard **Canadian** whisky, medium-priced, no better and no worse than an array of other such.

BLOODY MARY (COCKTAIL) This used to be the name of a person, but now it's the name of a drink made with tomato juice and vodka. Back in the 16th century, Bloody Mary was Queen Mary I of England, so called because, as a Roman Catholic, she was in favor of the blood of Protestants, shed, of course. Today's Bloody Mary is recommended as a morning-after potion, a restorative for the hungover. It probably won't cure anything at all, but go ahead, try it—there's no way on earth you can feel any worse.

The Rx:

2 jiggers tomato juice or V-8, 1 jigger vodka (or aquavit), juice of ½ lemon (or lime), dash or 2 of Worcestershire or L&P sauce, dash of celery salt, dash of Tabasco, twist of peppermill (optional).

Shake well with ice, strain, and serve in a 6-oz. or 8-oz. glass (Delmonico).

To make it even more nutritious, add a jigger of beef bouillon. And if that grabs you mightily, you should consider a bullshot which skips the tomato juice.

Hold the vodka and this makes a zesty and authoritative drink for your teetotaling great-aunt.

The British take a dim view of the American Bloody Mary—they prefer the life-depriving queen to the life-restoring potion—and one British author observes loftily: "The name is a typical straining for effect." Oh, yeah?

You can buy prepared Bloody Mary mixes, and they're quite adequate, though never as good as the freshly made concoction. The powdered forms are generally better buys than the liquid. The *poorest* buys are these liquids: Tahiti Joe, Schweppes, Holland House, Party Tyme.

One simple solution is Snap-E-Tom tomato cocktail, made not by Del Monte or Hunt's, but by Heublein, the giant wine and spirit conglomerate. All you do is add the vodka—and away, you're gone!

BOGGS CRANBERRY LIQUEUR It's probably the only cranberry liqueur in the world—and it deserves to be. Boggs simply doesn't make it. It's been heavily promoted by Heublein, but that only sells a liqueur—it doesn't render it good. Boggs Cranberry Liqueur is pleasant enough, but one looks for a lot more than that in a 40° domestic beverage selling for $12 (33.8 oz.).

BOLS LIQUEURS Bols is one of the oldest names in the history of liqueurs—and, in fact, in the history of commercial spirits. It was in 1575, more than 400 years ago, that a young man by the name of Lucas Bols set up a small distilling plant in the outskirts of Amsterdam.

The firm continued in the direct control of the Bols family until 1815, when the direct line died out. The name was then changed to Erven Lucas Bols, the Heirs of Lucas Bols.

Lucas Bols' original plant would probably fit into the tasting room of the Royal Distilleries Erven Lucas Bols of today. The huge, seven-story plant occupies many square blocks outside the little village of Nieuw-Vennep, near Amsterdam; it has a capacity of 250,000 bottles per day.

Bols has subsidiary plants all over the world—incredibly, in some 130 different countries: in Europe, Africa, Japan, the Philippines, Australia, New Zealand, and North and South America. Quality, however, is strictly controlled by the "Motherhouse" in Holland, and samples of the locally produced liqueurs must be sent periodically to the home plant.

In the U.S., Bols liqueurs are blended and bottled in Louisville, Ky., by **Brown-Forman Distillers Corporation** (properly speaking, the American firm producing the Bols liqueurs is the Erven Lucas Bols Distilling Co., a subsidiary of Brown-Forman). The master blender at the Louisville plant is, in fact, of Dutch nationality, and the quality of the liqueurs is strictly controlled by the central laboratory in the Netherlands.

No Holland - made Bols liqueurs are exported to the U.S., except special shipments for specific purposes. The only made-in-Holland Bols products exported to the U.S. are kirsch-wasser (90°, around $10 a fifth); Genever Gin (80° in stone crocks—around $8 a fifth); and a few deluxe packages such as a lovely ballerina bottle which comes in three different flavors, apricot, crème de menthe, and Gold Liqueur, at about $20 (pint); and two-and four-compartment bottles. Several two-compartment bottles are offered, with various liqueurs; they sell for $8 to $9 (14 oz.). The four-compartment bottle contains apricot liqueur, cherry liqueur, crème de menthe, and triple sec, and sells for about $19 (quart).

Bols is a 400-year-old name respected around the world. Koninklijke Distilleerderijen Erven Lucas Bols is not about to jeopardize any of that. Bols maintains high standards, even with their foreign-produced liqueurs and spirits. It's a name you can trust.

Should you happen to be wandering around Amsterdam anytime, be sure to find your way to the Bols tasting room near the site of the original plant of Lucas Bols. There you can sample the most renowned and perhaps the best of the Bols liqueurs, none of which are available in the U.S.: curaçao, advocaat, kümmel, and Half and Half (the last is half curaçao and half bitters—said to have been invented by mistake, by a careless workman adding the wrong liqueur to the right tank!).

BOODLES GIN This British product comes in a squat stylish bottle and advertises itself as "The World's Costliest Gin," and it may well be that, at around $7.75 (fifth). But Beef-eater (fifth) often sells for as much, as does Doornkaat (25.4 oz.), the German import. But note that Boodles is 94.4°, and Beefeater and Doornkaat are both 94°. (Most American gins are a miserly 80°.) Wherefore, computing ounce for ounce of alcohol, the latter two are sometimes more expensive than Boodles.

But the snob appeal evidently works, for some people, often more wealthy than wise, buy a thing precisely because it costs more.

Nonetheless Boodles is good gin. In blind tastings it usually ranks well. It is aromatic and tasty—as gins go, that is, which isn't very far in those two categories.

BOORD'S GIN . In . gins, there's Booth's and there's Boodles and there's Boord's. They are all quite distinct, not to be confused and confounded—yet they're all quite alike simply because all gins are quite alike. (For more on this subject, see gin.)

Boord's Gin originated, as did so many of the world's famous gins, in London town. The name Boord (or variations thereof) has been associated with the spirits and wine trade since the 14th century. In 1849, Joseph Boord of London devised the Boord's "Cat & Barrel" trademark which has since found its way around the world.

In 1924, Boord's became a part of the huge British spirits conglomerate Distillers Company Limited. Some Boord's Gin is still made in London, as also in New Zealand, but a great deal more is made today in the U.S.

Boord's makes two gins: "plain" Dry Gin, 80° and 85°; and Old Tom Gin, 85°, which has a mite of sugar (scarcely discernible) added. The principal difference between them is the label!

Boord's is standard, reliable, made-in-America gin. But more than that, it's a good value.

BOOTH'S GINS Booth is an old and respected name in the annals of gin. The Booth boys were distilling gin in London as early as 1740. John Wilkes Booth, the man who assassinated Abraham Lincoln, was a shirttail relative.

Booth's Distilleries Limited makes two principal gins: High & Dry, 90°; and House of Lords, 86°. High & Dry is the bread-and-butter gin, $5 to $6 (fifth). House of Lords is the prestige gin, about $7 (fifth). (Here's one of the few instances where the prestige brand is lower in proof than the "regular.") High & Dry is made in more than thirty countries around the world, including the U.S., and quality is controlled from London, says the company. House of Lords is made only in London, at the company's Red Lion Distillery.

All Booth's gins bear the proud, loud trademark of a red red lion; the House of Lords label has no fewer than six of the lions.

The company prides itself on High & Dry's extreme dryness —hence the name. Ideal for Martinis, is the pitch. But all gins today are extremely dry.

House of Lords Gin used to come with a slight golden tinge, first brought about by accidentally aging the gin in old sherry casks. Today it is still golden-tinted for the British market, but now comes water-white for the export market. The switch was made because people—Americans, in particular—wanted their Martinis crystal-clear.

Experts—and gin snobs— have long hailed House of Lords Gin as a superior beverage. One has no reason to disagree. However, experts have also been unable to detect House of Lords—or, for the matter of that, any other premium gin — from the more lowly, most inexpensive brands, when tasting them blindly. For the results of one such tasting, see *The Consumer's Union Report on Wines and Spirits* (Mount Vernon, N.Y.: Consumers Union, 1972), pp. 145–151.

BOOZE An opprobrious name for distilled spirits. But sometimes it's the only one that fits. When spirituous drinks are patently abused, that's *booze*. If intoxication is the goal, that's *booze*. Distilled spirits, because of their high alcoholic content, are obviously dangerous— sometimes lethal. They demand respect and restraint. Thus respected and cautiously enjoyed, they're one of the Creator's rarest gifts to toiling, moiling humankind. But when abused, they're not God's gifts—they're just plain *booze!*

BOULARD CALVADOS The label reads "Calvados Boulard" instead of "Boulard Calvados," because that's the way they do these things in France, but Boulard is the proper name and **calvados** the generic name for the world's most elegant apple-jack.

Boulard has been making calvados since 1825, and it shows. Boulard Calvados is one of the finest in the land. Two versions are available in Europe, a "regular" called Fine —say *feen*, not *fyne*—and Grande Fine, which has additional age. In the U.S., the most commonly seen Calvados Boulard is Arc de Triomphe, at $11 to $12 (fifth).

BOURBON It's as American as apple pie. Or more so. For millions of Americans, bourbon is whiskey, whiskey is bourbon, nothing else. Actually, bourbon is only *a* whiskey: one of some forty or more whiskey types made around the world.

Bourbon whiskey has an improbable history. First, it was "invented" in 1789 by the Reverend Elijah Craig, a Baptist minister. (With a name like that, what else could he be?) That's akin to the Pope inventing a new contraceptive device. Further, he made it in Bourbon County, Kentucky, which today—irony of ironies—is legally dry.

There is probably no subject on this benighted earth that is more encrusted with half-truths, untruths, myths, and misapprehensions than the subject of bourbon whiskey. Every drunk in every bar in the land has at least one illusion to promulgate.

For example, whiskey-wise people sometimes favor sour-mash bourbon as a superior beverage. They've been duped. "Sour-mash" simply means that the whiskey's been made with some of the leftover, "sour," mash of a previous batch: in

the trade, the "slop." It's no better and no worse than "sweet-mash" bourbon, and not even experts, tasting blindly, can distinguish sour-mash bourbon from the sweet-mash variety.

So also a myriad of myths envelops the subject of "aged" bourbon, and Americans have paid millions of extra dollars for those extra years the label proudly proclaims. They are mostly squandered dollars. The law requires only two years of aging, though most bourbons get four. So far, so good, but beyond four years, or six at the outside, it's mostly wasted effort. In fact, additional age may actually be harmful to the whiskey's flavor. There is probably some mellowing of the whiskey over a long period of time, but it's minuscule. It's simply a case of too long for too little. The proof of the pudding is in the eating, and expert tasters have been consistently unable to detect any taste difference between aged bourbons and youthful ones.

Another bourbon shibboleth is "bottled in bond." (The bottles are easily spotted: They have a green tax stamp over the stopper rather than the usual red one.) Such whiskeys were very popular thirty and fifty years ago—today the trend is toward lighter bourbons. "Bottled in bond" is sometimes invoked as a guarantee of quality. In effect it may well be such, but *per se* it is nothing of the kind. It means only that the whiskey is at least four years old and 100°, both facts assured by U.S. government supervision. But if you appreciate true bourbon flavor, these are the bottles you should seek, for they have more of that essential bourboniness; they are heavy-flavored, full-bodied potions.

Here are America's leading "bottled in bond" straight bourbons, in increasing order of price. These are the most bourbonish whiskeys you can buy. Be advised: *Buy the most economical!* There is no appreciable difference in taste between them. Prices are average across the continental U.S. for a standard fifth:

BOTTLED-IN-BOND STRAIGHT
BOURBONS

Haller's County Fair, $4.68
Old Log Cabin, $5.55
Hiram Walker Private Cellar, 6 years, $5.60
Old Heaven Hill, 4 years, $5.87
Barton's Ancient Bond, 8 years, $5.89
Fleischmann's, $5.89
Spring River, $5.89
Old Hickory, 6 to 7 years, $6.07
J. W. Dant, $6.25
Old Crow, $6.65
Old Kentucky Tavern, 8 years, $6.77
Old Forester, 6 years, $7.55
Old Fitzgerald, 6 years, $7.55
I. W. Harper, $8.16
Old Taylor, $8.22
Old Grand-Dad, $8.22

For a whiskey to call itself bourbon, only three things are required by law: (1) distilled at a maximum of 160°; (2) from a mash of at least 51% corn; and (3) aged a minimum of two years in new charred oak barrels. It does not have to be made in Kentucky. Like all American whiskey, it must be bottled at at least 80°, and 100° for bonded.

Most straight bourbon is *not* bottled in bond. It does not qualify to be bonded, either because it is less than 100° or because it is less than 4 years old. Such straight, nonbonded bourbons are the choice of most Americans. (There is also a "blended straight bourbon," which sounds like a contradiction in terms but isn't—it's just different batches of straight bourbon blended together. There isn't much of this around.)

If you are a bourbon freak and also like to save money, straight (nonbonded) bourbon is probably your jigger of whiskey, for this is still 100% straight bourbon—it lacks only the patina of government supervision and it is a lower proof. It should be noticeably less expensive than the bonded bottles, above.

Listed here are America's leading straight (nonbonded) bourbons. Again: Buy the most economical. It would take a professional taster—with divine guidance—to distinguish between most of them. Best buys are listed first. Prices are for fifths.

80° STRAIGHT BOURBONS

Glenmore Silver Label, $3.99
P.M., $4.19
Bourbon de Luxe, $4.39
Old Quaker, 4 years, $4.49
Sunny Brook, $4.49

Stillbrook, 4 years, $4.65
Old Stagg, 6 years, $4.72
J. W. Dant, 4 years, $4.82
Daviess County, about 4 years, $4.85

White Tavern, $4.85
Hill and Hill, $4.99
Colonel Lee, $5.00
Hiram Walker Ten High, 5 years, $5.12
Mattingly & Moore, 5 years, $5.15
Old Bourbon by J. W. Dant, $5.18

Bellows Club, $5.19
Antique, 6 years, $5.24
Bourbon Supreme Rare, 4 years, $5.37
Ezra Brooks, 4 years, $5.39
Early Times, 5 years, $5.50
Jim Beam, 4 years, $5.52
Old Crow, 6 years, $5.74
Old Taylor, 6 years, $5.99

86° STRAIGHT BOURBONS

Heaven Hill, 4 years, $4.44
Kentucky Beau, 4 years, $4.68
Olde Bourbon, by J.W. Dant, 4 years, $4.92
Hiram Walker, Ten High, $4.99
Hermitage, $4.99
Stillbrook, 4 years, $4.99
Barclay's Bourbon, 4 years, $5.05
Fleischmann's Select, $5.06
Old Museum Charcoal Filtered, $5.10
Heaven Hill Old Style, 6 years, $5.19
Antique, 6 years, $5.24
Ezra Brooks, 4 years, $5.39
Stitzel Weller's Canada Dry, $5.45
Bellows Club, 6 years, $5.47
Canada Dry, $5.49
J. W. Dant, 10 years, $5.55
Old Charter, 8 years, $5.60
Cabin Still, 5 years, $5.69
Yellowstone, 6 years, $5.69

Ancient Age, 5 years, $5.79
Old Hickory, 10 years, $5.79
Jim Beam, 4 years, $5.88
Old Taylor, $6.09
Henry McKenna, 6 years, $6.22
Virginia Gentleman, 4 years, $6.25
Walker's De Luxe, $6.27
Ancient Age, 10 years, $6.34
Old Charter, 7 years, $6.49
Evan Williams, $6.50
Old Forester, 6 years, $6.67
Rare Antique, 10 years, $6.75
Old Charter, 10 years, $6.75
Old Fitzgerald, Prime, 6 years, $6.94
Old Grand-Dad, $6.99
Old Hickory, 6 years, $7.00
I. W. Harper, 5 years, $7.00
Old Fitzgerald, 7 years, $7.17
Seagram's Benchmark, 6 years, $7.20
I.W. Harper, 10 years, $8.12
Wild Turkey, 7 years (86.8°) $8.32

90° STRAIGHT BOURBONS

Yellowstone 1872, 7 years, $5.98
Ezra Brooks, 7 years $5.99

Makers Mark Old Style, $7.36
The President's Choice, 4 years (90.30), $9.45

101° STRAIGHT BOURBONS

Makers Mark Limited Edition, $9.60

Wild Turkey, 8 years, $11.27

But if you're not really all that gung-ho over that deep-down bourbon flavor, then look for a bottle of American whiskey that doesn't have the word "bourbon" on it at all. It will say simply "American whiskey." But it's *practically* bourbon, made by the same basic process. It may not legally put the word "bourbon" on its label, however, for it was distilled at more than 160°, and that's the point where that bourbon flavor—whether you dig it or not—begins to fade away.

A blend must have at least 20% of 100° straight whiskey in it—that's not much. Neither is any aging period prescribed. So, if you descend to the very cheapest of these blended whiskeys, you may be buying some pretty gruesome stuff. Economical blends, yes—cheap ones, *no!*

With blends, distillers are allowed to use up to 2½% of "blending materials." The most commonly used is a special heavy type of sherry, but such goodies as prune juice and caramel are also used.

Tasting these blended whiskeys blind (labels hidden), no mortal man is able to distinguish between most of them. Ergo, *buy the most economical.* Brands are listed in price per oz. of alcohol (the only true *value* norm), best buys listed first.

BLENDED AMERICAN WHISKEY

Nuyens Blend, 86°, $0.38/oz.

Old Mr. Boston Pinch Bottle, 4 years, 80°, $0.39/oz.

Old Mr. Boston Rocking Chair, White Label, 4 years, 80°, $0.39/oz.

Old Thompson Premium, 4 years, 80°, $0.39/oz.

Sunny Brook, 80°, $0.39/oz.

Paramount Preferred, 86°, $0.40/oz.

White Tavern, 86°, $0.40/oz.

Philadelphia Gold Label, 86°, $0.40/oz.

Cream of Kentucky Double Rich, 80°, $0.40/oz.

Kentucky Gentleman, 86°, $0.41/oz.

Hallers Reserve, 8 years, 80°, $0.42/oz.

J. W. Dant Gold Label, 80°, $0.42/oz.

Park & Tilford Founders Choice, 86°, $0.43/oz.

Gallagher & Burton Black Label, 90°, $0.43/oz.

William Penn, 80°, $0.44/oz.

Governor's Club, 80°, $0.44/oz.

Paul Jones, 4 years, 80°, $0.45/oz.

Old Thompson Premium, 80°, $0.45/oz.

Mt. Vernon, 80°, $0.45/oz.

Park & Tilford Reserve, 80°, $0.45/oz.

Nichols Blended, 86°, $0.45/oz.

Bourbon de Luxe, 80°, $0.45/oz.

Barton's American Premium, 80°, $0.45/oz.

Fleischmann's Preferred, 4 years, 90°, $0.45/oz.

Kentucky Gentlemen, 80°, $0.46/oz.

Gallagher & Burton Black Label, 80°, $0.47/oz.

J. W. Dant Gold Label, 86°, $0.48/oz.

Wilson, 80°, $0.48/oz.

Bellows Reserve, 86°, $0.48/oz.

Kessler, 4 to 5 years, 86°, $0.48/oz.

Park & Tilford Carriage, 90°, $0.48/oz.

Bellows Partners Choice, 80°, $0.49/oz.

Carstair's White Seal, 80°, $0.49/oz.

William Penn, 80°, $0.49/oz.

Guckenheimer Reserve, 80°, $0.49/oz.

Schenley Reserve, 86°, $0.50/oz.

PM De Luxe, 80°, $0.51/oz.

Hill and Hill, 4 years or more, 80°, $0.51/oz.

Kessler, 80°, $0.51/oz.

Hiram Walker Imperial, 4 years, 80°, $0.52/oz.

Four Roses, 86°, $0.52/oz.

Calvert Extra, 80°, $0.54/oz.

Four Roses, 80°, $0.56/oz.

Seagram's 7 Crown, 80°, $0.56/oz.

Finally, if you *hate* the taste of bourbon, then your choice should be a light whiskey. These are virtually bourbonless bourbons—that is, the bourbon flavor has been almost completely eliminated by distilling the whiskey at a high proof. The label will read: "Light Whiskey," or "A Blend of Light Whiskeys," or "Blended Light Whiskey."

This is a new breed, introduced only in 1968. The genre arose because Americans seemed to be consistently opting for lighter and lighter drinks. The law was even changed to allow the producers to distill the whiskey differently from straight bourbon, and to age it in used cooperage, whereas straight bourbon must be stored in new oak barrels.

Surprisingly, light whiskey has not been nearly as successful as its producers had hoped.

Here are America's leading light whiskeys, in ascending order of price of alcohol per oz. Once again: *Buy the most economical*—as someone has said about our American politicians, there's not a dime's worth of difference between them.

LIGHT WHISKEYS

3 Feathers Superior Blended, 86°, $0.43/oz.

J. W. Dant, Premium, 4 years, 80°, $0.47/oz.

J. W. Dant Gold Label, 80°, $0.48/oz.

Old Mr. Boston, 80°, $0.49/oz.

Barton Q. T., 4 years, 80°, $0.49/oz.

Park & Tilford, 80°, $0.52/oz.

Royal American, 86°, $0.52/oz.

Crow Light, 4 years, 80°, $0.53/oz.

Melrose Rare, 80°, $0.54/oz.

In case you haven't already noticed it on the shelves, a glance at the above listings will tell you that there are many more 80° American whiskeys made today than there were just a few years ago. Distillers say it's because Americans are now preferring lighter alcoholic beverages. Possibly so, but it is also true that such whiskeys are cheaper to produce and the federal tax on them is also lower. So even if prices have

33 BRANDY

not risen—they haven't—in effect, you are getting less alcohol for your money.

Many and diversified cocktails are made from bourbon, and you could invent one of your own given five minutes and an array of mixes and liqueurs. But the really notable ones, where the whiskey is inspirationally married to the other ingredients, are few in number. The classic bourbon cocktails are: **Manhattan; Mint Julep; Old Fashioned; Sazerac; and Whiskey Sour.**

The truth is that bourbon is not a good mixer—Scotch is even worse. Perhaps that's why true bourbon lovers so often insist on taking their bourbon straight or simply with water. In fact, bourbon is famous for its affinity to limestone water, and American distillers boast of its presence in their whiskeys. "Bourbon and branch" is a byword among whiskey lovers, meaning bourbon and clear spring water. Purists—or snobs, if you will—insist that you should not use common ol' tap water—too "chemicalized" —to mix with good bourbon. Well, now . . . if anyone can detect the brand of water beneath a jigger or two of straight bourbon, they have the world's most educated palate!

Imbibed judiciously, bourbon can be a commendable aperitif, in cocktail form or in its virgin purity. Some recommend it for after-dinner sipping, but that's strictly for the stout of heart! Bourbon's best use is as a nightcap. And to all, saith America's favorite whiskey, a good night.

BOURBON de LUXE KENTUCKY STRAIGHT BOUR-

BON WHISKEY This label was first used in 1911, by L. Eppstein & Sons, in Fort Worth, Texas, and it has never been changed since that date. The label and the name were meant to convey the notion: highest possible quality. And they evidently do. Bourbon de Luxe is good whiskey, light in both flavor and aroma (80°). At $5.90 (quart) it is one of the best-priced of the quality straights. It also comes in a blended whiskey, available principally in the Western U.S. Since 1934, Bourbon de Luxe has been the property of **National Distillers Products Company.** Good whiskey, good price.

BOURBON SUPREME RARE STRAIGHT BOURBON This whiskey is made by the **American Distilling Company**, headquartered in Pekin, Ill. It was introduced in 1937, and is the company's best-selling whiskey: just under 500,000 cases per year. American also markets Stillbrook, Meadwood, and Guckenheimer, to mention a few.

Bourbon Supreme is noted for its smoothness and light body. It is charcoal-treated before it is aged. Also, the price is right: about $5 (fifth). Some claim that it is an excellent substitute for Jack Daniel's, which sells for around $8 (fifth) (Black Label).

There is also a Bourbon Supreme, 6 years old, 90°, which comes in an elegant, tapered "Eagle Bottle." It sells for about $1.50 more (fifth), and may be worth this difference if you collect elegant bottles.

BRANDY Brandy is probably

the oldest of all spirits, dating from the 13th century, and it is certainly the best. It is the noblest—there is no other word—of all liquors. It has been said that one of life's great moments is the first mouthful of a truly great brandy. One spirituous scribe waxes rhapsodic as he evidently begins his working day with a glass of brandy: "As the rare fumosity rises to penetrate the nostrils, an invisible fire tends to illuminate the mind, clearing the webs of thought to more concise articulation"—Robert Lawrence Balzer, *Book of Wines and Spirits* (Los Angeles: Ward Ritchie Press, 1973).

Oh.

But James Boswell in his *Life of Dr. Johnson* said it best: "Claret is the liquor for boys, port for men; but he who aspires to be a hero must drink brandy."

When the word "brandy" stands alone it means brandy made from grapes, just as the word "wine" standing alone means wine made from grapes, not dandelions. Brandy is distilled wine, and is called "the soul of wine." If you want to talk about a brandy made from fruit other than grapes, then you must call it a **fruit brandy.**

Everybody agrees that the greatest of all brandies is **Cognac,** followed closely by **Armagnac.** These are French brandies coming from very specific areas of France: Cognac, from the Charente district, not far from the famed wine district of Bordeaux; the ancient town of Cognac is the heart of the area. Armagnac comes from the hills of the same name in the southwest corner

of France, at the foot of the Pyrenees. There are good brandies made elsewhere in France, but they cannot use either of these hallowed names—they must be labeled simply "brandy." (See **France—brandy** for some of the other French brandies.)

Brandy is made wherever grapes are grown and wine is made, which is to say all over the world. By general consensus the best brandy comes from France, followed, in very vaguely descending order of excellence, from Spain, Portugal, the United States, Germany, Greece, Italy, and Peru. And if that listing doesn't start an international fracas, nothing's apt to. All the national brandies mentioned are individually treated in this book: just look under **Spain—brandy,** etc.

No two brandies are made in exactly the same manner, and, in fact, there are as many ways of making brandy as there are brandy labels. No other spirit has so many different methods of production—which explains why brandy comes in so many types and flavors, shapes and guises. Brandy is the most diversified, variegated spirit in the world. Only one thing is essential: it is a potable spirit distilled from wine.

Almost all brandy is aged at least three years before being bottled. It is matured in oak casks and it is said to improve "in wood" for some 50 years. In practice, the brandy you buy is almost always a blend of brandies of various ages and types.

Remember, however, that once brandy is bottled—like all other spirits—it ceases to improve. In fact, it may deteriorate—or more likely, it will eventually disappear, through evaporation. Those "Napoleon" brandies are pure myth (but note that there are some brandies with the name "Napoleon" on the label).

Brandies do pick up some coloring from the wood in which they are aged, but depth of color is no indicator of fullness of years, for most of the coloring is added artificially, by the simple addition of caramel.

Brandies, and especially Cognacs and Armagnacs, are the "sippingest" of all spirits. One can sip Scotch or rum or gin, it is true, but very few do, at least in these United States. But one should sip fine brandy. And millions do, to their spiritual advancement, the world over.

One caveat, however. Not in outsized balloonish snifters. Those bulbous monstrosities inhibit, not enhance, the bouquet of the beverage. Serve your brandy (Cognac, Calvados, marc, etc.) in a regular all-purpose tulip-shaped wine glass (4 to 11 oz.), or even better, in a normal brandy snifter with a rounded bowl; these range from a mere 2 oz.—quite adequate—to 8 oz.

The tradition of warming one's brandy by cupping the snifter in the palms is authentic and praiseworthy. Warming the spirit—unless you're at a Sahara oasis at 134°—enhances both the bouquet and the flavor.

Since brandies are so highly esteemed in their own right, they have not been incorporated into many cocktails and mixed drinks. But there are a few important brandy-based mixed drinks: **Brandy Alexander, Side Car,** and **Stinger.**

BRANDY ALEXANDER (COCKTAIL)

One of the most beloved of after-dinner drinks. It's also called simply an Alexander, but it's safer to give it its full name when ordering, because otherwise you may get it with gin instead of brandy, a less felicitous concoction.

The Rx: Equal parts of cream (light is heavy enough), brandy, brown crème de cacao. (For a less sweet drink, halve the cacao.) Shake with ice and strain—or blend quickly. For each drink use about 1 oz. of each of the ingredients.

You can buy a ready-made Brandy Alexander (Heublein) but don't. You get half as good a drink at twice as much the money.

BROWN-FORMAN DISTILLERS CORPORATION

George Garvin Brown was the man who started the business, in 1870, and George Forman was an early partner and chief accountant of the infant firm. The company had started as Brown-Thompson, but James Thompson sold his interest in 1890 to found the Glenmore Distillers, which that family still controls.

It is not accidental that a huge 100,000 gallon Old Forester bottle towers over the Brown-Forman corporate headquarters in Louisville, Ky. To the disappointment of visitors, the bottle contains only water. (If it contained Old Forester, it would afford about 8.5 million generous portions or three tall drinks for every single Kentuckian!)

There would have been no Brown-Forman without Old Forester. Old Forester Bourbon—it was originally spelled "Forrester"—was the original bourbon whiskey first made by George Garvin Brown, and it was this name that became the mainstay of the business (for more, see Old Forester).

Brown-Forman made a host of whiskeys in the early days, all of which have long since disappeared: Old Polk, Fox Mountain, White Mills, Gilded Age, and a gaggle of others. After Repeal, with the tremendous demand for whiskey, Brown-Forman, along with everybody else, bottled everything on hand, raw and immature as it might be. The brand names tell all: Here's Luck, Bottoms Up, Possum Ridge. Mercifully, the brands disappeared as quickly as the bad whiskey.

Brown-Forman is probably the only whiskey producer in America that insists on dropping the "e" from "whiskey," as the Scotch and Canadians do. It's Old Forester *Whisky* and Early Times *Whisky*. But they taste exactly like *whiskey!*

Today Brown-Forman is diversified—as is everybody else. Besides its staples, Old Forester and Early Times (the latter purchased during the depths of Prohibition to supplement diminishing stocks), the company also owns the Jack Daniel's Distillery Company of Lynchburg, Tennessee, and the Jos. Garneau Co. (N.Y.C.), which markets French Champagnes (Veuve Cliquot), Italian wines (Bolla and Cella), Anheuser German wines, and Cruse French wines. To add to the confusion, they also market the entire line of Bols liqueurs, Usher's Green Stripe Scotch, Ambassador Scotch, Old Bushmills Irish Whiskey, Martell Cognac, Pepe Lopez Tequila—among others!

BULLSHOT (COCKTAIL) This is a recently invented mixed drink, and a good one, one that was needed. In function it's akin to the **Bloody Mary** (see): a morning or morning-after beverage, a drink to revive one's flagged spirits. Essentially it's simply a long glass of beef consommé with a jigger of vodka. To add zest throw in a teaspoon of Worcestershire sauce, the juice of half a lemon, and perhaps a touch of Cayenne. Mix vigorously with lots of ice, strain, serve. Guaranteed to restore life to all but the extremely moribund.

BURNETT'S WHITE SATIN GIN Most of the famous names in gin are English, London-born. The bottle labels usually aspire to the British look, and most of them succeed. Burnett's is no exception. Its full name is Sir Burnett's White Satin Distilled London Dry Gin. "London Dry" is now simply a generic term, almost without meaning, used to describe the type of dry, not sweetened, gins made in England and the U.S. today.

Burnett's White Satin, like many another London-invented gin, is now American-owned and American-made. It comes from Baltimore, Md., and is made by Seagram's. It is good sound American gin, 86°, in the medium price range (about $5 for 25.4 oz., or fifth), no better and no worse than its competitors.

BUSNEL CALVADOS Some claim it is the oldest known brand of Calvados, and it may well be, for it clearly dates back to at least 1820. Today it is owned by **Ricard**, which makes the popular anise-flavored liqueur of that name. Busnel Calvados commonly comes in two versions in the U.S.: the "regular," La Normande, at about $12 (fifth), and Grande Fine, at $19 (fifth), specially aged and super-delicious. Enjoy, enjoy—if you can afford, afford.

BYRRH It's pronounced *beer*, but there the similarity ends. Byrrh is pure French, invented by a Pyrenees shepherd in 1866, very popular in its native land, and pretty vile to most American tastes. It's a wine-based aperitif laced with quinine and brandy, among other mysterious ingredients. It's bittersweet in flavor, dry and puckerish. No need to check brands—there's only one, still made by the family that first concocted it. It usually costs about $4.20 (fifth).

C

CACAO, CRÈME DE This is one of the world's most popular liqueurs, and small wonder, for it's chocolate-flavored, and chocolate is one of the world's most beloved flavors.

Cacao is three syllables, not two: *kah-kah-oh. Cacao* is simply Spanish for "cocoa," which is English for "chocolate"—approximately.

There are a score and more of chocolate-flavored liqueurs made around the world, of which crème de cacao is only one, although it is by far the most common. For a listing, see under **chocolate-flavored liqueurs.**

Crème de cacao is not precisely as simple a liqueur as it might appear; it is not made simply and solely from cocoa beans. In fact, it ordinarily has a number of other secondary flavoring ingredients, principally vanilla.

Crème de cacao is, of course, very sweet, soft, even heavy. American brands are all quite similar; further, it would be difficult, tasting them blindly (labels hidden), to distinguish between the domestic brands and the imported ones. But if they are carefully tasted side by side, differences are detectable. Thus, **Hiram Walker** Crème de Cacao is relatively bland; **Leroux** is more intense; Jacquin is lighter in body, but with good flavor. European

crèmes de cacao are slightly sweeter than American ones.

Since crème de cacao is almost always used in a mixed drink—or poured over vanilla ice cream, where it performs admirably—and since it varies little from brand to brand, it is probably advisable to buy the most economical.

American crèmes de cacao (mostly 50° or 54°) sell for around $5 (24 oz.). Imports vary from around $6 **(Cusenier)** to $10 **(Marie Brizard).**

CALVADOS It comes from Normandy, France, and it's the greatest apple brandy in the world. It's properly pronounced with the accent on the last syllable, but any reasonable facsimile will do, as long as you get what you're asking for: the genuine article. There are other apple brandies made around the world—our American **applejack** for one—but none of them compare with a fine, *vieux* (aged) "Pays d'Augée" Calvados.

Most Calvados coming into the U.S. has been aged in wood from 5 to 10 years, but you almost have to go to Normandy to get a really old one, 25 to 40 years of age, the optimum.

Calvados ranges in price from around $9 to $12, which is dirt cheap compared with the price of other real fruit brandies. The most common brands seen in the U.S. are **Bellows** (has a 5-year-old, about $9), **Busnel** (very important: has a marvelous Grande Fine, about $19), and **Boulard** Arc de Triomphe, (about $11, consistently excellent).

How to drink Calvados? Not as simple as you might think! See under **brandy.**

CALVERT EXTRA AMERICAN BLENDED WHISKEY The Calvert Distillers Company produces not only this whiskey, but also **Kessler, Four Roses,** Carstairs White Seal, Paul Jones, Antique, Henry McKenna, and Mattingly & Moore, to name only its bourbons and blends. And Calvert, in turn, is only a tiny part of that super-giant of the spirits industry, **Seagram.** Nothing is simple anymore!

If Seagram is adept at anything, it's blending whiskeys. In fact, Seagram got its start blending whiskeys, especially Canadian, in Canada, as far back as 1900. And blended whiskeys have been Seagram's forte ever since. In 1977 Seagram had four of its blends among the 20 top-selling spirits in the land: Seagram's 7 Crown (first), Seagram's VO Canadian (fourth), Kessler (sixteenth), and Calvert Extra (twentieth).

Calvert Extra is good blended 80° whiskey, but on the expensive side (listing under **bourbon**). And it is no better and no worse than—and practically speaking, no different from—almost any other blend. Blended whiskeys are notoriously alike, and it is even difficult to distinguish them, when tasted blindly, from Canadian whisky and American light whiskey.

CALVERT LONDON DRY GIN Calvert is a thoroughly American gin—it doesn't even try to look British, as most American gins do. The whole Calvert operation is a part of that mammoth enterprise, **Seagram Company Limited.**

Calvert gin is smooth, and extremely bland—the company prides itself on the fact that it goes through seven separate distillations in order to render it nonsweet and non-perfumey. English gins, by contrast, tend to leave more juniper and other flavors in the distilled product.

Calvert Gin is a good product, and a good value—it's priced a bit lower than other comparable American gins. You can buy tastier gins—if flavor is what you are after in your gin—but you can scarcely buy a safer and a smoother one.

CAMBAS Andrew Cambas is one of Greece's largest producers of wines and spirits. The firm's brandies are widely distributed. Besides a "straight" 10-year-old brandy (80°, around $8 a fifth), Cambas also makes a V.S.O.P., 15 years old, 80°, around $12.50 (fifth).

Also imported to the U.S. are several Cambas specialties. Their "Delicious" is patterned after the Greek **Metaxa** and is similarly flavored: sweet, heavy, aromatic. It sells for around $8 (fifth). The Mastiha, (see also **Mastika**) is technically a flavored gin, though it is consistently referred to as a brandy. It's flavored with mastic, a resin, just as is retsina, the Greek wine. Both are very much acquired tastes. Mastiha is 90° and sells for around $8 (fifth). Cambas also imports an ouzo, same proof, same price, as Mastiha.

CAMPARI Beyond question Campari is the world's favorite bitters. Angostura is internationally known, but it's used almost solely as an additive and spicer-upper—you splash it and dash it, but you *drink* Campari.

In all the world there are few—or no—bars or pubs worthy of the name where you cannot order Campari. Campari is exported to more than 150 countries around the world, and it is produced and bottled in twenty-six countries. (Bottled Campari is shipped from Italy to some countries, but to others, including the U.S., a high-proof concentrate comes from Campari headquarters in Milan, Italy.) Its sales have skyrocketed over the past several decades. For some unknown reason, Luxembourg leads the world in per capita consumption of Campari.

The founder of the firm was Gaspare Campari, who experimented in the 1860s with countless elixirs, liqueurs, and bitters, many of which he produced commercially until he and his successors finally settled on their single best seller, Bitter Campari. Campari first achieved fame when Gaspare served it in his fashionable café, the Campari, in the stately Galleria Vittorio Emmanuele, a stone's throw from the great Cathedral of Milan. It is there to this day.

Campari is the simplest alcoholic beverage in the world to describe—or the most difficult, as you will. All one can say, finally, is that it is a distilled spirit, with a blending of herbs and distilled water, plus a bit of natural coloring. Nobody is about to disclose what the herbs are—other than quinine and gentian, common to all bitters—so that's just about the limit of our knowledge. The extravagant folio anniversary volume published by Campari in 1960, in some 300 outsized pages, gives not one whit more information. The text only admits that "Bitter Campari is not a complicated preparation, but its recipe, the same as that invented by Gaspare Campari, is—however—jealously guarded and kept in the company's strong rooms."

Campari, like any other bitters, has a very distinctive taste: bitter, pungent, and aromatic, yet with an underlying touch of sweetness. It is also noted for its brilliant red color. Americans are sometimes a bit stunned at their first close encounter with Campari, but it's a taste that can quickly grow on one.

At least part of Campari's success around the world has been due to its extensive advertising, particularly by means of colorful and imaginative posters. For 50 years and more, eye-arresting posters by famous artists have made Campari a very "in" drink.

Besides the mainstay, Bitter Campari, there is Cordial Campari, a sweet, pale-yellow liqueur, with a raspberry base. It has never been nearly as successful as the Bitter Campari, and has been available only in Italy. However, the company is just now beginning to test market Cordial Campari on foreign markets. The firm is understandably moving slowly in this new venture, for fear of confusing the non-Italian drinking public.

Bitter Campari may be taken straight—some hardy souls with hair on their tongues do so consume it. But the vast majority of humankind prefer their Campari somewhat diluted, usually with soda or with sweet vermouth, as in the Americano and Negroni cocktails. In Italy and Switzerland, in fact, Bitter Campari sells by the millions of bottles in small single-measure flasks with the soda already premixed. This is (logically enough) labeled Campari-Soda. The company claims that all the bottles of Campari-Soda produced in Italy in a single year would encircle the entire coastline of Italy—and that's standing the bottles upright. Include Sicily too. Even more incredibly, it is said that a bridge could be built between Europe and the U.S. with all the bottles of Bitter Campari produced throughout the world in three years—and these figures are as of 1960. Today the bridge could probably be a divided highway, with a 20-foot median.

Campari is 48° and sells in the U.S. for about $6.50 (fifth).

CAMUS COGNACS These are excellent French Cognacs ("French Cognac" is at least *somewhat* tautological, as all Cognac, by definition, comes from France), more popular around the world than in the U.S. A recent Camus magazine ad said that in 1976 only 4,116 bottles of Camus Cognac were sold in the U.S.

Best buy is the Celebration, around $13, better than most 3-star Cognacs.

CANADIAN CLUB CANADIAN WHISKY This is the whisky that made Hiram Walker famous. Or more accurately and more simply, that *made* Hiram Walker. The great Canadian enterprise of Hiram Walker–Gooderham & Worts Ltd. would never have come to pass except for Canadian Club.

Hiram Walker, an inventive and enterprising young New Englander, began making his smooth and distinctive whisky near Ontario, Canada, in 1858. He first named it simply Club Whisky to indicate that it was good enough to find acceptance in the most exclusive of men's clubs. When American competitors complained that Walker was being deceptive by not indicating that his popular whisky was Canadian-made, he added "Canadian" to the name. And it proceeded to sell even better! When the Hiram Walker Company changed hands in 1926 at a price of $14 million, $9 million was for the magic name of Canadian Club.

Canadian Club is still the mainstay of Hiram Walker, selling around 4 million cases per year. It is exported to more than 150 countries, and at the present time it is number four on the American market. Year after year, Canadian Club continues to be one of the best-selling whiskies around the world. It may be the most "called-for" name in spirits on this earth.

And with some reason. Canadian Club is one of the smoothest whiskies in the world. It's somewhat more expensive than most Canadians: around $8 (fifth) vs. mostly $5 to $6, but then it's 86.8°, where most are 80°, and it's aged a full six years, though the minimum requirement for Canadian whisky is only two years. It is not guaranteed, however, to either inspire or enable you to do all those wild and glamorous things that the Canadian Club ads depict so matter-of-factly.

It is also true—and this bears constant repetition—that among whiskies of the same type, in this case, Canadian, there is usually scant difference between them.

CANADIAN LTD. CANADIAN WHISKY

It's owned by Fleischmann, it's 80°, it's a good Canadian whisky, and at about $5 per fifth, it's an excellent value.

CANADIAN MIST CANADIAN WHISKY

This good Canadian whisky recently became the property of that formidable distiller of Kentucky bourbons, Brown-Forman, producers of Early Times and Old Forester, to mention only its two best sellers.

Canadian whiskies are all very much alike within a given type, and Canadian Mist is no exception. It would be virtually impossible to distinguish it from other Canadians in a blind tasting. But that is not to say it is not good whisky; it is. It is medium-priced: about $5.50 (750 ml—2 oz. less than a fifth).

CANADIAN WHISKY

If you are not exactly wild about the taste of whisky—few people *really* are—Canadian whisky

may be your kind of ardent spirit. It is the lightest-bodied, mellowest of all the world's whiskies.

American blends and "lights" are light whiskey, certainly, but there is a difference: these American brews are made "light" mainly by the addition of neutral grain spirits, which have no flavor whatever—like vodka—but Canadian whisky uses no neutral spirits at all. It's a 100% grain whisky.

Canadian whisky has become increasingly popular in the U.S. in recent years. Part of this has been the American trend toward lighter drinks. But another part has been the simple fact that Canada makes fine whisky: distinctive, delicate, decorous.

As with bourbons, scotches, and blends, there is not a great deal of difference between Canadian whiskies of the same proof: in fact, they are virtually indistinguishable one from another. Be therefore sagely advised: Buy the most economical.

Here are the leading Canadian whiskies imported to the U.S. in increasing order of price; best values first:

86.6° CANADIAN WHISKIES, (FIFTHS)

Kings Crest, $5.80
Old Mr. Boston Canadian River, $6.39
Seagram's V.O., $7.47
Canadian Club, $7.65
O.F.C. by **Schenley**, $8.25

80° CANADIAN WHISKIES (FIFTHS)

Canadian River, $4.49
Canadian Rare Mark IV, $4.49

Laird's Premium Canadian, $4.75

Barton's Canadian, $4.89

Canadian Breeze, $5.26

Canadian Ltd., $5.27

Canadian Host, $5.49

Canadian Supreme, $5.49

MacNaughton, $5.59

Canada House, $5.60

Canadian Mist, $5.64

Hudson's Bay Canadian, $5.64

Hiram Walker Special Canadian, $5.65

Windsor Supreme, $5.69

James Foxe Canadian, $5.69

Grande Canadian, $5.75

Black Velvet, $5.89

Paddington of Canada, $6.02

Lord Calvert Canadian, $6.15

Seagram's Crown Royal, $10.87

Canadian Masterpiece by **Lord Calvert,** $11.46

CASSIS, CRÈME DE *Cassis* means "black currant" in French, and crème de cassis is a very sweet, low-proof liqueur made from these little black berries. Black currants are grown in the U.S., but the best come from France, particularly the Burgundy region —even more specifically, from the Dijon area. The best cassis liqueurs, likewise.

Cassis (the abbreviated form of the name) is rarely consumed on its own. Its principal use is as a mixer. It is used in two very popular and very happy combinations: Combined with dry (French) vermouth, it becomes Vermouth Cassis; combined with any dry white wine it becomes Kir. Both are the soul of simplicity.

Vermouth Cassis (also called Pompier or Export-Cassis) is the most famous *tall* drink in all of France. Thus:

1 part crème de cassis, 1 part dry vermouth, 1 part soda water, 1 ice cube (no more, no less)

Stir gently, sip gratefully. If you prefer a less sweet drink, of course, the cassis may be halved or quartered (as in hung, drawn, and . . .).

Kir is simply a little cassis mixed with quite a lot of dry white wine. Many toss in an ice cube. Vary the amount of cassis according to your taste. Four parts of wine to one of Cassis is the classic proportion, but that makes a rather sweet drink. Most people prefer about seven to one. Kir is very "in" these days as an aperitif—it's virtually displaced those paralyzing Martinis that used to inundate the scene.

Cassis is an exceptional cordial in several respects: it is extremely low-proof, and it is short-lived. Most liqueurs, even after being opened, will last virtually forever. Not cassis. With its low alcoholic content, it will deteriorate relatively rapidly. After three or four months, it will begin to fade, and in a year's time it will be blaaaah.

Most major American liqueur firms make a crème de cassis, most of them 40°, usually priced from $5 to $6, generally 24 oz. (The lower proofs —Dubouchette and **Leroux,** 35°, Garnier, 36°—should be somewhat cheaper.) These American cassises, to invent an outlandish plural, are not bad, but they are not very good either. European imports are distinctly superior— and distinctly more expensive: $9 to $10 (24 and 25 oz.) (**Cusenier,** at a low, low 30°, is an exception at about $6, 24 oz.). The two oldest and still the best are L'Heritier-Guyot, 36°, and Lejay-Lagoute, 40°, both around $9 (24 oz.).

And let it be noted that black currants are higher in vitamin C than any other fruit. Wherefore if you feel a cold coming on, you are advised to seek solace and healing not in vapor rubs and cold remedies, but in crème de cassis.

CEREMONY BRANDY It comes in two versions: a 5-year-old and an 8-year-old, both "straight" brandies, that is, the product of a single year's harvest and not sweetened, smoothed, or "rectified" in any way. Most California brandies are blends (of various batches) and are rectified by such agents as sugar, prune juice, and sweet wine. This is not necessarily bad, but these are not "pure" or "straight" brandies. Ceremony Brandy is straight, pure, hearty. Also, both versions are made from Flame Tokay grapes—also a plus.

If you like a sweet brandy (Christian Brothers, for example), Ceremony may not be to your taste, not your snifter of the water of life. Ceremony Brandy is on the dry side, particularly the 8-year-old. It is smooth, not soft; heady, not dainty.

The 5-year-old sells for $5.59 a fifth (California) and the 8-year-old for $6.89 a fifth (California), both excellent values.

But having said all this, we return, perforce, to the most basic and most important truth about brandies—indeed, about all distilled spirits: It usually takes an expert (plus a liberal sprinkling of divine guidance) to discern the subtle differences between various brands of brandy. Our most elemental, most earthy advice is simply to buy the most economical.

CHARCOAL - FILTERED Some bourbon labels loudly proclaim that the whiskey has been "charcoal-filtered." They —the labels and the distillers —seem to be saying this with some measure of pride, judging from the prominence of the words on the label. But it really isn't that big a deal. Many spirits—bourbon, vodka, rum, okolehoa (a Hawaiian spirit)—are filtered through vegetable charcoal in order to purify them and remove unwanted congeners, such as fusel oils, various acids, and aldehydes. But other means are equally effective, and charcoal filtering may not be an unmixed blessing, for if the process is too thorough, it may remove some of the desirable congeners, which give that particular spirit its distinctive taste and character.

CHARTREUSE Two of the world's greatest liqueurs, Benedictine and Chartreuse, were invented by cloistered monks, which goes to prove either or both of two things: (1) that monks don't spend all their time telling their beads, and (2) that unto those who seek first "the kingdom of God, and his righteousness, all these things shall be added" unto them (Matthew 6:33).

Benedictine is no longer produced by the Benedictine monks themselves, but Chartreuse, to this very day, after almost 400 years, is still made under the direct supervision and according to the ancient secret formula of the Carthusian monks. The label still says, "Liqueur fabriquée par les Pères Chartreux."

The name "Chartreuse" means three things, in this chronological order: (1) a mountain range near Grenoble, France; (2) A huge Cistercian monastery built there in 1084; (3) a celestial herbal liqueur, yellow or green in color, created and produced there by the monks. The basic formula was given to the Carthusians by a military officer in 1605. That recipe is still in use today, but it has also been added to and improved upon over the course of centuries.

Perhaps the most astounding truth about Chartreuse is that some 130 different herbs, flowers, and fruits are used in its production. Many of these herbs can be found only in the mountains, and when the monks first produced their Chartreuse in Tarragona, Spain, from 1903 to 1938 (after being expelled from France —for the second time), it was said to be decidedly inferior. Today, Chartreuse is produced in both Voiron, near Grenoble, and in Tarragona, but from the identical herbs. In fact, the three monks who are in charge of the French production travel periodically to Spain to supervise the operation there. Today the two liqueurs are identical.

The Spanish - made Chartreuse is sold only in Spain and Latin America. It is not exported to the U.S. The label is the same as the French one except that it says "Chartreuse sae Tarragona."

Chartreuse is made with a base of fine old brandies, and it is aged for at least several years in oak vats. All these things add up to make it one of the world's most noble liqueurs—some say the greatest, bar none.

On the second floor of the distillery at Voiron is the "Herb Room." Only monks ever enter this room. Here is the heart, the secret essence of Chartreuse. Three of the brothers work here daily, tending and blending their myriad herbs, fruits, spices, and flowers. These three alone know the formula for Chartreuse.

Chartreuse is made in two styles: yellow and green. The green is the original, and the stronger of the two, a walloping 110°, the most potent liqueur in the world. The green is also the more complex of the two (it uses some herbs and spices not used in the yellow version). The yellow is sweeter and softer, as well as less expensive, and for both these reasons it is often preferred.

French production alone of Chartreuse is over 1 million liters per year, about two-thirds being green Chartreuse and one-third yellow. And nobody appreciates Chartreuse as Americans do. For many decades now the U.S. has been the world's biggest consumer of the monks' magic medicine.

Several special variations of "standard" Chartreuse have been made down through the years:

A white Chartreuse, very potent, very elegant, was made until 1900. It was called "Elixir des Pères Chartreuse," and today a bottle is worth a king's ransom.

Elixir Vegetal is the original medicinal tonic and digestive, made according to the original 1605 formula, and it is still made today. At a numbing 142° it's guaranteed to effect something and to cure almost anything. It can be purchased at the Chartreuse Distillery, Voiron, France, but it's sold primarily at pharmacies throughout France. Because of its strength it cannot be imported to the U.S.

CHARTREUSE V.E.P. *Vieillissement exceptionnellement prolongé,* "aged exceptionally long") is a mere 108° (compared with the green at 110°), and it's at least 12 years old. V.E.P. is made only in small quantities, and isn't always available. When it is, it sells (in the U.S.) for around $22 (quart). A yellow V.E.P. is also made, at 84°, but it is rarely seen in the U.S.

Chartreuse Orange and Chartreuse Myrtille are two new liqueurs recently created by the monks. They are a sobering, lowly 34°, and are made from green Chartreuse mixed with orange juice for the one and blueberry juice for the other. To date they have not been imported to the U.S.

The celibate, vowed-to-silence Carthusians have never allowed Chartreuse to be advertised by the use of a female, either pictorially or verbally. But today, ironically, the year-around tours of the distillery and aging cellars at Voiron are conducted by "Green Angels" —women clad in sporty light-green outfits, looking more like airline stewardesses than monastery guides.

As elegant as Chartreuse is, you will want to consume it straight up, but somewhat chilled—around 50° is fine—or on the rocks, though even this seems a rather sinful dilution.

But if Chartreuse is simply too stout, especially the green, for straight sipping, you will probably delight in Chartreuse Royale which is simply a good German white wine (Blue Nun will do fine), perhaps 6 to 8 oz., with a bit (a jigger or so) of green Chartreuse added.

And if you want to sink to the ultimate sacrilege you can indulge in a swampwater, an abominable commingling of canned pineapple juice, lime juice, and green chartreuse. Preferably you drink your Swampwater from a mason jar—if no rusty old tin can is handy. It's all quite "in" these days with affluent young people, and it certainly figures to be the most expensive Swampwater to be found this side or the other side of the Slough of Despond.

Yellow Chartreuse (80°) sells in the U.S. for around $12 (23.6 oz.), green (110°) for around $13.50 (both 23.6 oz.). In a Limoges decanter, the green comes to about $25 (23.6 oz.).

CHERI-SUISSE LIQUEUR The label tells most: Swiss chocolate cherry liqueur, from Switzerland. What it does not tell is that this is a superb after-dinner liqueur. It's an enticing cherry-pink in color, it is not cloyingly sweet, it is light-bodied, and it has a wondrously intense cherry-chocolate flavor. It comes in both 52° and 60° and sells—now the bad news—in the U.S. for about $12 (23.6 oz.).

CHERRY LIQUEURS AND BRANDIES Cherries are

found around the world, and so are cherry liqueurs. They are among the world's most popular fruit cordials.

Cherry liqueurs are usually deep red in color—almost always derived from the cherries themselves, not artificially induced—and have a rich cherry flavor, frequently with almond undertones. Various varieties of cherries are used, but the best are the small black bitter Marasca cherries of Europe.

There is one cherry liqueur that goes by a different name: **maraschino.** It's made from the same marasca cherries, tastes much the same as other cherry liqueurs, and is, in fact, simply a cherry liqueur. The only difference—and it's purely accidental—is that cherry liqueurs are usually red, while maraschino is colorless.

The cherry "brandies" of the U.S. and England are not true brandies at all—in fact, the U.S. product must always be labeled "Cherry-Flavored Brandy." The only true cherry brandy commonly available in the U.S. is **Kirschwasser;** it is made wholly from fermented cherries and is high-proof, dry, colorless.

Cherry-flavored brandies are more liqueurs than they are true brandies: they are sweet, deeply colored, relatively low in proof and price.

Almost all American liqueur firms make both a cherry liqueur and a cherry-flavored brandy. They are very similar in taste, composition, and price ($5 to $6, fifth). The liqueur is usually the sweeter of the two, and the lower in both proof and price (by a few cents).

These American liqueurs and "flavored brandies" are not up to the standards of the European imports discussed below. They do not make good after-dinner sipping liqueurs. But for mixing (in cocktails) or flaming (in Cherries Jubilee) they are wholly adequate and admirably economical.

The best-known and probably the best cherry liqueur in the world is Peter F. Heering Cherry Liqueur (Denmark), until recently known the globe around simply as Cherry Heering. (Note: Heering, two e's, not Herring, two r's, the latter a cold dead fish.) Today's label reads simply "Peter Heering Liqueur." It's 49° and sells for around $9 (23 oz.).

And speaking of things Danish, there are some lovely cherry wines imported to the U.S. from Denmark. They're less than half the price of Peter Heering, and they have the same distinctive cherry flavor. One popular brand is Cherry Kijafa, about $4.50 (Western U.S.).

Almost as famous and almost as good—some say better—is Cherry Rocher, made for the past couple of centuries by Rocher Frères of France. The cherries—they use several varieties—together with the pits are steeped in the spirit base for a full two years.

Another excellent cherry liqueur is Luxardo Cherry Brandy, Sangue Morlacco (60°), from Italy. (It's not a true cherry brandy in American terms, but rather a liqueur.) This fine liqueur is not to be confused with **Luxardo Maraschino,** the original liqueur that made the name of Luxardo famous. The Maraschino is made by *distilling* the Marasca cherries (with their pits), and the finished beverage is water-white, whereas the liqueur is made by *infusing* the cherries and pits in brandy, and the beverage is a deep ruby color. Luxardo Cherry Brandy sells for around $9 (25 oz.).

The British are great lovers of cherry liqueurs—they call them "brandies," which they are not. The best-known (and the only one commonly available in the U.S.) is Grant's Morella Cherry Brandy. Grant is the name of the inventor—Thomas Grant, 1774—and Morella is the name of the cherry. It comes in two styles: sweet, labeled "Queens," and dry, labeled "Sportsman."

Another French offering available in the U.S. is Cherry Marnier, 48°, made by the same folks who produce the illustrious Grand Marnier. It's a fine liqueur, with good brandy and almond flavors beneath the cherry. It's a sippin' beverage—and it should be at the price, about $12 (more in the Eastern U.S.), for, note, 22 oz., not the usual 24 oz. or 25.6 oz. (fifth).

Also from France, excellent and moderately sweet: **Marie Brizard** Cherry, 50°, about $10 (23.6 oz.) on the West Coast.

Eastern Europeans are also fond of their cherry liqueur, and from Poland comes Polmos Wisniowka, 80°, at around $10 (fifth), and Polmos Wisniak, 48°, about the same price. Both have a hint of spiciness; the Wisniak is the sweeter of the two. Both are excellent.

From Italy comes Cheristock, 50°, deep red in color, with good cherry flavor. It's a brand name, of course. It sells in the U.S. for around $8.50

for 24 ounces (New York State; 50¢ less in the West).

Another Danish import is Cherry Karise, 49°, by **Leroux**. It's a new creation: semisweet, with a nice aromatic cherry flavor. It goes for about $10 (Western U.S.; add $1 in the East [¾ quart]. Leroux used to make a domestic version of Cherry Karise, also 49° (fifth), at about half the price.

Cheri-Suisse comes from Switzerland, and is often classified as a chocolate Liqueur, as it has a combination chocolate-cherry flavor. But unlike most chocolate liqueurs, the chocolate does not predominate. *Mirabile dictu,* the cherry flavor wins out, making it a beautifully balanced, nonsugary, very tasty beverage. Cheri-Suisse—now the bad news—sells for around $12 (23.6 oz.).

As an economical substitute you might try Hiram Walker's Chocolate Cherry (around $6, 28 oz.), considerably sweeter, and more chocolaty, but at less than half the price, quite admirable withal.

And if none of the above appeals to you, you can always make your own cherry liqueur. One book, *Liqueurs for All Seasons,* by Emilio Cocconi (Wilton, Conn: Lyceum Books, 1975), pp. 38-41, lists no less than five different recipes, and for several of them you need no cherries at all—only cherry leaves!

CHIVAS REGAL SCOTCH WHISKY This is an astounding whisky—with the Scotch-whisky market generally declining, and the higher-priced bottled-in-Scotland Scotches especially hurting, here is this high-priced, premium, 12-year-old whisky gaining in sales. Some of this is certainly due to spirits snobbery, plus a lot of astute advertising — it's the property of super-astute Seagram—but quality would also seem to be a factor.

Chivas is named after James Chivas, the man who first started blending this whisky, around the turn of the century, in Aberdeen, Scotland. It was introduced in the U.S. in 1909, but didn't really catch on until after World War II. Today, Chivas is universally hailed as one of the very finest of Scotch blends. It is currently selling—rather incredibly, at its premium price—a cool million cases a year in the U.S.

Chivas is 86° and sells for around $13 (fifth), expensive even for a 12-year-old. It is evidently worth the difference to its many loyal admirers. And if one sips one's Scotch neat, the difference in quality and finesse *may* be detectable—it certainly will not be in a cocktail, or a long tall Scotch-and-water.

CHIVAS ROYAL SALUTE SCOTCH WHISKY It comes in a *royal* Spode of England bone-China flagon, and has a *royal* price tag, about $42 (fifth). Chivas Royal was created in 1952 to honor the coronation of Queen Elizabeth II. The 21 years of aging parallels the 21-gun salute due to a head of state. The aging of a spirit for such a length of time is, of course, a very costly project. Besides the enormous amounts of capital thus tied up, there is a huge loss of precious liquid due to evaporation and leakage. In 21 years there is more than a 60% loss. It is 80°.

It would seem advisable to sip your Chivas Royal very carefully, very appreciatively, very grudgingly.

CHOCLAIR This is a chocolate-coconut liqueur made under the Arrow label, the property of that giant of the spirits industry, Heublein. It's Heublein's answer to a number of chocolate-coconut liqueurs recently being imported to the U.S. Heublein is apparently rather proud of its Choclair, and has even distributed a glossy booklet filled with glamorous recipes using Choclair. But it's difficult to determine what they're so proud of, for Choclair is a very nondescript liqueur. The heralded coconut flavor is virtually absent. Choclair simply tastes like a second-rate crème de cacao, with some unidentifiable off flavors. It is 54° and sells for around $6 (¾ quart).

CHOCOLATE - FLAVORED LIQUEURS Chocolate has been one of mankind's favorite weaknesses since Columbus brought the first cocoa bean from the New World quite some years ago. Small wonder, then, that chocolate-flavored liqueurs are, overall, probably the most popular of all the world's liqueurs.

The most common is crème de cacao, but there are many others, most of them combining chocolate flavor with one other predominant flavor. Here is a partial listing of those commonly available in the U.S.: Afri-Koko (Chocolate-coconut; Africa), **Choclair**, Choclait (straight chocolate, Switzerland), Chococo (chocolate-coconut, Virgin Islands),

Chokalu (straight chocolate, Mexico), Marmot Chocolate, Sabra, Vandermint, and Veraña (chocolate-orange-citrus, Spain).

These are all "given," proprietary names. Besides these there are a myriad chocolate-with-something combinations that American firms have been coming out with. Hiram Walker has Chocolate Cherry, Chocolate Mint, and Swiss Chocolate Almond, the best of which, and very good it is, is Chocolate Cherry. Leroux has five different chocolate-flavored liqueurs in its repertory: Chocolate Mint, Chocolate-Raspberry, Chocolate-Cherry, Chocolate Banana, and its most popular, Chocolate-Amaretto—these are over and above their regular white and brown crème de cacao. The most chocolate-happy firm of all is the House of Hallgarten, London, Purveyors of fine German wines, which makes an array of no less than seven chocolate liqueurs, its "Royal" line: Royal Banana-Chocolate, Royal Cherry-Chocolate, Royal Ginger-Chocolate, Royal Lemon-Chocolate, Royal Mint-Chocolate, Royal Orange-Chocolate, Royal Raspberry-Chocolate. These are among the world's finest chocolate liqueurs. Hallgarten produces only one other liqueur, Glen Mist.

CHRISTIAN BROTHERS BRANDY In the U.S.A. the name Christian Brothers is associated as much with wine and brandy as it is with the Roman Catholic Church and Christian education. The Christian Brothers, or more properly, the Brothers of the Christian Schools, are a teaching order of the Catholic Church, founded in France in 1684, but the average American associates the name first with spiritous beverages, and secondly, perhaps, with Christian pedagogy.

The Christian Brothers make a lot of both wine and brandy. In fact, the brothers' regular brandy is not only America's largest-selling brandy, incredibly it is the biggest-selling brandy in all the world.

The brothers must be doing something right. More specifically, they're doing two things right: making two good brandies, both of which have been extremely successful.

The long time mainstay of the brothers' brandy production has been their "regular" brandy, first produced in 1945. It is not a great brandy by any stretch of the most soaring imagination, and brandy connoisseurs tend to scowl at the name, but it suits the taste of most non-brandy-leaning Americans: definitely on the sweet side, soft and mellow, with lots of grapiness. It's aged an average of four years.

At the same price, about $5.75 (25.4 oz.), there are better California brandies (see the Listing under United States—brandy) and there are worse ones. But there are none so popular.

A few years ago Christian Brothers introduced a "super-brandy," the X.O. Rare Reserve. The price is a bit super too: about $9 (fifth), by far California's most expensive brandy. X.O. Rare has had a lot of promotion, plus a good press, and even some rave reviews. It is clearly the closest thing to real Cognac ever produced in these United States.

X.O. is made by the old-fashioned pot-still method which produces a full-flavored, heavy-bodied, complex beverage: a boon to true brandy lovers, but qualities that will probably be lost, or abhorred, by the neophyte. In sum: Brandy freaks, rejoice; non freaks, reject.

CIAO LIQUORE This is a light-colored Italian liqueur, with a brandy base, made with an assortment of herbs and spices according to a secret formula—every liqueur in the history of mankind has been made according to a secret formula. It has a slightly bitter, flat, herby taste. The best thing about Ciao is the bottle it comes in: a handsome elongated hourglass type. The liqueur is, well, blaaah. It's 80°, about $10 (fifth).

COATES PLYMOUTH GIN Plymouth gin is so called because, of all things, it originated and is still made in Plymouth, England. Good thinking. Thus, there is Plymouth gin as contrasted with London (dry) gin. Today, however, the distinction is somewhat blurred, and British gin is pretty much British gin. And, truth to tell, gin is pretty much gin. The Plymouth variety, however, is slightly more "juniperish" than London gins—more "ginny" one might say, as juniper is gin's distinctive and distinguishing taste characteristic. Coates is the only distillery in the world making Plymouth gin today.

Coates Plymouth Gin has a long and interesting history. It was first made in 1798, in a Dominican monastery — whether or not it was actually made by the Dominican friars is not clear. A portion of the monastery still adjoins the Coates Distillery.

The Royal British Navy has long appreciated Coates Gin, and at one time every ship leaving Plymouth took aboard 200 cases of the giggly stuff. It is said that the stock was always depleted by the time the ships reached Gibraltar.

Some insist that the only proper way to make a Pink Gin, "Pinkers" to British salts, is with Plymouth gin. So be it.

Coates Plymouth Gin is good, even superior gin. Devotees say that its excellence is due to the softness of the Devon water (Plymouth is in Devonshire County). But for ordinary quaffing or mixing or slurping, Coates Plymouth Gin will go mostly unappreciated, for the differences between gins—Plymouth or London, British or American—are infinitesimal. Coates is 94.4° and sells in the U.S. for ca. $7.50 (fifth), a premium price for a premium label, which very few will duly appreciate.

COCKTAIL Today "cocktail" means simply a mixed drink. A few years ago it meant a short, potent mixed drink, usually sweet. A few years before that it meant a spirit mixed with a little bitters, water, and sugar. Before that it meant a hot drink such as a toddy or shrub (rum or other spirit mixed with fruit juice and sugar).

Nobody knows how the term originated, although there are as many theories—most of them wholly implausible—as there are cocktails. The first printed reference seems to be in an American periodical in 1806, which describes a cocktail as "a stimulating liquor, composed of spirits of any kind, sugar, water, and bitters—it is vulgarly called *bittered sling*, and is supposed to be an excellent electioneering potion."

If the origin of the name is unknown, the origin of the reality is not. The cocktail, at least as we know it today, clearly originated in the U.S. in the late 19th century. (Folks, of course, had been mixing and heating wines and spirits, herbs and spices, from time immemorial, but these were not "cocktails" in our sense of the word.) It was during Prohibition that cocktails skyrocketed in popularity, and the reason was obvious: *Something* had to be done to all that vile bootleg booze to make it quasi-palatable.

The number of cocktails is endless, almost infinite. There are as many as there are heads to invent them, and mouths to drink them. New cocktails are invented daily. The producers of spirits stay awake nights imagining fanciful new cocktails. These days it's mixed drinks that sell spirits—witness the incredible surge in tequila sales in the past decade, due almost wholly to the popularity of the Margarita and the Sunrise. Some years ago the United Kingdom Bartenders' Guild listed more than 8,000 known cocktails and mixed drinks. A recently published American bar guide (*Jones' Complete Barguide*, by Stan Jones, Barguide Enterprises, L.A., 1977) lists—with recipes—more than 5,000.

Almost any alcoholic beverage can be mixed with any other alcoholic beverage, and/or with spices or bitters or sugar or herbs, and the result will not be undrinkable. But it will usually be highly forgettable. Over the course of the decades, only a handful of truly memorable cocktails have been invented. All of the great, classic cocktails will be found in this book, plus a sprinkling of recent creations. They are as follows:

Whiskey (bourbon, rye, blend) base; **Manhattan, Mint Julep, Old Fashioned, Presbyterian, Sazerac, and Whiskey Sour.**

Scotch base: **Rob Roy** and **Rusty Nail,** and **Scotch Cooler.**

Rum base: **Bacardi, Banana Cow, Cuba Libre, Daiquiri, El Presidente, Hot Buttered Rum, Mai Tai, Piña Colada, Planter's Punch, Rum Cooler, Rum Punch,** and **Rum Swizzle.**

Brandy, (Cognac, Armagnac, Pisco) base: **Brandy Alexander, Pisco Sour, Portuguese Coffee, Side Car,** Pisco Punch (see under **South America** brandy), and **Stinger.**

Gin base: **Gimlet, Negroni, Pink Gin, Ramos Gin Fizz,** and **Singapore Sling.**

Vodka base: **Black Russian, Bullshot, Dry Martini, Harvey Wallbanger, Moscow Mule, Screwdriver, Seattle Mist,** and **Sundowner.**

Tequila base: **Freddie Fudpucker, Margarita, Sangrita, Tequila Sour,** and **Tequila Sunrise.**

Other base: **Black Velvet** (Champagne), **Glogg** (aquavit), **Golden Cadillac** (Galliano), **Grasshopper** (Crème de menthe), **Irish Coffee** (Irish Whiskey), **Jordan Blend** (Kahlúa), and **Pink Squirrel** (Crème de noyau).

COFFEE LIQUEURS Coffee has long been one of mankind's favorite beverages, but only recently have coffee-flavored liqueurs begun to keep pace. In the past several decades, coffee liqueurs have become extremely popular, and brands, both domestic and imported, have been proliferating like amebae.

Coffee liqueurs are both diversified and distinctive — because coffee is so diversified and distinctive. For example, chocolate is pretty much chocolate, and chocolate liqueurs are really pretty much the same. But coffee is not simply coffee. There are almost as many different coffees as there are coffee brands, and there are almost as many different coffee liqueurs as there are brands.

Here are a few of the names under which coffee liqueurs are sold in the U.S. today:

Bahia (Brazil)

Brazilian Gold Coffee Liqueur (Brazil)

Café (France; Marie Brizard brand)

Café de Love (Mexico)

Caffe Lolita (U.S.)

Coffee Espresso (Italy; Stock brand)

Coffee House Liqueur (U.S.)

Coffee Liqueur (U.S.; De Kuyper brand and Bols brand)

Crème de Café (U.S.; Arrow brand, Leroux brand)

Crème de Mocha (or Moka)

Espresso Coffee Liqueur (Italy)

Galacafe (Italy: Stock brand)

Gallwey's Irish Coffee Liqueur (Ireland)

Kahlúa (Mexico)

Koffie Mente (U.S.; De Kuyper brand)

Liquore di Coffee (U.S., Mohawk brand)

Mocaffee (Holland; Bols brand)

Pasha (Turkey)

Royal Irish Coffee Liqueur (Ireland)

Sabroso (Mexico)

Tia Maria (Jamaica)

Besides all of the above, plus those not listed, there are a host of coffee-flavored brandies, almost all of them American-made. They are virtually all 70°, and that is one of two principal differences between them and coffee liqueurs: their higher proof. The second major difference is that they are not as sweet as the coffee liqueurs, and for this reason they make for better straight-up sipping than do the liqueurs. Practically every major American liqueur firm makes a coffee-flavored brandy, and there is not much to distinguish between them. This is not to say that they are poor beverages. It is to say that they are all equally good beverages. Coffee-flavored brandies sell in the U.S. for between $5 and $6.

In fact, coffee-flavored brandies—sometimes they're called "Coffee & Brandy. (To totally muddy the waters, J. W. **Dant** markets a "Coffee Liqueur & Brandy," which should be classified as a coffee liqueur, not a coffee-flavored brandy, at least because of its low proof, 42°)—are consistently your best buys among coffee-flavored beverages. The coffee liqueurs are almost always considerably more expensive, and they're not all that much better.

Since coffee liqueurs and even coffee-flavored brandies are quite sweet, it is important that they be served icy-cold if you're taking them straight. A little heavy cream floated on top makes the host a connoisseur. If you do it too often, a fat connoisseur.

The best-known cocktail using a coffee liqueur is the **Black Russian**, and it was this drink alone that has accounted for the recent ascendancy of Kahlúa in the land.

There are many other coffee-liqueur cocktails, from the Dirty Mother (equal parts of brandy and coffee liqueur) to the Xochimilco (2 parts of coffee liqueur to 1 part of cream), for the hardy (or fool-hardy) and intrepid (or trepid) souls.

Coffee liqueurs vary as much in price as they do in quality. The American-made ones, of course, are generally cheaper than the imports, ranging from as low as $4 **(Bols)** Coffee Liqueur (fifth) to as much as $10 (Leroux Crème de Café, Stone Jug, quart). Imports vary almost as much in price, ranging from around $7 **(Sabroso,** 23 oz.) to a high of $11 or more (Pasha, fifth, and Gallwey Irish Coffee Liqueur, 23 oz.)

Excluding coffee-flavored brandies—which, as mentioned, are probably your best value of all—here is a listing of some of the most commonly available domestic and imported coffee liqueurs, listed in descending order of excellence: (best listed first) Café de Love, (Mexico), Tia Maria, Pasha, Kahlúa, Galacafe, Sabroso, Bahia, El Toro.

COGNAC The name resounds of red-velvet elegance and expensive cigars. Cognac is the classiest of the world's classy drinks. It is almost universally acclaimed as the finest of the world's brandies, of which there is a mighty horde — here's one of mankind's most distinguished spirits.

Cognac is a proud and noble name and it can be used only of the brandy produced in a very specific delimited area of southern France, the Cognac region. All Cognac is brandy, but not all brandy is Cognac—it only wishes it were.

Cognac is the most expensive spirit in the world for two principal reasons. First, because it's expensive to make; it takes at least ten bottles of wine to make one of Cognac. The distilling process is slow and exacting. Second, Cognac is expensive to keep. It costs money to store anything—hippopotami, whiskey, diamond earrings—and it costs lots of money to store Cognac because of the unconscionable length of the time involved, up to 50 and even 100 years for some of the very rare ones, and because of the tremendous loss due to evaporation. It is estimated that in the Cognac region 25,000 bottles evaporate every single day—the "angel's share."

Even standard Cognacs are at least 5 years old when they go to market, and 20 years is not at all exceptional.

There is no place in the entire world where the human nose is more esteemed and honored than in France's Cognac region. Cognacs are commonly a blend of dozens of different spirits—at times, even hundreds—and it is the human nose that must detect the subtle differences between batches and vintages, must select the ultimate "perfect" blend. Cognacs are endlessly swirled and sniffed and inhaled—and spat out—drat!—by expert tasters. In no other business on earth are machines and computers more useless than here. Only the highly trained, acutely sensitive human proboscis is effective in the land of Cognac. Alas, poor Cyrano, if he had only known . . . but then, who nose?

Liquor and wine labels the world over are notorious for their impreciseness and confusing jargon, especially when they happen to be in a foreign tongue. But none can be more mysterious, at least to the "foreigner," than Cognac labels, with their stars, their alphabetical abracadabra, their invocations of the name of Napoleon, and their calling themselves "Champagne."

First, the word "Champagne" on a Cognac label has nothing whatever to do with that esteemed bubbly wine from the northern reaches of France. "Champagne" on a Cognac label goes back to the fact that *champagne* in French originally meant simply "field" or "area." The Cognac district is divided into six subdistricts, carefully defined by French law. These are officially ranked, from first to sixth place, according to the excellence of the Cognac they produce. The two highest-ranked districts are (in order) Grande Champagne and Petite Champagne. If a Cognac is produced in either of these specified areas, it may put that designation on its label. More often, however, it will be a blend from the two regions and will call itself "Fine Champagne" (pronounced *feen,* not *fyne*).

The other districts, in decreasing order of excellence, are Borderies, Fins Bois, Bons Bois, and Bois Ordinaires. These lesser designations are only rarely seen on a Cognac label.

The alphabet soup on the Cognac label? Surprisingly, the letters stand for English words, not French. It all started back in the 17th century when Britain became France's most important market for Cognac— which it still is, two centuries later:

The alphabet:

C—Cognac

E—Especial

F—Fine (pronounced "fine," not "feen")

M—Mellow

O—Old

P—Pale (paradoxically used for the oldest Cognacs, which are also the darkest in color— evidently paleness was highly esteemed back in the 17th century)

S—Superior

V—Very

X—Extra

You may find the letters in almost any combination on a label: V.S., Very Superior; X.O., Extra Old; S.F.C., Superior Fine Cognac. But the most common combination is V.S.O.P., Very Superior Old Pale.

There is no French law governing the use of this alphabetical mishmash, so a firm may actually use the letters according to its own whim. In practice, however, the usage is pretty well standardized, and you may trust any given combination of letters to denote one specific *type* of Cognac. Thus V.S.O.P. almost universally denotes a firm's *ordinary* top-of-the-line Cognac, on a par with its "Fine Champagne." Note the word "ordinary"—most of the large Cognac firms make a small amount of very special, very aged Cognacs—commonly up to 40 years, and even up to 100—often in special crystal decanters, and extremely expensive. Hennessy has its X.O. Decanter bottle (average age, 35 to 50 years) at about $37; Martell, its Cordon Bleu Baccarat Decanter at $75; Gaston Briant Le Paradis Grande Champagne (75 to 95 years old, rarely available—luckily) at over $100; and undisputed victor, Rémy Martin with its 250th anniversary bottle (average age over 50 years) at a tidy $280.49. (These prices are all per 25.6 oz., a fifth, not per case!)

V.S.O.P. denotes a well-aged Cognac, of the 20-year-old type. Experts say that despite its lofty price tag (around $17) V.S.O.P. is a good value, for you're getting twice as good a Cognac for only a few dollars extra.

Cognac's stars are probably the most misunderstood of all the abracadabra. The stars do not indicate the age of the Cognac, at least not directly. Different firms use the stars differently, but there is a general consensus that three stars designates the firm's "standard" Cognac, a Cognac usually about 5 years of age. Some American brandy producers (see **United States—brandy**) have adopted this sorry starry business, but it's even more meaningless there.

As for the name of Napoleon on a Cognac label, forget it; it's pure hokum, or fancy. It's a prestige word without any real significance. It does not denote a Cognac, or even a type of Cognac that Napoleon favored, much less one that existed during his lifetime. (If it had been in the barrel since 1821, it would have long since evaporated, and if by some miracle it had been in a bottle these 150 years, it would be no better and no worse than the day it was bottled, for Cognac, like all spirits, ceases to change, for better or for worse, once it is corked and bottled.)

The word "liqueur" on a cognac label does not mean that this is a sweet beverage, in the manner of a true liqueur, but only that this is a well-aged Cognac. But they all are!

A final word of caution: Once opened, do not keep a bottle of Cognac too long, especially if the air space in the bottle is large. It will slowly—over several years' time—lose some of its zing and/or zang. The experts' stern advice: Drink up!

Having said all these good things about the noblest of all spirits, it must be confessed that Cognac is often an acquired taste, particularly for Americans, who today favor light drinks. Cognac is intensely concentrated, fiery and heady in both bouquet and flavor. The Cognac fumes are such that people working in the *chais* where it ages are in constant danger of being overcome by the heaven-ascending vapors.

Speaking of things celestial, the area of the *chais* where the very finest, most ancient Cognacs are stored is called *Le Paradis.*

If you are a sincere searcher

after Cognacs, the place to start may be with brandies, especially French or American ones, which are essentially mild forms of the more intense and austere French masterpiece.

Cognac abounds in famous names: Martell, Hennessy, Courvoisier. This is one spirit, perhaps the only spirit, where the name on the label is the best assurance of quality. Here are the biggest, most famous, most reliable Cognac firms, in alphabetical order: Bisquit (pronounced *bis-kwee;* has nothing to do with the thing you eat), Courvoisier (pronounced *koor-vwahs-yay*), **Delamain, Denis-Mounié,** Gaston de la Grange, **Hennessy, Hine, Martell, Monnet,** Baron **Otard** (pronounced *oh-tar*), and **Rémy Martin.**

There are other, lesser-known firms that also produce excellent Cognac, and these you can research yourself by the tasting thereof!

Fine Cognac, of course, is to be sipped slowly, lovingly, meditatively, appreciatively—it must never be demeaned by adulteration in a cocktail! For information on how to drink Cognac, type of glasses, etc., see under **brandy.**

Cognac is the best of all spirits to cook with. At the price, however, you won't want to use it to flame your lowly hamburgers. But remember your Cognac with roast duck, Tournedos, Steak au Poivre, Cherries Jubilee—almost any fine food will be improved with a jigger or two of Cognac. For a culinary spectacular, heat the Cognac, toss it over the dish, light it—and step back.

COINTREAU Cointreau is both the name of a French liqueur firm and the given name of an orange-flavored liqueur—really a triple sec—which is the specialty and best seller of the firm of Cointreau. For details on the liqueur, see under **triple sec.**

The firm of Cointreau was founded in Angers, France, in 1849. Today, it is worldwide, with thirteen distilleries, and with sales in more than a hundred countries.

A full line of cordials under the Cointreau label used to be produced in the U.S. in Pennington, N.J. This was discontinued in 1970, and the Cointreau line was merged with the Regnier line, a label the company had already been using around the world. Today the Regnier labels still bear the name of Cointreau, but only in small print, at the very bottom.

COLLINS A Collins, in today's usage, is a tall drink, with lots of ice, lemon juice (usually), and a sweetened spirit. The best-known is the **Tom Collins,** made with gin. A John Collins is the same drink, but made with true Holland gin. (Some also use the term for the same drink when made with bourbon or blended whiskey, but this is really a misnomer.) Any spirit may be used, however, and then it becomes a Rum Collins, Bourbon Collins, etc.

COLONEL LEE KENTUCKY STRAIGHT BOURBON WHISKEY Bourbon fanciers have often hailed this whiskey as being a good value and possessing good quality, though more skeptical souls might question the validity of any such value judgments when it comes to bourbons of the same type. Some claim they can taste the limestone flavor in Colonel Lee. Maybe. But in any case, the price is right, about $5 (25.4 oz.) and it is good standard Kentucky bourbon, but note also that it is only 80°.

CONGENERS (OR CONGENERICS) This is a very important word in the world of spirits, for congeners are what give a particular spirit—Scotch, rum, bourbon, whatever—its own individual taste and character. When ads boast of a particular beverage's "smoothness" or "deep flavor" they are talking about the presence or absence of congeners.

Chemically, congeners are an extremely diversified gang and include such questionable individuals as aldehydes, ketones, fusel oils, esters, and furfural.

If a spirit is distilled at very high proof—190° and over—almost no congeners are "brought over." The result is neutral grain spirits: "neutral" because lacking in all taste, odor, and color. This is virtually pure ethyl (beverage) alcohol. If you give a Russian-sounding name to it, you've got vodka. If you give it a wee flavoring of juniper, you've got gin.

If a spirit is distilled at a low proof, 160° or less, it will be loaded with congeners and you will have a heavy-bodied, distinctively flavored spirit such as bourbon, malt whisky, or tequila.

Congeners can be removed by various processes such as charcoal-filtering, or they may be "improved" by aging the beverage in wood.

CONTI ROYALE BRANDY It's a full ten years old, made by the East-Side Winery of Lodi, Calfironia, the heart of California's brandy industry. (The romantic name of the winery, East-Side, comes from the less romantic fact that the winery is located on the eastern side of the town). This brandy is 80° and has a nice aroma and good rich flavor. It sells for around $8 (fifth) in California, but is not often available elsewhere.

CORDIAL MÉDOC The name means, more or less, a liqueur from Bordeaux (France), and that's pretty much what this is: a French liqueur made in Bordeaux (by J. A. Jourde). It's made with aged claret, an English name for red Bordeaux wine, blended with **Curaçao, crème de cacao,** and a bit of brandy (or Cognac); it's further flavored with herbs and fruits. Cordial Médoc is reddish in color, sweetish in taste, with the cacao (chocolate) flavor predominating over the Curaçao (orange).

For the record, "cordial" is a synonym for 'liqueur," and Médoc (pronounced **May-dock**) is synonymous with great wine. It is perhaps the most important wine district of the most important wine country in the world.

Cordial Medoc was formerly known as Jourde's Liqueur. It sells in the U.S. for around $10 (24 oz.).

CORDIALS The word is precisely and exactly synonymous with **liqueurs.** "Cordial" was once more commonly used than "liqueur," but today the opposite is the case. A few American liqueur producers still use the word on the labels of some of their products.

CORN WHISKEY To most Americans, corn whiskey means simply *bad* whiskey. It reeks of secret mountain stills, Georgia moonshiners, pursuing revenooers. We know where the homebrew comes from, but where the corn whiskey comes from is a secret still.

This popular picture is not entirely unfounded. Much moonshine is corn, and a lot of legitimate commercial corn whiskey is pretty raw stuff. Some good corn whiskey does get made, though—it's light, yet distinctive. It should proudly proclaim its age. If it does not, beware and eschew!

To qualify as corn whiskey it needs only to be made from at least 80% corn (maize), and to be distilled (like all whiskey) at less than 190°. No aging period is required (as it is with bourbon: two years minimum), nor must it be stored—if it gets stored at all—in new charred barrels, as must bourbon and rye. "Corn Likker's" most commendable feature is undoubtedly its lowly price.

Corn whiskey comes in all manner of ages, proofs, and shapes. Here are America's leading brands listed according to price per ounce of alcohol. Notice the wide variation, mainly due to the age of the whiskey.

A.M.S. Kentucky Straight, 86°, $0.43/oz.

Southern Pride Straight, 100°, $0.44/oz.

Georgia Moon, 30 days, 80°, $0.48/oz.

Platte Valley Straight (stone jugs), 7-9 years, 86°, $0.60/oz.

McCormick Platte Valley Straight (corn jugs), 6 years, 86°, $0.72/oz.

CORONET V.S.Q. BRANDY It looks for all the world like a high-class imported brandy or Cognac, and is often mistaken for precisely that, but it's as American as apple pie— or bourbon whiskey. It's made by the giant Schenley Distillers, headquartered in Fresno, California.

The V.S.Q. on the label is about as esoteric as R.F.D. and means, in American, Very Special Quality. Coronet's Very Special Quality is that it's a very light brandy, slightly sweet, nicely grapy. It mixes well—indeed, Schenley advertises that it's "made for mixing."

Coronet Brandy is neither better nor worse than a host of other California brandies at about the same price, about $5 (somewhat more in the Eastern U.S.), but is a rip-off at $6 (fifth) or more.

COURVOISIER COGNAC Cognac and brandies are constantly invoking the name of Napoleon. Most of this is sheer Madison Avenue. Courvoisier used to put both the name and figure of the Little Corporal on every single bottle of Cognac they produced, some 20 million per year. Every label boasted: "The Brandy of Napoleon." Today only the top-of-the-line labels call upon the name and/or silhouette of Napoleon. But is it the brandy of

Napoleon? Was it? It isn't—no brandy in the world today dates back to the days of Napoleon (d. 1821).

Was it? Was it Napoleon's choice? A weak "perhaps." It's possible—remotely. Nobody is quite certain whether the emperor was enamored of the brandies (today, say Cognacs) of Emmanuel Courvoisier. It is certain, however, that the Courvoisier empire was founded during the days of the First Empire

With such a romantic background—whether true or false—it seems almost sacrilegious that today Courvoisier is the fief and domain of the giant Canadian spirits firm of **Hiram Walker**. But so it is in this age of conglomerates.

Such amalgamation by a huge parent concern is not necessarily bad; sometimes it is even helpful. In the case of Courvoisier it has been neither good nor bad. Courvoisier Cognac has simply continued to be its old reliable, refined, tasteful self since Hiram Walker took over in the mid-'60s.

Courvoisier does not make its own Cognac—it buys Cognacs, mostly young ones, from others and then blends and ages these spirits in its own *chais*. Courvoisier distills not a single drop of Cognac—nor, for the matter of that, do they own a single grapevine. Courvoisier is strcitly a *negociant*: a merchant-producer.

In this case this seems to be advantageous, for it allows them to devote more time and attention to the blending and aging of Cognacs.

Courvoisier Cognac come in four different grades. Three Star, V.S. (Very Special) is

popular and good, with a touch of sweetness; costs about $12.50 (fifth). V.S.O.P. is aged 4 to 5 years and is "bigger" than the V.S.; it costs about $15 (fifth), and for Cognac-fanciers, is worth the difference. Napoleon Fine Champagne averages 15 to 20 years old and is a fine bottle of Cognac, but at the price, about $27 (fifth), there are others (e.g., Camus Napoleon) that are better. Extra Vielle—it means "Extra Old"—is about 50 years old. And it has a price to match: about $50 (fifth). It's an elegant, snobbish bottle of spirits, but not in the top ranking of Cognacs in this high-society price range. If you're on the market for a Cognac of this super quality, you might look for **Hennessy** Extra, a mere $37 (25.4 oz.) or **Martell** Cordon Argent, around $68 (fifth).

CRÈME It's French, it's pronounced *krem,* and it means "cream." It originally meant "the best," as in "the cream of the crop," but today, as applied to liqueurs, it simply means one of exceptional sweetness.

There are innumerable crèmes produced around the world. Here is a sampling of the more readily available ones:

crème de almond
crème de ananas (pineapple)
crème de banane (banana)
crème de cacao (chocolate)
Crème de café (coffee)
crème de cassis (black currant)
crème de celery (celery seeds)
crème de fraises (strawberry)
crème de framboise (raspberry)

crème de mandarine (tangerine)
crème de menthe
crème de mocha (or moka)
crème de noyau
crème de prunelle (plum)
crème de recco (tea)
crème de roses
crème de thé (tea; pronounced *tay*)
crème de vanille (vanilla)
crème de violet
crème d'Yvette (violet)

CRESTA BLANCA BRANDY

Cresta Blanca is an old and respected name in California wines—the label has been around for almost 100 years. Cresta Blanca Vintage Brandy was the company's first venture into the world of spirits, and it was well ventured, for this is an excellent California brandy. A vintage brandy is a rarity anyplace in the world—in California it is wholly unique.

The first bottling was in 1966, and that is still the current vintage. Supplies are getting low, however, so look for a 1969 Cresta Blanca Vintage Brandy to appear sometime in 1979. The winery feels that '69 was the best vintage year for brandy since '66. *Videamus*—Latin for "we'll see."

None of this is to say that a vintage brandy is necessarily better than a nonvintage one. It is only to say that a vintage brandy is necessarily different. Since brandy is made wholly from grapes, and grapes do differ vintage to vintage, there is a difference between brandies of different vintages. But this is necessarily a minuscule difference, detectable perhaps to an expert, but scarcely to the ordinary consumer.

On the other hand, the fact that the winery has taken the trouble to produce its brandy wholly from the grapes of a particular vintage is proof positive that the producer considers this beverage something special, and we may legitimately presume that he has lavished special love and care upon it.

Cresta Blanca Vintage Brandy is made entirely from Flame Tokay grapes—another plus—and comes in an attractive champagne-shaped bottle. Like all California brandies, it retains some of the sweetness of the fresh grapes; it is balanced and has good flavor. It is aged in both new and used cooperage (American white oak), and this seems to contribute to the brandy's smoothness.

Cresta Blanca Vintage Brandy sells for around $7.25 (fifth). There are good California brandies available for less, but this one seems to be worth the difference.

Convinced that one good brandy deserves another, in 1977 Cresta Blanca came out with a companion brandy to its Vintage: St. Emilion Brandy. The name derives from the fact that the brandy is 100% from St. Emilion (or Ugni Blanc) grapes. That's already a step ahead, for this is the grape primarily responsible for the greatest of all the world's brandies: Cognac. Further, this brandy is 100% pot-stilled, as Cresta Blanca proudly points out. Pot-stilled means that the brandy is made in old fashioned, inefficient pot stills, as contrasted with modern, continuous (or column) stills, which are much more efficient but produce a more *dispirited* spirit, a blander, less tasteful beverage. Further, this new brandy is priced exactly the same as its kissin' kin brandy, Vintage, about $7.25 (fifth).

If you're looking for a typical bland, slightly sweet, soft brandy, choose the Vintage. If you are a two-fisted, cigar-chompin' brandy freak and lover of Cognacs, the St. Emilion is your potion.

CRIBARI BRANDY This is a new brandy from an old winemaker. Cribari has been making wine in the U.S. since approximately the year 1—that's only A.D., however, not B.C.—but came out with this brandy only in 1976. Cribari Brandy is light, slightly sweet, quite decent. It's one of California's most economical brandies, a good value at about $5 a fifth (in California).

CROW LIGHT WHISKEY Light Whiskey was introduced in 1972 to meet the growing demands of Americans for lighter spirits. Light whiskey is milder than American blends, but for some reason, light has never quite caught on. One of the mere handful of lights that "made the cut" was this youthful, not Old, Crow. (That's not to say that Crow Light is not a mature whiskey —it's a full 4 years old.) It was probably the familiar name of Crow that enabled Crow Light to survive at all.

Light whiskies are notoriously alike—they are even difficult to distinguish (tasted blindly) from American blends and from Canadian whiskies. They all sell for about the same, about $5 (fifth), and are of like quality. Crow Light is 80° and is no better and no worse than its partners and peers. Which is to say, it's good light whiskey, reliable, light-bodied, tasty enough.

CUBA LIBRE (COCKTAIL) This is simply a glorified Rum-and-Coke, but long live the difference. The Cuba Libre is the only civilized way to combine rum and cola—it's the presence of the lime that makes all the difference. The recipe for the authentic article:

> 1 jigger rum (light or dark; some recommend mixing them), juice of ½ lime (squeeze by hand; mechanical squeezers get too much oil from the rind), rind of the lime (just toss it in), ice cubes. Cola—fill tall glass to top
> Salud!

CUBA—RUMS These used to be among the finest rums in the world. No longer, because Cuba—or Cuber, as Jack Kennedy used to say—is now populated by bad guys, and Cuban rums no longer find their way to the U.S. Well, *verdad* to tell, Cuban rums have changed not one whit. They're still excellent, light-bodied, golden-colored, tasty. But you'll find a lot more Cuban rums in Moscow than you will in Phoenix or Peoria.

(JOSE) CUERVO TEQUILA Only a few years ago, to Americans Jose Cuervo Tequila was not simply *the* tequila—it was tequila itself. There was virtually no other. Today, with tequila's sudden rise in popularity and the proliferation of brand names, this is no longer the case. Cuervo Tequila is still the *numero uno* seller in the U.S., it is true, but consumers are surrounded by a sea of other brand names.

Much of Cuervo's success has certainly been due to incessant promotion on the part of Heublein, Inc., its sole importer. When Heublein acquired Cuervo some dozen years ago, it was selling in the neighborhood of 20,000 cases per year—in 1976 it sold something like 500,000 cases!

Nobody denies the purity and excellence of Jose Cuervo Tequila—it's universally acclaimed—but two things need to be noted. First, Cuervo Tequila, ounce for alcoholic ounce, is among the highest-priced in the land (see table under **tequila**). After all, *somebody* has to pay for all that advertising. Second, it is unquestionably true that all tequila imported to the U.S. is reliable and *sabroso,* and there is scant difference between brands. Ordinarily—especially if you're going to be making Margaritas and Sunrises—buy the most economical.

Cuervo comes to the U.S. in the two standard versions: White, 80°, selling for around $7 a fifth (somewhat cheaper on the West Coast), and Gold, Cuervo Especial, 86°, around $7 (fifth) in California (more on the East Coast). Also available on occasion is Jose Cuervo 1800, a beautiful and aged tequila, at around $11.50 (fifth).

CURAÇAO Curaçao is first of all the name of an island off the coast of Venezuela (formerly the Dutch West Indies), and then it is the name of one of the world's finest orange liqueurs.

Curaçao is the progenitor of all orange liqueurs, for it was the first one ever made, almost 300 years ago, by the Dutch from bitter oranges from the island of Curaçao. Gradually the liqueur came to be called by the name of the island, and finally Curaçao has bcome a generic name for a type of orange liqueur, even when the fruit from which it is made does not come from the island.

Originally the liqueur was made from the entire orange, but today only the peel is used. The orange is not the sweet one Americans are accustomed to, but the bitter orange, which quite illogically is green-skinned even at maturity. The skins are often dried and shipped abroad, especially to Holland and France, where the best Curaçaos are still made. The Dutch are mad about their Curaçao and make it in a variety of colors, one for every mood: blue, green, brown, orange, red, and water-white. The normal and natural color, however, is reddish-brown.

Curaçaos are made with various spirits as their base: rum, brandy, even port wine, but most commonly with a high-proof alcohol.

American-made Curaçaos are generally as good as European-made ones. (This is a happy exception to the rule; other European liqueurs are invariably superior to their American-made counterparts.) In fact, many European liqueur firms—**Bols, De kuyper,** Garnier—make a Curaçao for the American market in their subsidiary plants in the U.S.

Here are some of the made-in-the-U.S. Curaçaos: **Leroux,** Garnier, **Hiram Walker,** Dubouchette (all 60°); **Old Mr. Boston** (54°); **Arrow** makes a blue Curaçao besides a regular (both 54°), as does **Bols** (both 60°) and **De Kuyper** (orange, 60°, blue, 54°). All of these Curaçaos sell between $6 (24 oz.) and $7 (fifth) in New York State, and about a dollar less in California.

From Europe we have **Marie Brizard** (France), at about $10 (23.6 oz.) in the Eastern U.S., but not that much better than American versions. **Cusenier** (France) has an 80° Curaçao, an excellent value at about $6 (24 oz.). Garnier (France) has a 60° Curaçao, at about $10 (24 oz.) compared to their American-made product at half the price, and the European-made Curaçao is nowhere near twice as good as the American version.

Some liqueur firms make a citrus liqueur they call simply "Orange." In effect it is a Curaçao. Marie Brizard has one, 76°, around $10 (24 oz.).

Cusenier's Orange, 80°, is both old and famous. It uses Armagnac as its base, making it akin to Grand Marnier, but here the orange flavor predominates, not the brandy. At about $6.50 (24 oz.), it is a marvelous value. Leroux has a new import (from France) entitled Cognac with Orange, 80°, for around $10—it deserves to be snifter-sipped. Dolfi has the best of both nomenclatures, calling their product Curaçao Orange Sec, packaged in a little brown jug.

CUSENIER LIQUEURS In 1857, Eugene Cusenier started making liqueurs in his home at Ornans, a small town in the Jura Mountains of eastern France, an area noted for its fruit orchards. Today Cusenier (*key-zen-yay*) liqueurs are known around the world. Cusenier products now flow from five different distilleries scattered across France, though the liqueurs come solely from the main plant near Paris.

Two Cusenier liqueurs are particularly famous: **Freezomint,** a great favorite in Britain, and Orange, perhaps the only liqueur that truly challenges Grand Marnier. Cusenier liqueurs are rather difficult to find in the U.S., but they're usually worth the effort.

CUTTY SARK SCOTCH WHISKY "Cutty Sark" first means "short skirt" in the dialect of the Scots. Secondly it is the name of a famous sailing vessel, the last of the great clipper ships, those lean, graceful, bygone greyhounds of the sea.

The Scotch whisky that now bears that name was first called Berry Brothers Scotch, after the Berry Brothers who had been making it in London since the mid-19th century. George Berry had come up from Exeter to London in 1803, to take over his grandfather's coffee mill at No. 3 St. James's Street. The Berrys are still there (today it's Berry Brothers & Rudd). And it's still a fashionable spot.

In 1923 the Berrys were casting about for a more dashing name for their whisky, when the *Cutty Sark* came into port. At lunch that day at No. 3 St. James's Street, Francis Berry declared that "Cutty Sark" would be the new name. The Scottish-born American artist, James McBey was there, and he immediately sketched the clipper on a sheet of yellow paper, together with the old fashioned, rough lettering, "Cutty Sark Blended Scots Whisky." Not "Scottish" insisted McBey, but "Scots," the more correct adjective.

Cutty Sark has been under full sail ever since. From 65,-000 cases shipped to America in 1951, this Scotch—whoops, Scots—whisky sold more than 2 million cases in the U.S. in 1977. It has suffered some slippage, however, in recent years—along with other bestselling Scotches such as J&B, Dewar's, and Johnnie Walker Red—and, in fact, it lost its position of No. 1 Scotch in the U.S. to J&B in the early 1970s. In 1977, Cutty was in third place, behind J&B and Dewar's, but sales are now holding steady.

Berry Brothers & Rudd Ltd. has always prided itself on Cutty Sark's lightness in both color and taste. Indeed, these qualities seem to have been precisely what has endeared it to the American drinking public. Cutty Sark is an elegant, light-bodied whisky. It's 86° and is priced along with other quality Scotches: around $8.50 (fifth).

There is now a sister ship to Cutty Sark: 12-year-old Cutty 12, appropriately priced at around $12 (fifth). The Company boasts that it too is light and smooth, "with finesse and gentility." Rex Harrison says he likes it—he's grown accustomed to the face, and taste.

And, the original *Cutty Sark*, refurbished and sparkling, is still to be seen, in all her 19th-century splendor, on the River Thames at Greenwich near London.

D

DAIQUIRI (COCKTAIL) The Daiquiri is perhaps the most popular of all rum drinks—in the U.S. it certainly is. And happily so, for it's one of the simplest and best: rum, lime, a bit of sugar, that's it. The name comes from the Daiquiri iron mines of Santiago, Cuba, where American laborers, around 1900, invented this inspired admixture to restore their flagging spirits and aching backs after a hot day in the mines.

There are two versions of the Daiquiri: the "plain" and the "frozen." The plain is made with cracked ice and then strained; the frozen is made in a blender with cracked ice and blended at high speed until it is slushy. Almost everybody nowadays prefers the slurpy frozen version:

1 jigger light rum (Puerto Rico, Virgin Islands), Juice of ½ lime—never lemon! ½ cup or more cracked ice.
Put into a blender, blend at high speed until slushy.

To add variety to your Daiquiri diet, you can add an exotic touch by simply adding a little something to the basic recipe—or invent a Daiquiri of your own, like a Rutabega or Irish Potato version.

Peach Daiquiri: Add ½ fresh peach, sliced—you don't even have to peel it.

Mint Daiquiri: Add 6 fresh mint leaves.

Pineapple Daiquiri: Add canned pineapple: 4 chunks, or 6 tablespoons of crushed.

Banana Daiquiri: Add 1 banana sliced.

DAMIANA First the name refers to a small Mexican shrub (*Turnera aphrodisiaca*) said to have aphrodisiac properties. After that, it's the name of a Mexican liqueur, with the same kind of a reputation. You can believe that as you will, and you may also feel deeply about flying saucers and Easter bunnies.

As a liqueur, damiana has all the forcefulness and potency of a marshmallow. It's one of the most nondescript, effete liqueurs in the history of distilled spirits. Happily, it is not imported to the U.S. It's popular in Mexico, however—they work hard down there on their *machismo*—and one popular brand, Guaycura, made in Guadalajara, has two very *macho* Indian braves on the label.

(J. W.) DANT Al Capone may have been less secretive about his liquor operations than are the J. W. Dant people. They make an array of spirits and liqueurs, but they're not talking. Not even the parent Company, Schenley, is that close-mouthed! And Dant has some good spirits at some good prices. Most notable perhaps is

66

their Olde Bourbon by J. W. Dant, a straight bourbon which comes in both 80° and 86°. Their J. W. Dant Charcoal Perfected also comes in both 80° and 86°; it is technically not a bourbon according to the Treasury Department; it is a consistent best-seller though it has suffered some slippage in recent years, as have so many straights.

Dant also makes a Bottled-in-Bond Bourbon—100°, selling for around $6.25 (fifth), and a blend, J. W. Dant Gold Label, 80°. The firm also markets a Canadian whisky called, again, J. W. Dant, and a Scotch answering to the same name. Besides all these whiskies, Dant also has a complete line of liqueurs which are safe, standard American cordials, rather economically priced.

DAVIESS COUNTY KENTUCKY STRAIGHT BOURBON WHISKEY Knowledgeable bourbon lovers have long hailed this whiskey as one of the best values around. It's light-bodied, mild in flavor, with a touch of sweetness. If you're not a seeker after big brawling bourbons, Daviess County may be for you. It's 80°, owned by **Fleischmann**, and sells for about $5 (fifth).

DE KUYPER LIQUEURS It's pronounced dee-Ky-purr. The name and antecedents are thoroughly Dutch: Johs. de Kuyper & Zoon was founded in Rotterdam, Holland, in 1695. Today the firm is located in Schiedam, Holland, and it is still producing liqueurs and Dutch gin, just as it has for the past 280-plus years.

The De Kuyper liqueurs seen in the U.S., however, are Dutch only in name. All are made in the U.S., in Cincinnati, Ohio. The American De Kuyper Co. is a division of **National Distillers Products Company.**

De Kuyper makes a full range of liqueurs, plus a few unique ones: Delecta Liqueur, 65°, an imitation Benedictine; Lemonique Lemon Liqueur, 45°, made from tangerines; and the latest offering, Wild Strawberry Liqueur, 45°.

De Kuyper liqueurs are dependable, moderately priced, wholesomely and wholly American. You can buy better—if you're willing to pay twice the price—and you can buy for less, if you're venturesome.

DELAMAIN TRÈS BELLE GRAND CHAMPAGNE COGNAC ("PALE & DRY") The name of Delamain is an old and revered one in the Cognac world. Delamain is a relatively small operation, and only one of its Cognacs is commonly available in the U.S., the Pale & Dry. But it's well chosen, for this is a fine bottle of Cognac. It seems specifically designed for the connoisseur: extremely dry, elegant, with a lovely finish. It's about 30 years old, sells for about $20 (fifth). In its price range (the same as **Courvoisier** V.S.O.P. or **Hennessy** Bras d' Or) it is a "best value."

DEMERARA RUMS Here are rums that don't come from a Caribbean Island. But almost. Demerara rums come from Guyana, formerly British Guiana, a small land on the eastern (Caribbean) coast of South America. The rum is named after a river running through the land. Some of these, like some Jamaican rums, are shipped to London for aging, and then they're called London Dock rums. They're very fine.

Demerara rums are one of the darkest of all rums, but don't let the darkish hue deceive you, the rum is rather light-bodied, lighter in flavor than most Jamaican rums. Demerara rums are delicate and fruity, especially flavored with fruits and spices. At one time raw meat was tossed into the brew to enhance the flavor. Don't depart this world without having tried a tot of Demerara rum.

DENIS-MOUNÍE GOLD LEAF COGNAC For the price, around $10, this is a good value in Cognac, the finest of the world's brandies. It's light, slightly sweet, almost oily. Denis-Mouníe is a French firm, with some 150 years of Cognac experience. Its products are better known abroad (especially in England) than they are in the U.S. They also make a V.S.O.P. Grand Fine Champagne Cognac, about $12 (fifth) also a good value.

DETTLING KIRSCHWASSER Dettling is a respected name in the world of premium eaux-de-vie. Three Dettling products are commonly found in the U.S.: a "regular" kirschwasser, 92° and 96° (about $20 a fifth), a 12-year-old Reserve Exceptionnelle Kirsch, 86° (about $25 a fifth), and an Elixir William's

Pear Liqueur, 70° (about $18 a fifth). These are all top-flight beverages, with top-flight prices to match.

DEWAR'S WHITE LABEL SCOTCH WHISKY It's pronounced *Doo-ers* and its always been a pronounced success. It all began in 1846 when John Dewar, a part-time distiller and full-time shopkeeper, decided to sell his own private distillation from a small shop in Perth, Scotland. Dewar's Whisky was soon recognized in surrounding towns and villages, then throughout Scotland, and finally, the world. Dewar is said to have been the first man to bottle his whisky—up to that time retailers stocked whisky in barrels and customers brought their own containers to be filled.

Dewar's today is owned by the giant spirits conglomerate **Distillers Company Limited,** of London. It is imported and distributed in the U.S. by Schenley.

Dewar's label boasts that the whisky has received "50 Gold & Prize Medals," beginning in 1886, and extending to 1930. Probably any Scotch that's been around as long as Dewar's could say much the same thing. Nonetheless, Dewar's White Label Scotch is excellent whisky. The company boasts that White Label is a blend of more than forty "fine mature whiskies drawn from the hundred distilleries throughout Scotland." Dewar's is not an economical Scotch: it sells for about $8.50 (fifth). It's 86.8°. Dewar's top-of-the-line is its 12-year-old **Ancestor,** a kindred spirit.

DISTILLERS COMPANY LIMITED This is a giant international spirits conglomerate, founded in 1885, based in Edinburgh, Scotland, and in London, England. It has assets of almost $1 billion.

The public ordinarily thinks of various brands of spirits as being locked in ferocious rivalry. This is often the case. But far from always. There are many huge spirits conglomerates around the world, owning numerous "competing" brands. Distillers Company Limited is one such.

The various brands are ordinarily independent operations, and even compete with each other, but they are commonly owned and directed.

The Distillers Company Group includes, among others, these brands of gins: **Booth's High & Dry, Booth's** House of Lords, **Gordon's London Dry, Tanqueray Special Dry,** Boord's Dry, and Boord's Old Tom.

The principal Scotch whiskies owned by the D.C.L. Group are these: **Johnnie Walker, Dewar's White Label, Vat 69, White Horse, Haig & Haig, Black & White,** and **King George IV.**

One of the subsidiaries of Distillers Company Limited of Edinburgh and London is Distillers Company, Limited, of Delaware. It has distilleries in Linden, N.J., Plainfield, Ill., and Union City, Calif. This is a wholly owned subsidiary of the parent company; its best-known products are **Gordon's** Gin and Vodka, **Booth's** Gin and Vodka, Boord's Gin and Vodka, and Black Cat Gin.

Distillers' darkest day came in the late 1960s, when a terrible outcry against the firm was heard throughout all England. The outrage was directed against Distillers as the former distributor of the tranquilizer thalidomide, which caused mothers who had taken the drug during pregnancy to give birth to deformed babies. The drug was withdrawn from the market in 1961, but some 400 deformed "thalidomide" babies had already been born. The subsidiary pharmaceutical company has since been sold, but only after much foot-dragging and legal maneuvering. Distillers eventually paid more than $50 million in damages.

DRAMBUIE The name sounds the way it tastes: exotic, very Scottish. Drambuie smacks of honey and whisky, is redolent of heather and perfume. The name is an abbreviated form of the Gaelic "The drink that satisfies." That it does.

Drambuie probably has the most romantic history—fact or fable, it matters not—of any beverage known to man. The story is that Prince Charles Edward Stuart—*his* liqueur, it says on the bottle—better known as Bonnie Prince Charlie, pretender to the throne of Great Britain, when fleeing for his life after the battle of Culloden Moor in 1746, was befriended by and hidden in the home of a certain Mackinnon family on the Isle of Skye, part of the Hebrides, in the northwest corner of Scotland. Charlie eventually made it to France and safety, and to repay the Mackinnons, the prince gave them the only thing of worth he possessed after his headlong flight, the formula for the royal family's private liqueur. For some 150 years the

Mackinnons guarded their secret formula, making Drambuie—the name wasn't registered until 1892—only for themselves. It was only in 1906 that the Mackinnons began to produce Drambuie commercially. To this day a Mackinnon is still at the head of the Drambuie Liqueur Co., Ltd.

And if there is anything that the firm is insistent upon, even today, it is the fact that the Drambuie formula is a deep dark never-revealed secret. Certainly Drambuie Ltd. is not about to publicize its prize recipe, but this is true of every major (and minor) liqueur in the world. These are carefully guarded trade secrets. It is said that the late Mrs. Gina Mackinnon, head of the firm, mixed the "essence" of Drambuie in her own home, with her own hands, and then carted it to the plant. She evidently had a very large kitchen, not to mention very large hands, for Drambuie is Great Britain's largest-selling liqueur, as well as the U.S.'s largest-selling imported liqueur.

Beyond question, Drambuie is one of the world's most elegant liqueurs. It has often been imitated, but never exactly duplicated. The imitations—Glen Mist, Glayva, and Lochan Ora, to name three that are imported to the U.S.—are also fine liqueurs, quite similar to Drambuie, yet different.

Drambuie is made of the finest ingredients: excellent aged Scotch whiskies (mostly malts), heather honey, and a host of secret herbs.

There is only one Drambuie, of course—it is a patented, invented name—and it is 80°. It sells for right around $12 (23 oz.). It is too good to sub-

merge it in some nameless, formless mixed drink. With only one exception: the Rusty Nail, where it is enhanced by Scotch whisky.

DRY MARTINI (COCKTAIL)

This dainty, innocent-looking little cocktail is probably the most famous mixed drink ever blended by the human hand— and one of the most paralyzing, ounce for ounce. It is no more intoxicating, of course, than any other drink with the same amount of alcohol—it only seems so! But remember that using a 90° gin, and mixed at 8 to 1, you are imbibing a straight 84° drink! That scarcely qualifies as a "mixed" drink.

It is well named, the *dry* Martini, for it consists wholly of dry gin, with a bit of dry vermouth. And over the course of the years it's become ever drier and drier, with less and less vermouth, more and more gin. It started out, back in Prohibition days, as a 1-to-1 mixture: half gin, half vermouth. The traditional proportion through the '40s and '50s was 3 to 1, and today it's 8 to 1 or even 12 to 1. Worse yet, true Martini freaks pour the vermouth over the rocks, throw away the vermouth, then pour their gin over the aromatized rocks! Some bartenders use an eyedropper or an atomizer for the vermouth. Others, it seems, pass the vermouth cork over the gin, or whisper "vermouth" over the glass. Indeed, one gin ad pushes the ultimate Martini: all gin, forget the vermouth. That is at least logical, even if it isn't civilized. Straight gin is what it is and let it be called that, and know that it is one of the most barbarous drinks known to man.

Small wonder then that the once sovereign Martini has begun to decline in popularity. Or more accurately, Gin on the Rocks has continued to decline and true Martinis have almost ceased to be made.

When the Martini was in its heyday, people used to speculate endlessly about its origin. Today nobody much cares. But that history may be served, let it be noted that most authorities agree that the first Martini was assembled in 1862, by one Jerry Thomas, in Martinez, California, across the bay from San Francisco. It was first called the Martinez. But after two Martinezes, it came out *Martini*—or *Tee Martoonis*.

A Martini is a concentrated little spitfire of a drink, even when made in its proper classic proportions. Proceed with caution. With its faint touch of vermouth, it's a sophisticated, intriguing glassful, deserving of its bygone glory. Tastes differ of course, as to the "correct" proportion of gin vs. vermouth, but the Martini is not true to its noble heritage if the proportion is more than about 10 to 1.

Nobody in the world is fussier about the mechanics and ritual for making a mixed drink than Martini fanciers. Here is the only proper and civilized procedure for assembling the true, the classic Dry Martini: 1. Refrigerate the gin and vermouth beforehand—a Martini must be bitingly cold. 2. Chill stemmed 3-oz. cocktail glasses. 3. Fill a pitcher with dry, hard—frozen ice cubes or cracked (not crushed) ice. 4. Pour gin over ice—it should smoke if all's right. 5. Pour dry vermouth over ice. 6. Stir vigorously—this is important. 7. Quickly strain into frosted glasses. 8. Garnish with a stuffed green olive. 9. Consume enthusiastically, if gingerly. P.S. Add a cocktail onion instead of a green olive, and you've got a Gibson.

DUBONNET   (COCKTAIL)
Classic and good. Thus:

1 jigger red Dubonnet, ¾ oz. gin, dash orange bitters (optional), ice cubes (3 or 4) Stir, strain into chilled cocktail glass (4 oz.). Garnish: twist lemon peel.

E

E & J BRANDY The E. and J. are, of course, Ernest and Julio Gallo—who else? It was inevitable that the giant Gallo Winery (Modesto, Calif.) would someday get into the brandy business, and that someday was 1977. E. & J. was introduced in typical big-time, high-splash Gallo fashion, with a media blitz the likes of which no brandy of this world has heretofore enjoyed.

The label says "Extra Smooth" and, yea, E. &. J. is that. Like all Gallo products, E. & J. is made to please the mass of humankind, not the connoisseurs and "freaks." It's soft, smooth, with noticeable sweetness, the epitome of all that is good in California brandies. At about $5.50 (fifth), it is in the moderate price range, slightly cheaper, for example, than Christian Brothers and Paul Masson. Good California brandy, decently priced.

EARLY TIMES KENTUCKY STRAIGHT BOURBON WHISKY Nobody knows where the name came from, for this is a very old whiskey, dating back at least to 1860, and probably beyond that. The label is now owned by the Brown-Forman Distillers Corporation (Louisville, Ky.), famed for its Old Forester brand. Early Times was purchased at a most unlikely time:

in the depths of Prohibition (1923). Brown-Forman had been granted a license to sell "medicinal" whiskey to wholesale druggists, who in turn could sell it to anyone who could pry a prescription from a physician. A veritable epidemic seems to have followed, for medicinal bourbon was in great demand. To augment their dwindling supplies, Brown-Forman purchased the entire stock of Early Times Whisky, along with bottles, packaging, and labels.

Note that Early Times is a "whisky," not a "whiskey." Only Canada and Scotland ordinarily drop the "e." But Brown-Forman does it with both Old Forester and Early Times, for no demonstrable reason.

Early Times is the second-best-selling bourbon in the world (after Jim Beam), with sales of over 2 million cases per year. Bucking a persistent trend over the past 5 years, Early Times is one of the very few bourbons that has increased its sales. The increase was probably due to its being heavily promoted as an ideal mixer. Early Times is medium-bodied, smooth, well matured. It is 80° and sells for somewhat under $6 (750 ml, 2 oz. less than a fifth).

EAUX-DE-VIE The singular

is eau-de-vie and it's French for "water of life." The plural is eaux-de-vie, and both are pronounced *oh-deh-vee*. It was the first name given to brandy. Today the word "brandy," standing alone, usually means brandy made from grapes. If it's "brandy" made from some other fruit—cherries, plums, raspberries—it's called eau-de-vie in Europe (or *alcools blanc*, "white alcohol," as they're colorless), and fruit brandy in the U.S.

Eaux-de-Vie are elegant, dry, fiery, and expensive. For more, see fruit brandies.

EGGNOG It's historical, it's American, it's festive, and it's delicious. The Eggnog was invented in the U.S. of A., back around 1775; The name probably was originally 'Egg-and-Grog."

There are unnumbered Eggnog recipes around, and everybody and his or her great-aunt has his or her favorite. All are good, certainly, for any Eggnog is better than no Eggnog. But most of them can be reduced to two basic Eggnogs, the Single Eggnog (makes one drink) and the Holiday Eggnog to serve many.

INDIVIDUAL EGGNOG

Combine:

1 egg, 1½ tsp. powdered sugar, 1 oz. rum (preferably Jamaican), 1 oz. blend (or bourbon), 4 to 6 oz. milk, 3 or 4 ice cubes

Shake or stir vigorously, strain into a chilled highball glass. Sprinkle with ground nutmeg.

You can use almost any liquor—brandy, Cognac, applejack, gin—or such wines as Madeira, sherry, or port, or any combination of any of the above. The traditional spirits are brandy and rum, and as of the 20th century, whiskey.

EL PRESIDENTE (COCKTAIL) This Cuban drink, fit for a president, comes in two versions, one with sweet (Italian) vermouth, the other with dry (French) vermouth. Savor and see which you prefer.

Combine in a medium-sized glass:

1 jigger light rum, ½ oz. Curaçao, ½ oz. sweet or dry vermouth, dash Angostura Bitters, 3 or 4 ice cubes

Stir vigorously. You can twist a hunk of orange peel over the glass, for the oil, but don't add it to the drink.

EL TORO COFFEE LIQUEUR On the label it has a stirring picture of a fearless matador and charging *toro*, surmounted by the word "Genuino." And it's about as genuino as tequila made from daffodils. If you continue reading to the bottom of the label, and if you have at least 20-20 vision, you'll read, in infinitesimally minute print, that *genuino* El Toro is "prepared and bottled by the American Distilling Co., Inc." of Pekin, Ill., etc.

El Toro is, of course, a direct imitation of that illustrious Mexican liqueur, Kahlúa. But a sad, pale imitation. It has some coffee flavor, of course, but the off flavors, especially in its bitter aftertaste, are glaring. It is 53° and sells for some $3 less than Kahlúa (about $7, ¾ quart) but is no bargain. And would not be at half that price.

EL TORO TEQUILA Even gringos know that the name means "The Bull." But it's no bull the way this Mexican tequila has been growing in popularity. It must be the quality, at least in part, for it's not the price: El Toro sells for the same as Jose Cuervo (around $7.50 a fifth). El Toro is indeed good, reliable tequila. But it's no better and no worse than a score of other tequilas, almost all of them selling for less. (For a complete listing, see under **tequila**.) It's 80°, comes in both White and Gold.

EVAN WILLIAMS KENTUCKY STRAIGHT BOURBON Black Label. Here's a sleeper, one to look for. Evan Williams is fine Kentucky bourbon, decently priced for a straight 90° (around $6 for 25.4 oz.) It's made by the Heaven Hill Distilleries, Inc., of Bardstown (Nelson County), Ky., one of the very very few independent whiskey makers left in the U.S. The name comes from the man sometimes credited with building the first distillery in Kentucky. It is clear that Williams began making whiskey as early as 1783. Sophisticated bourbon freaks give Evan Williams high marks, and the mere fact that it is an independent brand is somehow bracing. On the other hand, one must always remember that the differences between bourbons of the same type (straight, blend, whatever) and the same proof are few and slender.

F

FIOR d' ALPE This name, meaning "Flower of the Alps," has a thousand variants—Fior di Alpi, Flora di Alpi, Flora Alpina, Fiore d'Alpe, Fiori Alpini, Fior d'Alpi, Flora della Alpi, and more, but you get the idea.

By whatever name, "Flower of the Alps" is a rather sweet, aromatic, slightly pungent, gold-colored Italian liqueur in a tall white bottle, with a "Christmas tree" inside: a small twig with crystallized sugar clinging to it.

The name is a generic one, not a proprietary (privately invented and owned) one. Which is to say: various firms make Fior D'Alpe. The best known, and probably the best, and the only one commonly imported to the U.S., is Fior d'Alpe from Isolabella, 92°, selling for $9 to $10 (23 oz.)

Fior d'Alpe is a most pleasant liqueur, lacking perhaps the stature of greatness, but smooth, appealing, refreshing. Some say it is reminiscent of yellow Chartreuse.

FLEISCHMANN DISTILLING COMPANY Fleischmann's has been making whiskey—and yeast—since the end of the Civil War. The first plant was in Riverside, Ohio; today there are Fleischmann plants and distilleries in Ohio, New York, New Jersey, Pennsylvania, Maryland, California, Kentucky, and Nova Scotia.

Fleischmann's purchased the name, stocks, and assets of the reputable Daviess County Distilling Company of Owensboro, Ky., in 1940, when their own stock of aged whiskey was running low. Today all Fleischmann whiskeys are produced at Owensboro.

In 1929, Fleischmann's became the property of the giant conglomerate, Standard Brands, purveyors of such well-known goodies as Planters Peanuts, Royal Jell-O, Baby Ruth, Butterfinger, etc.

Besides the Fleischmann-brand products (whiskey, vodka, and gin), and Daviess County Bourbon, the Fleischmann Distilling Company today markets these brands of spirits: Canadian Ltd. Canadian Whisky, Capercaillie Malt Scotch, Churchill Scotch, Fonda Blanca Tequila, Numero Uno Tequila, Romanoff Vodka, Ron Trigo Rum, White Tavern Vodka, and White Tavern Scotch.

Among imports the firm markets Gaston Cognac, potcheen (Irish whiskey), Duval Vermouth, and the entire line of Garnier liqueurs.

FLEISCHMANN'S GINS Fleischmann's has the distinction of being the first American firm to distill dry gin on American soil—that was in

1870, at Riverside, Ohio. And Fleischmann's has been doing commendably ever since. The firm makes two good Gins: Fleischmann's Dry Gin, 86°, at around $5 (fifth), and White Tavern, 80°, at around $4 (fifth), an exceptional value.

FLEISCHMANN'S KENTUCKY STRAIGHT BOURBON WHISKEY

Though the Fleischmann Distilling Company is now diversified, marketing all manner of spirits and liqueurs, its heart still seems to be with its bourbons and blends. At least that's where it appears to do best. All Fleischmann whiskeys are made in Owensboro, Ky., though they are bottled and blended in various plants, east and west.

Fleischmann's makes two straight bourbons: a 100° Bottled in Bond, and an 86° Fleischmann's Select. These are two good bourbons, both economically priced. Fleischmann's Bond sells for about $6 (fifth), and the Select for around $5 (fifth).

FLEISCHMANN'S PREFERRED BLENDED AMERICAN WHISKY

Though its sales had been declining a few years ago, this venerable blended whiskey has recently begun to show some growth, and it is still one of the best-selling blends on the American market. It is also one of the very few blends still being marketed at 90°. It is medium-priced (see comparative listing of blends, by price, under **bourbons**).

Fleischmann's Preferred is good American blended whiskey—some claim it is as good as Seagram's 7 Crown— and even at 90° it sells for less, about $5 (fifth), than does the 7 Crown at 80°, about $5.50.

FORBIDDEN FRUIT

This citrus-flavored liqueur is one of the very few American-born-and-bred liqueurs. Almost all of the world's great liqueurs originated in Europe—Forbidden Fruit is a notable exception. And notable it is, for this is a fine beverage.

Forbidden Fruit is made principally from the shaddock (or pummelo), a citrus fruit, close kin to the grapefruit. (Originally it was made wholly from the shaddock; today other citrus fruits as well as apples are used.) Forbidden Fruit has a brandy base and is infused with honey; it is reddish brown in color and has a bittersweet taste. It is moderately sweet. Ironically, Forbidden Fruit is more popular in Europe than it is in the land of its birth.

It is sold in a unique round bottle the shape of a grapefruit and encircled with golden filigree. In the U.S., Jacquin Forbidden Fruit, 60°, sells for $7.95 (fifth) in California, somewhat more in the Eastern U.S.

FOUR ROSES AMERICAN BLENDED WHISKEY

Nobody knows how the name arose—no pun—though there are legends aplenty. All of the stories have red roses playing a leading role.

Four Roses has been a popular blended whiskey for almost 90 years. It was first produced by the Frankfort Distilling Company of Kentucky, and was sold, very literally, lock, stock, and barrel to the Seagram organization during World War II.

This is good, dependable blended whiskey. Unfortunately it is among the most expensive of our American blends (see the listing of blends by price per ounce of alcohol, under **bourbon**). Remember that there is almost no humanly discernible difference between brands of blended whiskey.

Four Roses is available in two proofs, 80° and 86°. The 80° sells today for almost $6 (fifth), rather much for a blend.

FRAISE (or FRAISE DE BOIS) It's pronounced *frez*, and in French it means simply "strawberry;" fraise de bois (prounounced *deh bwa*) means "wild strawberry." But it is also the name of a rare, expensive, fragrant **fruit brandy** from Alsace, made from strawberries. Strawberries do not readily lend themselves to distillation, and true fraise—not simply a strawberry liqueur — is light, subtle, gentle, and very expensive.

FRAMBOISE It's pronounced *frahm-bwahz*, and basically it means "raspberry," but in this case, it means brandy made from raspberries. Framboise is a true **fruit brandy**, not merely a liqueur made from neutral grain spirits and flavored with raspberries. That's why it's colorless, just as all distilled spirits are when first produced. Framboise is not aged.

Framboise is becoming increasingly popular in the U.S., and a few brands are now being imported, principally from Alsace. At its best, framboise is a smooth, richly fla-

vored spirit—small wonder Americans are now beginning to pursue it. Sad to relate, however, it comes dearly: $15 (fifth) and upward.

FRANCE — BRANDY Almost everybody agrees—except some ardent and loyal producers of American brandy— that France makes the best brandies in the world. That's overall. But that is not to say that every bottle of French brandy is better than every bottle of American brandy. There are individual bottles of American brandy that are far superior to particular bottles of French brandy. Clear? (If not, forget the whole thing, and just remember that French brandies are the world's finest—most of the time.)

The two greatest names in French brandy are **Cognac** and **Armagnac.** Cognac and Armagnac were places, geographic locations on a map, long before they became Brandies. Which is another way of saying that only brandies produced in those very specific, delimited areas can call themselves by those two hallowed names.

But there are many other brandies produced in other parts of France. They call themselves simply brandy. They can be excellent—and they can be terrible. They are, of course, half or a quarter of the price of most of the illustrious Cognacs and Armagnacs, and they can be marvelous values.

Here are some fine French brandies to get you launched, until you discover your own favorite: Cusenier ($6.29 a fifth; *kee-sen-yay*), Duvet ($5.63 a fifth; *doo-vay*), Garnier ($6.12 a fifth; *gar-nee-yay*), E. Martin

(10 years, $6.49 a fifth), and
St. Rémy Napoleon ($6.85 a
fifth).

To learn how to drink
French brandy, see under
brandy. See also **Calvados;
marc**.

FRANZIA BRANDY The
name of Franzia is synonymous with economical California wines: standard, uninspired,
uninspiring. The same may be
said for Franzia Brandy: adequate and unmemorable. Franzia's is one of California's most
economical brandies—around
$4.50 (fifth). It's definitely on
the sweet side, and for this
precise reason will be pleasing
to some palates and distasteful
to others.

**FRAPIN GRANDE FINE
CHAMPAGNE SUPREME
COGNAC** It goes for around
$15 (fifth), but it goes well, for
this is excellent French Cognac.
In one public tasting, Frapin
placed first. It has a marvelous,
huge bouquet, yet is soft and
gentle on the tongue.

Frapin also makes a super-
Cognac, but don't ask the
price—it's like that yacht: if
you have to ask the price you
can't afford it. It's made from
grapes from a single vineyard,
and it's called Chateau de
Fontpinot. Ah . . .

**FREDDIE FUDPUCKER
(COCKTAIL)** Even if it were a
vomitous concoction—it isn't—
this tequila cocktail was an assured success the moment it was
christened. Freddie Fudpucker
. . . someone stayed up nights
to name it. People will order
it, sight unseen, just for its
joyousness on the tongue. But
a twist of the tongue could be

calamitous. After two Fud-
puckers, best to order Sunrises.

The Freddie Fudpucker is
simply a **Tequila Sunrise** with
Galliano instead of grenadine.
Or, if you will, a **Harvey Wallbanger** with tequila instead of
vodka.

Take one glass (6 oz. or so)
of orange juice, add some ice
cubes, mix in a jigger or two of
tequila, and about one jigger of
Galliano.

Hail to Freddie, the
Fudpucker!

FREEZOMINT This is the
"given" name of what some
consider the best mint liqueur
in the world. "Freezomint" is
the invented, patented name
that the French liqueur firm of
Cusenier gives to what we in
America would call their crème
de menthe. It is probably the
world's best-known mint
liqueur. It is especially popular
in England.

In fact, the mint for
Freezomint is imported from
England to France. Other
herbs—their identity a trade
secret, of course—are also used
in the production. Like our
American crèmes de menthe,
Freezomint is best appreciated
Frappé (over shaved or
cracked ice). It sells in the
U.S. for around $6.50 (24 oz.),
a very reasonable price for an
import of this quality.

FRUITY BRANDY When the
word "brandy" stands alone it
usually refers to, and should
always refer to, the distilled
spirit made from grapes and
grapes alone. If the spirit is
produced from some fruit other
than grapes, it is called a fruit
brandy. The French name is

eau-de-vie (plural: **eaux-de-vie**), "water of life."

None of this is to say that fruit brandies are in any way inferior to grape brandies—they're simply different. Indeed, fruit brandies can be of the very highest quality—can be, and often are.

Probably the best-known fruit brandy in the U.S. is the French spirit made from apples: **Calvados,** and its American counterpart, **applejack.** But there are a jolly assemblage of other fruit brandies available in America—they're made from plums, cherries, berries, and pears.

But don't confuse fruit brandies with liqueurs. Fruit brandies are not sweetened. Liqueurs are. Fruit brandies are higher in alcohol (around 90°, but going as high as 150°) than liqueurs, which hover between 30° and 80°. Fruit brandies are colorless, or virtually so—hence their common French name, *alcools blancs;* liqueurs are almost always artificially colored, white crème de menthe and white crème de cacao being notable exceptions.

To add to the confusion, enter American enterprise! Many of America's largest liqueur producers—Hiram Walker, Arrow, Old Mr. Boston—make a whole line of "fruit-flavored" brandies. These are not true brandies, since they are not made simply from the specified fruit. Calvados (France), for example, is distilled from apples —it is not beverage alcohol flavored with apples. These "fruit-flavored brandies" are not distilled from the specified fruit—they are flavored therewith somewhere along the line. This is why the labels of these beverages may not read, by American law, "peach brandy," for example, but must read "peach-flavored brandy." Even this term is accurate only in that they're peach-flavored; they're not true peach-brandies, for brandies are distilled only from grapes or fruit.

Fruit brandies, speaking broadly, are more "natural" than liqueurs—they are not arbitrarily flavored. They are more "authentic," for their flavoring comes wholly from the particular fruit from which they are distilled. Liqueurs, essentially, are simply alcohol which has been specially flavored, with fruit, seeds, herbs, plants.

None of this, of course, is to denigrate liqueurs—they can be the most exquisite, most palatable, not say the most beautiful to behold, of all the world's great alcoholic beverages. But this is to express the nonpareil excellence, the uniqueness, of true fruit brandies.

True fruit brandies are always expensive for the simple reason that it takes a huge amount of fresh and perfect fruit to make them. Also, the fermentation process is exceedingly protracted, often up to a year and more.

Fruit brandies have many uses in cooking and in mixed drinks, but perhaps they are most appreciated when sipped, well chilled, after dinner. Be sure to enjoy their enormous bouquet by serving them in tulip-shaped glasses.

Here are the world's greatest fruit brandies: **applejack** (apples), **Calvados** (apples), **fraise** (strawberries), **framboise** (Raspberries), **kirschwasser** (cherries), **mirabelle** (plums), **poire**

Williams (pears), **quetsch** (plums), and **slivovitz** (plums).

FRUIT-FLAVORED BRANDY

Beverages calling themselves apricot- or pear- or blackberry-flavored brandy are found only in the U.S. of A. The term was invented by and is prescribed by the Federal Alcohol Administration, in order to distinguish these beverages from true **fruit brandy**. True fruit brandies are made wholly from the fruit in question. Fruit-flavored brandies are true liqueurs, actually, as they are made from a base of a distilled spirit—brandy in this case—and the flavoring fruit is then added. They are then sweetened, filtered, and bottled. Thus they are true liqueurs: highly flavored, sweet distilled spirits.

Most American liqueur firms produce a complete line of fruit-flavored brandies, almost all of them 70°, the minimum demanded by law. The list includes apricot, blackberry, peach, and cherry—these are the big sellers—and sometimes also coffee, ginger, and apple.

Many American firms make both fruit-flavored brandies and fruit-flavored liqueurs. The practical difference between them is that the brandies are drier, and higher in proof: 70° vs. 40° to 60° for the liqueurs.

Fruit-flavored brandies, no matter how you approach them or where or how or when you take them, are simply not fine liqueurs. They are not elegant sipping beverages. But then they're not made to be. They're made to splash in a mixed drink, pour over ice cream, or soak a layer cake.

Here are some of the domestic names: **De Kuyper,** Arrow (by **Heublein**), Regnier (by **Cointreau**), Connoisseur, Garnier, Dubochette, Jacquin's, **Leroux, Bols, Hiram Walker,** Mohawk, Chateaux, Nuyens.

Fruit-flavored brandies are not expensive: they're priced today between $5 and $6 (24 oz.), and a few (e.g. Connoisseur, Jacquin's) are considerably cheaper.

FUNDADOR (PEDRO DOMECQ) BRANDY

It's distinctly Spanish in flavor: sweet and earthy, quite different from French brandies and Cognacs, and even further removed from American brandies, though both tend toward sweetness. Fundador, however, is not a "pleasant" brandy. It's assertive and distinctive, but with an underlying bitterness. Fundador sells in the U.S. for around $8 (fifth), but at that price it's not really recommended, unless you simply want something different.

G

GALACAFE This is a coffee-flavored liqueur made by the giant Italian spirits firm of Stock, and imported by Schenley. It is definitely on the sweet side—even for a liqueur, even a coffee liqueur. (In this respect it is on a par with Kahlúa, also very sweet). It is surely a good reliable beverage, but by no means outstanding. There are better coffee liqueurs at a comparable price—and there are worse.

Galacafe is 53° and sells in the U.S. for around $7.50 (fifth), a fair price for a fair beverage.

GALLIANO This smooth, rich, golden-hued Italian liqueur is often thought of as a newcomer to the American drinking scene, but it's been around for more than half a century, introduced in 1925, and was created almost a full century ago, in 1894, in Leghorn, Italy.

The "inventor" named it after an Italian military hero, one Major Giuseppe Galliano, who defended Fort Enda Jesus in Ethiopia against insuperable odds, during the Ethiopian War of 1895-96. The fort, a stolid, stupid, pillbox kind of affair, is pictured on the Galliano label, along with the figure of Major Galliano, or one of his subalterns or drinking buddies. The name of the inventor is also there: "Ditta [Firm of] Arturo Vaccari."

Liquore Galliano (its full name) reached its present eminence in the U.S. thanks mostly to American salesmanship. The McKesson Liquor Company (New York, N.Y.), Galliano's sole distributor in the U.S., has promoted this Italian immigrant with devotion and vigor. During the '60s, McKesson ran an intensive advertising campaign to promote the Harvey Wallbanger cocktail. Galliano now sells more than 4 million bottles per year in the U.S.

Galliano is said to be made from as many as eighty different herbs, fruits, and spices; it goes through several distillations and is aged for up to six months in glass tanks. It is repeatedly filtered before being bottled.

Liquore Galliano is deservedly popular—ironically, more so in the U.S. than in its native land—for it can be numbered among the world's great cordials. It is spicy yet smooth, aromatic yet soft. And it has a wonderful anise and vanilla penumbra that envelopes all.

Galliano's slender tapered bottle is well known—in fact, it's a patented trademark.

Galliano imitations have inevitably begun to appear—some Italian-produced, some American-made. Two from Italy are Liquore Roiano, made by Stock, and Liquore Gaetano, both 80°, and both considerably cheaper than Galliano. The Roiano sells for around $9 (fifth, California), compared to Galliano at around $12 (23 oz.). The U.S. has entered the lists with at least two pseudo-Gallianos: Florentino Liqueur and Neapolitan Liqueur. Florentino sells for around $6 (fifth), and Neapolitan for around $7 (fifth).

All of these imitations are palatable and quite adequate for mixing. None of them is as smooth and complex as Galliano. The Roiano is clearly the best of the lot; it has a good anise aroma and flavor. The Florentino, strictly Chicago-born and -bred, tries hard to look Italian—and it succeeds: It looks exactly like a bottle of fine Italian olive oil!

But if they're going to be submerged in a torrent of orange juice and vodka, these Johnny-come-lately imitation Gallianos will serve admirably. Who needs twice-the-price Galliano just to bang walls?

Innumerable mixed drinks employing the services of Galliano have arisen over the past decade. One book lists eighteen starting with the word "Golden"! Most are eminently forgettable. The most memorable are these: **Freddie Fudpucker, Harvey Wallbanger,** and **Golden Cadillac.**

Galliano is also recommended in the kitchen. For a complete article on the subject, see *Vintage* magazine, September 1975, p. 44.

GAVILAN TEQUILA Good, reliable tequila, almost always a bargain in the Western states, at around $5.25 (fifth) for both Gold and White, but considerably higher in the East, when available there.

GEORGE DICKEL TENNESSEE WHISKEY It's often called "the other Tennessee Whiskey," after Jack Daniel's and that's a pretty apt description, as George Dickel Whiskey has been *after* Jack Daniel's in almost every respect. It was created after Jack Daniel's: George A. Dickel was wholesaling his whiskey in 1870, but Jack Daniel was retailing his a decade earlier. The George Dickel black-and-white label is something of a look-alike of the Jack Daniel's label. Jack Daniel's has Old No. 7—George Dickel has Old No. 8 and Old No. 12. George Dickel Whiskey comes after, way after, Jack Daniel's in sales.

But this is all historical precedence—George Dickel Tennessee Whiskey is not *after* Jack Daniel's Tennessee Whiskey in taste and quality. It is fine whiskey, rather full-bodied, smooth, almost sweet, and every bit as good as Jack Daniel's, which is good indeed. If fans of Jack Daniel's challenge these assertions, bet your bottom dollar that they cannot distinguish between the two whiskeys when they are tasted blindly (labels hidden). Mere luck, of course, gives one a 50-50 chance, so repeat the tasting a number of times. The more times the experiment is repeated, the less will be the chances of guessing correctly. And if the tasting proceeds far enough, it will be impossible to distinguish anything from anything.

The George A. Dickel Distillery of Tullahoma, Tenn., is today the fief and domain of Schenley Industries, Inc.

George Dickel Old No. 8 Sour Mash, 86.8°, sells for about $7 (fifth), and Old No. 12 Sour Mash, 90°, for about a dollar more (fifth).

GERMANY BRANDY The German people are very fond of their native brandy, and with good reason—it is a most creditable beverage. Despite the vast quantities of wine grapes produced by Germany, virtually all the grapes used to make German brandy are imported. The simple but ironic fact is that German grapes are too valuable to be used for distillation. They are much more valuable when used to make those precious and delightful German white wines.

German brandy is soft, slightly sweet, not highly flavorful—quite similar, in fact, to American brandy.

Only one German brandy is imported to the U.S. in any quantity, **Asbach Uralt** (80°), but it's not exactly peasant fare—it sells for around $11 (fifth).

GILBEY'S LONDON DRY GIN The Gilbey brothers, Alfred and Walter, began their spirituous careers as wine merchants in London, later expanding into Scotch whiskies and Irish whiskeys, but it was their last venture of all, in 1872, that was their most successful: the making of gin. To this day the name Gilbey stands first for gin. In fact, in the U.S., Gilbey's Gin is the second-best-selling gin in the land (Gordon's is No. 1), with sales

of well over 2 million cases per year.

Gilbey's is 86° and sells for around $5 (fifth), about the same as other standard American gins: **Fleischmann's, Gordon's, Calvert,** Canada Dry, **Hiram Walker, Burnett's White Satin, Schenley's, Seagram's.** And no expert on earth can distinguish between them tasting them blindly (labels hidden). These are good, standard American gins, all made in almost precisely the same manner, all flavored almost exactly alike, and all emerging from their respective distilleries exactly alike. The differences between them are so infinitesimal that, like all those medieval angels, they can be placed on the head of a pin.

GILBEY'S VODKA Gilbey's began as, and still is, a British firm, but today it is part of a large diversified British corporation. Gilbey's began by making gin, in 1872. Now Gilbey's Limited, London, handles many other spirits and Liqueurs.

The American firm, **National Distillers Products Company,** now produces the Gilbey products for the American market. The line includes not only the original gin, but Gilbey's Vodka, introduced in 1956, and Gilbey's Rum, introduced in 1974.

The gin, of course, is the best-selling of the Gilbey products (more than 2 million cases per year), but the vodka is also doing well, with sales of almost a million and a half cases annually. In their promotional literature for Gilbey's Vodka, the producers challenge the consuming public to blind-taste their product alongside other vodkas. That's a brave gambit, one not often tried in the world of spirits, or even, for the matter of fact, in the field of alcoholic beverages generally. The company confidently believes and boldly proclaims that in such a blind tasting its vodka, Gilbey's, will be selected as the smoothest of the lot, regardless of price, imported vodkas included. In several blind tastings, Gilbey's Vodka has placed well, not because it was the smoothest, but because it was the tastiest. All of which goes to show—*again*—that vodkas are all very much alike, particularly when one compares American vodka against American vodka. Gilbey's is 80°.

GIMLET (COCKTAIL) This beguiling little summertime drink originated in the Far East —Singapore or Hong Kong, probably, invented by British Colonials there. Nobody knows how it got its name. A gimlet is a small boring tool, resembling a corkscrew, but how to connect the cocktail with the instrument? Perhaps it was that ol' "gimlet eye," the piercing glance that this drink either caused in the eye of the consumer, or thwarted on the part of one's enemy.

At all events, the Gimlet began as simply gin and lime juice, and that's the way it should remain.

Combine: 1 jigger gin (vodka is often substituted, but the classic Gimlet was strictly gin) and 1 oz. Rose's lime juice (if you want to use fresh lime juice, use the juice of one lime and add 1 tsp. powdered sugar). Shake well, or stir thoroughly. Strain into a chilled cocktail glass, or serve on the rocks. Garnish with a slice of lime.

GIN This colorless, almost tasteless, innocent-looking spirit has had the most checkered, most flamboyant career of any distilled spirit known to man. It's been in and out of civilization's good graces since the day it was invented. That was some 350 years ago, by a Dutch physician. It was in excellent repute then, for the good doctor only wanted to make a simple, cheap, universal medicine. And he succeeded! Gin— or *genievre*, as he called it— was an instant success and it cured whatever you happened to have.

But nothing stays the same. Only decades later gin reached England, and by the middle of the 18th century, gin was a very dirty word. As well it deserved to be, for the Dutch doctor's simple medicine came closer to devastating the British nation than the Jutes or Hitler's buzz-bombs ever did.

In those raucous rollicking days, gin sold for next to nothing, and was overpriced at that, for most of it was utterly ghastly stuff. And it was everywhere—not sold simply in licensed premises, but by grocers, tobacconists, barbers, even peddled on the streets and door to door. The poor swilled the stuff down by the hogshead—to forget their miseries —and so added one more. The upper classes disdained it. William Hogarth's paintings, captivating and revolting at the same time, tell all: "Gin Lane," "A Harlot's Progress," "A Rake's Progress."

But by 1900, gin had regained its respectability, even

in England. It was the invention of the cocktail in America that wrought the transformation. Gin, at least the English variety, is a nonaggressive beverage, a natural mixer. Damned as "Mother's Ruin" a century before, it was wholly proper in such decorous cocktail drinks as the **Tom Collins**, **Gin and Tonic**, and especially that distinguished lord of all mixed drinks, the **Dry Martini**.

But ah, respectability can be such a capricious thing. In 1920 came the Great Experiment—or more accurately, the Great Fiasco, or more commonly, Prohibition. Lo, wonder of wonders, the more gin was forbidden, the more did it abound. Gin is the easiest to make of all spirits, for it is nothing more than neutral grain spirits—pure ethyl alcohol—with some flavorings, especially juniper berries.

And made it was from 1920 to 1933, by the million of gallons, hundreds of thousands of bathtubsful. The poor thirsty masses made their gin from homemade distillates, from medicinal grain alcohol, even from commercial alcohol. Most of it was not merely vile, head-splitting stuff—some of it was literally lethal. This was bathtub gin, a fitting name for an unfit drink. Born in the bathroom, it should have been disposed of *ibidem*. And now in these latter days, beginning with the repeal of Prohibition in 1933, gin is again quite respectable, even faddish. The consumption of gin in the U.S. has risen steadily if unspectacularly over the past 40 years. Only in very recent years have gin sales begun to level off. It has now been replaced as the

most popular of "white spirits" by vodka for the obvious reason that vodka is an even more neutral mixer; it is totally tasteless. For the past few years vodka has outsold gin in the U.S. and by a progressively larger margin.

Technically it's almost impossible to define gin, for it can be made in a number of different ways, from a number of different ingredients, including molasses, of all things. But why define it? Just enjoy it. Only one thing is essential: the flavoring with juniper berries.

Dutch, English, and American distillers put a variety of weird substances—"botanicals," they call them—into their gin to flavor it: tree barks, assorted peelings, ginger, licorice, etc. But it is the essential oil of juniper that must predominate, else it's not gin. Call it what you like, vodka, slivovitz, it's not gin in the popular esteem.

Gin is probably the most widely used spirit in the entire world. It is gin's sociable nature, a good mixer, that makes it so, for it is seldom appreciated straight.

Except by the Dutch—to them "neat" is the only civilized mode of consumption. And those Dutchmen just may have something there, for Dutch gin—they call it Genever or Hollands or Schiedam—is distinctly removed from the emasculated gin Americans consume. It's made differently: distilled at a low proof so that it does retain some character. It's heavy-bodied, full-flavored, with a slight malty quality. It's worth a try, but it's not for mixing.

And if you don't like the taste of Genever neat, use it in

your cooking. Gin's not often taken into the kitchen, and that's a pity, for in some times and climes it works wonders! Gin is the perfect topping for pistachio ice cream. Sounds abominable, tastes marvelous! It is also a "natural" with all manner of pork and most types of sausage. Toss a jigger or two or three into the pan with your pork chops, pork sausage, or pork roast. It also has a natural affinity for sauerkraut: Just add a shot or two to the pot. And it simply *loves* all manner of fish. Do it with a flair: warm a couple of jiggers of Genever, toss it over the fish, and flambé it. Voilà! Use your most flavorful gin in cooking, preferably the Dutch or German types.

Very little Dutch gin finds its way to America—only the best class of liquor stores carry it at all. What 99% of Americans drink is London dry gin. It's so called because London's where it was originally made, and it's dry in contrast to Old Tom gin, a sweetened gin, very popular a century ago, but scarcely to be found in these latter days. The name "London Dry" on a bottle today, whether from England or the U.S., has no significance whatever: more London dry gin is made today in Peoria, Ill., than anyplace else in the world! Ditto for "English Dry Gin" or simple "Dry Gin": the words mean nothing.

There is perhaps a subtle difference between English and American gins, but only a professional taster could distinguish the one from the other, tasting them blind—well, with a little bit of luck, perhaps he could. The British variety is somewhat less highly distilled, and therefore retains a whisper more of flavor.

There is also a Plymouth gin, again named after the British city of its origin, but today only one distillery makes it: Coates. In taste, it is somewhere between London dry and Dutch gin, but the casual drinker will scarcely note any difference between the two. There are a few true Plymouth freaks in the world, however, who will drink no other gin. It is said that Plymouth is the only type of gin to mix with Angostura bitters to make Pink Gin. The Germans also make a gin, Steinhäger (or Steinhaeger), much like the Dutch type, with a distinctive taste of juniper. It's not cheap, but it's good. It comes in "stone" bottles—the most commonly seen name in the U.S. is Doornkaat.

There are also flavored gins—orange, lemon, pineapple, whatever—which are simply ordinary gins with the addition of the particular fruit flavor. And sloe gin is not a gin at all, but a cordial.

Gin is ready to drink the moment it is bottled—age makes it older, not better. In fact, it is against U.S. law to put any statement regarding age on a gin label. A small amount of American gin is aged, however, in wooden casks and it takes on a light-yellow color from the wood. It's called golden gin and is exactly the same as "plain" gin, only prettier.

Which type of gin should you buy? The fancy cellophane-wrapped $7.75 import or the $4.50 domestic? There is as much snobbery and cultism in the world of gin as in the rest of the "spirit world" —perhaps more. Expensive British gins happen to be "in" today; the big names at the moment are Beefeater, Boodles, Tanqueray, and Booth's House of Lords. Is there any significant difference between these premium-priced bottles and the economical domestics? Not really—only the price! Buy the most economical and challenge your snobbish friends to distinguish Boodles ("The World's Costliest": $7.75) from the American made White Tavern ($4.25). But note that British gins are almost all of higher proof than American: 90° to 96.6° vs. American gins at 80° to 86°. And of course the higher the proof, the more gin, not water, you're buying.

Gin is used in more mixed drinks than any other spirit in the world. It would require a small book to list them all. To begin with, gin mixes well with any fruit juice—and there are a few hundred of those around the world—and especially with citrus fruit juices. A handful of gin-based drinks have become internationally famous over the course of the centuries. Here are the truly great ones: Dry Martini, Gimlet, Gin Swizzle (see under Rum Swizzle), Negroni, Ramos Gin Fizz, Singapore Sling, and Tom Collins.

GINGER-FLAVORED LIQUEURS AND BRANDIES

Ginger-flavored liqueurs and brandies were more appreciated by our forefathers, especially in Colonial times, than they are by us, and they are more appreciated today by the British than they are by Americans.

Nonetheless, most American liqueur firms make a ginger-flavored brandy, usually 70°, selling for $5 or $6, and all of them are nicely gingery, not too sweet, and a vast improvement over ginger ale! Jacquin makes a particularly good ginger-flavored brandy. But the best ginger liqueur, hands down, is King's Ginger Liqueur, made in Holland, with a Cognac base. Unfortunately it is not imported to the U.S.

GLAYVA

Glayva means (in old Gaelic) "Very Good," and that it is. It's an elegant liqueur, made with fine matured Scotch whiskies as a base. Glayva is an obvious imitation of Drambuie, made only since World War II. In taste, it is quite similar to Drambuie (and Glen Mist and Lochan Ora—it's kissin' Scottish cousins), though it is a trifle sweeter. (Glen Mist is the driest of the lot). The flavor of the basic Scotch whisky comes through more forcibly in the Drambuie, and for that reason might be more appreciated by Scotch lovers.

The label bears the crest of the Borthwicks, one of Scotland's oldest families. Just what the connection is, nobody seems to know, or cares to tell. Perhaps it signifies that if the ancient Borthwicks had known of Glayva, they would have loved it. Indubitably. Aye.

Glayva is made by Ronald Morrison and Co., Ltd., of Edinburgh, Scotland, which has been making fine Scotch whisky for more than a century. It is 80° and sells for about $1 less than Drambuie (about $11 for 23 oz.), and it's every bit as good, though different.

**GLENFARCLAS MALT
SCOTCH WHISKY** This es-
teemed Scotch malt whisky is
not to be confused with **Glenfiddich**, though both are made
by a Grant Company of the
Scottish North Highland. This
whisky is made by J. & G.
Grant Ltd. and Glenfiddich is
made by William Grant & Sons
Ltd. Nor is it to be confused
with the **Glenlivet**, though it
actually has that name in hyphenated form on the label:
it's officially Glenfarclas-Glenlivet. All three are prized pure
malt whiskies, made within a
few miles of each other, in the
"whisky belt" of the Highlands.
J. & G. Grant Limited was
founded in 1836 by Robert
Hay. He ran the firm for some
30 years and on his death it
was sold to a farmer by the
name of John Grant, who established the firm and whose
descendants still run the business.

Glenfarclas 15-year-old Malt
Whisky (91°) received a prestigious award in 1972: a Gold
Seal from the highly regarded Club Oenologique of London. The 12-year-old came
home with a Bronze Seal in
the same competition. It was
said to have "great character
and subtlety." Glenfarclas is
great malt whisky. It is matured in aged sherry casks. The
12-year-old is normally shipped
to the U.S. at 104°, but to California at only 91°; it sells for
$13 to $14 (fifth). Glenfarclas
is a single malt.

**GLENFIDDICH MALT
SCOTCH WHISKEY** Malt
Scotch whisky, virtually unknown in the U.S. a scant decade ago, is today one of the
nation's "in" drinks. The "big

three" malts in the U.S. today
are The **Glenlivet, Laphroaig**,
and Glenfiddich. In 1974,
Glenfiddich overseas sales top-
ped 1 million English pounds.

Glenfiddich had its beginning in 1886 when William
Grant, a veteran of the Battle
of Waterloo, founded the
whisky company that still bears
his name. Within a year he
and his seven sons had built
the Glenfiddich Distillery stone
by stone. The first whisky ran
from the stills on Christmas
day, 1887.

The site, just outside of
Dufftown, Banffshire, in the
Scottish Highlands, was originally chosen because of the
Robbie Dubh spring there, the
purity of whose water had long
been appreciated by smugglers.
The company did so well that
five years later, the foundation
stone was being laid for another distillery, Balvenie, a
little way down the hill, also
on the River Fiddich. The
name Balvenie derives from the
medieval castle, now in ruins, a
stone's throw from the distillery. In 1963 a grain-whiskey
distillery was built in the quiet
Ayrshire hills near Girvan, and
a few years later, the Ladyburn
Lowland Malt Distillery nearby.

The unique triangular bottle
used for all the Grant whiskies
was introduced in 1957.

Glenfiddich is one of the
very few single-malt whiskies
available in the U.S. A "Single"
malt differs from a "plain"
malt in that the whisky comes
from a single distillery, and is
not blended with malt whiskies
from other distilleries. Every
drop of whisky in that Glenfiddich bottle came from the

Glenfiddich distillery, Dufftown.

Glenfiddich is a premium malt whisky, 86°, one of the very finest. The 8-year-old version received a notable award, a silver seal from the highly regarded Club Oenologique of London, in 1971. And if that doesn't impress you, know that it is Liz Taylor's favorite whisky. Like all malts, it is totally "Scotchy"—it's what makes Scotch an elixir to some, an abomination to others. *De gustibus* . . . And premium whisky, premium price tag: Glenfiddich 10-year-old sells in the U.S. for around $14 (fifth). There is also an 8-year-old, somewhat cheaper, and a 10-year-old "Stillmaster Crock" at around $17 (25.4 oz.).

Balvenie Pure Malt Whisky is not imported to the U.S. Though the two distilleries are only a stone's throw apart, and though both use the same famous water and the same ingredients, it is the company's boast that the two whiskies are distinctly different. (Aside: a soft-spoken, but distinct *Perhaps!*)

THE GLENLIVET MALT SCOTCH WHISKY It's *The* Glenlivet. Not simply Glenlivet. This is the original, the only Scotch in the world that has the right to call itself The Glenlivet. The Thing. That was established by law in 1880. Other firms may use a hyphenated form of the name— some thirty do so—but no other whisky may call itself simply The Glenlivet.

The Glenlivet calls itself "the greatest whisky in the world," and there are many who would agree. The Glenlivet is, indeed, the father of them all, the original unblended Scotch, from the oldest licensed distillery in Scotland.

This is pure malt scotch whisky, quite different from the blends that most Americans know as Scotch whisky. But it has been the blends that have made Scotch so popular in the U.S. Before blending began— around 1900—Scotch whisky was simply malt whisky, nothing else, and it was known virtually only in Scotland.

All the popular brands of Scotch that line our retail shelves are blends: Black & White, Chivas Regal, Cutty Sark, Johnnie Walker, J & B, and a thousand others.

Scotch malts are just beginning to find their way to the U.S. Only a decade ago, 12-year-old The Glenlivet sold only about 2,000 cases per year in the U.S. In 1977 it sold better than 30,000 cases. In 1978 it sold at a monthly growth rate of approximately 50% over the corresponding month in 1977.

For more than 200 years the Glenlivet area has been known for its fine malt whisky. The Scots have always said that the best whisky comes from the Highlands, and the best of the Highland malts is The Glenlivet. This remote glen, tucked away in the rolling hills of the central Highlands, seems heaven-blessed for the making of great whisky. The Scots say that four things are essential to create a fine whisky: good barley, good water, good peat, and "cunning chemists." This glen, the Glen Livet, has them all: the deep fertile fields of the Laichs of Banff and Moray to grow the choicest barley; from the Cairngorms heights towering over the glen there springs "the fairest and purest water on earth," which tumbles down the mountainside for 1,200 feet; conveniently nearby is the celebrated Faemussach moss, a seemingly inexhaustible deposit of high-grade peat; and as for the "cunning chemists," every inhabitant of the glen seems to have a natural proclivity toward the making of good malt whisky.

In its relative inaccessibility, Glenlivet became the last stronghold of the smugglers when illicit distilling had ceased throughout the rest of the Highlands. Those "good old days" at Glenlivet are described by one author as a time of "incessant struggle and strife, of marchings and countermarchings, desperate battle, fierce pursuits, and perilous escapes" (*Glenlivet*, Glenlivet Distillery, Scotland, 1966, p. 14).

Yet, ironically, Glenlivet was the first distillery to go "legit." In 1824, George Smith, the king of the local smugglers and the man who is hailed as the founder of Glenlivet, took out a license for his "bothy" (illegal distillery).

Thus the Glenlivet Distillery came into official existence. George Smith died in 1871 and was succeeded by his son, John Gordon Smith. The two names are still on the Glenlivet label.

The Glenlivet Malt Scotch Whisky has been universally acclaimed for more than 150 years. Sir Walter Scott and George Saintsbury have sung its praises. It's the quintessence of what Scotch whisky is all about. It is immoral—and

should be illegal—to drink The Glenlivet in any manner other than by sipping it neat. It is 86° and sells in the U.S. for around $15 (25.4 oz.). There is also a 25-year-old at around $31 (25.4 oz.).

GLEN MIST Four liqueurs with Scotch whisky as their base are imported to the U.S.: **Drambuie** is the oldest and most famous. Glen Mist is the second oldest; then comes **Glayva**, introduced after World War II, and the baby of the foursome, **Lochan Ora**.

These latter three are obvious imitations of the original Drambuie. And pretty good imitations they are. They're similarly produced, and contain similar ingredients, namely aged Scotch whiskies, honey, herbs, and spices.

Glen Mist is the driest of the three. Like Drambuie, it is matured in whisky casks.

During World War II, because of the shortage of Scotch whisky, production of Glen Mist was moved to Ireland, using Irish whiskey as a base. Today production is back in Scotland. Unlike Drambuie, Glen Mist is wholly produced and bottled in Scotland.

Glen Mist is rather hard to find in the U.S., but worth the search. It sells for around $11 (fifth).

GLENMORE DISTILLERIES COMPANY Glenmore Distilleries of Louisville, Kentucky, markets a few spirits by the name of Glenmore, but ten times as many with other names —such as **Mr. Boston, Old Mr. Boston**, Kentucky Tavern, **Yellowstone**, George Moon, Desmond & Duff. Further, the company takes more pride in these latter products than it does in its Glenmore products. Or at least it works harder to promote them. Right now Glenmore executives are staying up nights devising ways to promote these products in particular:

Amaretto di Saronno
Desmond & Duff Scotch
Mr. Boston Cordials and Cocktails
Kentucky Tavern Bourbons
Yellowstone Bourbon

Glenmore is obviously a very big operation. Total sales in the 1977–78 fiscal year were almost $200 million, and net earnings more than $4 million. The products bearing the name of Glenmore have become only a small part of the total operation.

The acquisition of the Mr. Boston line in 1968, and of Foreign Vintages in 1970, has caused Glenmore some growing pains. The company fell on some lean and difficult times through the early 70s because it tried—laudably but disastrously—to remain a family operation, honest and open. Such old-fashioned attitudes don't make for great success in today's cutthroat liquor marketplace! Aggressive merchandising and marketing are the name of today's ruthless game.

Two years ago things and people were reshuffled at Glenmore, and it's become a tighter ship, and the ledgers are looking rosy —or rather, blackish—once more. Some 900 items—not brands—were dropped. For example, sometimes there were five or six different proofs of the same spirit, and four or five different sizes of each of the proofs. Paul Casi, new president of Glenmore, came in with a

scimitar, and the magic word has been "Cut!" Casi hopes to drop another 300 to 400 items within the year.

In the meantime, back at the distillery, Glenmore Silver Label Kentucky Straight Bourbon seems to be the only bourbon still being made under the Glenmore label. And it's been a good potion down through the years, and a good value, and still is. It comes in 86°, 90°, and 100° bottled in bond. Glenmore vodka, rum, gin, and brandy are also produced, and though they're not everywhere available, they are economical, reliable, good.

GLÖGG ALSO GLÜGG OR GLÖG, OR OMIT THE UMLAUT,   GLOGG. However you pronounce it—preferably *gloog,* or *gloooog,* or permissively, *gluhg*—it's one of mankind's happiest combinations of disparate wines and spices. Glögg is a Swedish mulled wine punch, historically a Christmas drink, but a marvelous inspiration any time of the year, and particularly in cold weather.

Here's how to bring unbounded Yuletide joy to the hearts of twenty-five or thirty people at Christmas time, or other time:

In a stainless steel or enameled pot—wines are allergic to other types of cookware—put:

2 bottles (fifths) California Burgundy—it's inexpensive, 1 bottle California Muscat de Frontignan—or Muscatel, or Moscato di Canelli, or Muscat Blanc, or anything similarly named, 1 bottle medium or sweet sherry—California-made will do fine (real Span-

ish sherry is considerably more expensive), ½ bottle (pint) sweet vermouth—California-produced is adequate, 2 tbsp. Angostura Bitters

Put the following spices in a cheesecloth bag and add them to the wines—or you may simply dump these into the wine without benefit of the cheesecloth, but warn your celebrants not to mistake cardamom seeds for golden raisins!

Peelings of one orange—or 2 tbsp. dried orange peel, 12 whole cloves, 1 2-inch piece of fresh ginger—or 1 tsp. powdered ginger, 1 2-to-3-inch stick cinnamon, 12 whole cardamoms, slightly crushed, 2 cups of golden raisins.
Cover and let the mixture stand for at least 12 hours.

Before serving, add 1½ to 2 cups sugar, stir well, and bring to a boil over high heat. Remove immediately, add 2 cups of blanched, slivered almonds. Pour the Glögg into cups or mugs and serve with a small spoon to extract the almonds and raisins.

You may add brandy or aquavit (about 12 ounces) when you add the sugar, but the drink really doesn't need it: it's already potent enough and tasty enough.

Some insist on flaming the Glögg, but why burn up all that alcohol you've paid good money for?

GOLDEN CADILLAC This is strictly an after-dinner libation, and it's quite as rich as it sounds. You can blend it in a blender or shake with ice

and then strain: 2 oz. cream (light or heavy), 1 oz. Galliano, and 1 oz. white crème de cacao.

One could replace the Galliano with one of its more economical substitutes (see under **Galliano**), but when you're constructing a Golden Cadillac, economy is not a valid consideration!

(DANZIGER) GOLDWASSER
The name means "goldwater" and that's exactly what this is: a liqueur filled with bits of gold. When you shake the bottle, the clear liquid comes alive with suspended flakes of 22-carat gold-leaf flakes.

The golden particles are entirely harmless, as well as tasteless. Unfortunately, they're also noncurative. It was once thought that gold, that rare and precious metal, was a true all-purpose curative. Gold dust was sometimes sprinkled on the food of royal guests, both to impress and to cure.

The name "goldwasser" is often preceded by "Danziger" (or Danzig) because that was where the beverage originated: in the ancient Free City of Danzig (now the Polish city of Gdansk). That was back in 1598; it was made by the firm of Der Lachs, "The Salmon," and to this day, almost 400 years later, the salmon is still on the label. Today Der Lach Goldwasser (80°) is produced in West Berlin according to the original Danzig formula. It sells in the U.S. for almost $7.50 per pint. Polmos, the Polish firm, also makes a goldwasser (80°), imported to the U.S. It sells for somewhat less than does Der Lachs. Both are excellent.

In France they simply translate "goldwasser" into French and call it "liqueur d' or." Garnier makes one, 86°, about $11.50 for 24 oz., an excellent value. Bols of Holland labels its "Gold Liqueur" for the American market; it's 60°, sells for a hefty $12.50 (pint).

Occasionally goldwasser is labeled "Eau de Vie de Danzig," or simply "Eau d' Or."

Goldwasser's flavor comes from three diverse agents: orange peels, caraway seeds, anise—but not the gold flecks; they're strictly for show. Kümmel is a kindred spirit.

A "silberwasser" used to be made, but it lacked the necessary glint and glitter.

Goldwasser is best appreciated when consumed straight. It's sweet, rich, and tasty. Sip carefully. The price alone should make you do that. And be sure to shake well before pouring . . . behold, a golden snowfall!

GONZALEZ BYASS BRANDIES Gonzalez Byass is an old and established sherry firm which also makes some commendable brandy. (Their sherries are also recommended.) Their two most popular brands, both of which are imported to the U.S., are Soberano—the name has nothing to do with "sober"; it means "Sovereign"—and Lepanto. Soberano is 86°, between 2 and 3 years old, and sells for about $7 (fifth). Lepanto is the "top of the line"; it's 82°, aged a full 15 years, and sells for about $19 (fifth). These are good brandies, typical of Spanish brandy: somewhat sweet, full-bodied, earthy.

GORDON'S LONDON DRY GIN Gordon's Gin is the biggest selling gin not only in the U.S.—almost 3 million cases annually—but also in the United Kingdom, and, in fact, it is the largest selling gin in all the world. And should you happen to think that perhaps our world is getting too serious and sober in these latter days, consider the fact that throughout the world two bottles of Gordon's Gin are consumed every second of every day and night.

It all started in Britain, of course, with Alexander Gordon, a Scotchman by birth, who built a distillery in London in 1769. Things have gone smashingly, spiritedly ever since.

In 1898, Gordon's Gin joined forces with another winner, Tanqueray Gin, to form Tanqueray, Gordon & Co. Ltd. To complicate matters still further, this firm is now part of the huge Distillers Company Limited; the alliance took place in 1922.

Today there are Gordon distilleries all over the world, including three in the U.S. (Linden, N.J., Plainfield, Ill., and Union City, Calif.). The London plant is the largest gin distillery in the world.

No matter where it is made, Gordon's Gin is said to be precisely the same the world over, for it is always made exactly according to the same original formula used by the London distillery. Ingredients are selected and blended in London for use by overseas distilleries. Samples of the gins produced are sent to London for final approval. Perhaps this is one of the reasons for Gordon's success. Plus the fact that it got off to a good, early start. And Gordon's is fine gin. It is only infinitesimally different from other comparably priced 86° gins. But it is still good gin.

GRAND MARNIER Along with a scant half-dozen other names, Grand Marnier is one of the great, romantic, classical names in the world of liqueurs. Even the name (pronounced *grawn-marn-yay*) exudes superiority and flamboyance. Some call Grand Marnier simply the greatest liqueur in the world. It is certainly one of the greatest.

Grand Marnier is orange-flavored and made with Cognac—not mere brandy—as its base. Only bitter oranges are used, from Haiti. In contrast, Grand Marnier's great sister spirit, Cointreau, uses both bitter and sweet oranges. More precisely, bitter and sweet orange peels—the flesh of oranges is rarely used in the making of orange-flavored liqueurs.

Grand Marnier is made by the firm of Marnier-Lapostelle of France. The firm makes a few other products besides Grand Marnier, but 80% of their production consists of this noble liqueur. It is the most widely exported of all French liqueurs.

It would not seem to be any longer necessary, but Grand Marnier is still extensively and internationally promoted, and this, of course, adds to the price tag. It sells in the U.S. today for $13.50 to $15 (23 oz.), not precisely a peasant brew. If you prefer it in an opaline decanter, $30.24, please . . . and only 23 oz. yet!

Actually there are two forms of Grand Marnier, though Americans think of it as a single entity, as only one version is seen in this country: Grand Marnier Cordon Rouge ("Red Ribbon"—it has a red sash tied around its neck). A second form, less expensive, Cordon Jaune ("Yellow Ribbon") is available in continental Europe.

Grand Marnier is less sweet than most liqueurs, especially American-made ones; it is dry and pungent, with wonderful oranginess—the Cognac base is unmistakable. Grand Marnier makes for marvelous sipping, preferably straight up. It is famous for its use in the kitchen, and is absolutely mandatory for Crêpes Suzette and Soufflé Grand Marnier.

GRAND OLD PARR SCOTCH WHISKY The most distinguished feature of this whisky is its name. It's named after a redoubtable old Englishman, Thomas Parr (1483-1635), who was reputed to have lived to the full round age of 152 years. His longevity was heralded throughout all of England, particularly when he did public penance at the age of 105 for his sexual excesses! To honor his long life, not to say his prowess, he was buried in the Poets Corner of Westminster Abbey. Parr enjoyed his daily ration of Scotch whisky, and so it was only logical that a Scotch whisky should one day be named in his honor.

Old Parr is a deluxe whisky, 86.8°, 12 years old, especially popular in Japan, Mexico, and South America. It comes in an odd shaped, squarish bottle, said to be a faithful replica of the actual bottle used by "Old Parr," as he was known. This sells in the U.S. for about $10 (fifth). It also comes in a stoneware flagon for about $3 more. Old Parr is good, aged Scotch, but for 99% of humanity it will be mostly indistinguishable from other like-bodied Scotches.

GRANT'S SCOTCH WHISKY

Grant's Scotch is inextricably intertwined with Glenfiddich Scotch, for they were both "invented" by the same man, William Grant, and both are still made by William Grant & Sons Ltd. Distillers, Glasgow, Scotland.

William Grant's first whisky was Glenfiddich (1886), a pure malt whisky, and it wasn't until the turn of the century that he began blending some of his malt whiskies with grain whisky to produce Grant's Blended Scotch.

Grant's and Glenfiddich were successful whiskies from the day of their birth—but principally in their native land. It has been only in the past 25 years that worldwide sales have skyrocketed. In 1956 a huge bottling plant was opened at Paisley, near Glasgow; from here Grant's is shipped to 190 markets around the world. As of 1965 the company has a wholly owned subsidiary company in the U.S., William Grant & Sons, Inc., of New Jersey. Scotch whisky is not made here, of course—it can be made only in Scotland—but a wide range of spirits are bottled here: cordials, cocktails, gin, vodka, brandy, rum, bourbon, and, of course, a good deal of Scotch.

Clan MacGregor, a blended 80° Scotch whisky owned by the William Grant Co., is shipped to the U.S. in bulk, as are many Scotches these days, and bottled at the New Jersey plant. This represents considerable savings both in shipping costs and taxes. This is not harmful to the whisky in any way, nor are such whiskies per se inferior to those bottled in Scotland. What difference does it make if the distilled water is added (to lower proof) in Scotland or the U.S.? Clan MacGregor is, in fact, a rather good buy in Scotch whisky: about $5.50 (fifth).

Grant's Scotch Whisky comes in several versions these days, all 86°, and all in the singular, triangular bottle. First there is Grant's 8, an 8-year-old at $7 (New York) or $8 (California) a fifth. Then there is Grant's Stand Fast (the ancient battle cry of the clan), not imported to the U.S., but known around the world, usually as simply "Grant's." This is actually the firm's "regular" Scotch. In the deluxe category there is Grant's Royal, a 12-year-old, at $10 (New York), to $12 (California) a fifth, and Grant's Own Ancient Reserve, 20 years old, at around $19 (California) a fifth. This whisky, made only in very small quantities for sale in the U.S. (and, for some strange reason, Alberta, Canada), will soon be discontinued, and replaced by an even more expensive, even older, blend.

These Grants whiskies are excellent blends. All contain a good, though varying, portion of Grant's two famous malt whiskies, Glenfiddich and Balvenie. (The latter is not presently imported to the U.S., but if the market for single-malt scotches ever becomes strong enough, it certainly will be.) All are on the expensive side, but may be worth the price—if you're going to sip them delicately, soberly, and unadulterated—the whisky, not you.

GRAPPA A Frenchman would define grappa as the Italianized version of the French marc. An Italian would say that marc is the Gallic version of grappa. Anyhow, they're very similar: brandies made from wine pomace, the solids (pips, stems, gook) after the juice has been expressed. Sounds rather dreadful but grappa, particularly those exported, can be very good.

Grappa is still something of an acquired taste, for it is sharp and fiery, at least when unaged. Some say it tastes more like the stem of the grape than the grape. But when well aged, grappa can become quite domesticated, almost mellow in the mouth. Hemingway appreciated grappa, and his characters are continuously consuming it. Even California produces a small amount of Grappa.

Here are some Italian grappas you can rely on: Stock, Martini & Rossi, Sembenotti, and Cavaglio.

Grappa should be drunk like brandy.

GRASSHOPPER (COCKTAIL) This is not the green, jumpy kind, but the green, slurping kind, one of the most popular of American after-dinner drinks. And one of the best "spirited" digestives.

The makings: 1 pony (¾

oz.) green crème de menthe, 1 pony white crème de cacao, and 1 pony cream—or a bit more to taste. Shake with ice, strain—or blend quickly in a blender. It tastes better in a shallow sherbet-type glass.

A variation, called the Coffee Hopper, or anything similar, substitutes a coffee liqueur for the crème de cacao, and uses (if available) white crème de menthe instead of the green.

To expedite the concocting of Grasshoppers, you can buy special "Grasshopper" bottles containing both green crème de menthe and white crème de cacao. Bols has an imported version, with 7 ounces of each, at an impressive $10, or thereabouts. The domestic versions are more reasonably priced, and the liqueurs are just about as good: Mohawk has such a two-compartment bottle, with 7½ oz. of each liqueur, at around $8. Jacquin has a four-compartment contrivance, containing, beside the Grasshopper innards, **Forbidden Fruit** and blackberry-flavored brandy—6 oz. of each—price, $14 or more.

To simplify things still further, some liqueur firms do everything for you but drink the Grasshopper. They bottle the whole thing: bottled Grasshopper. All you have to do is pour and drink. Heublein has one, 30°, at about $4.50 (24 oz.), and Bols (domestic) one, 55°, about $5 (24 oz.). Both are quite adequate, but you'll have a better drink at half the price if you make your own Grasshopper from scratch.

GREECE — BRANDY The Greeks enjoy their brandy, and they make a lot of it, both for home consumption and for export. But the Greeks are fond of adulteration—only of their beverages, of course. They add resin to their wines, and they add a variety of "botanicals" to a lot of their brandies. Their two most famous brandies, metaxa and ouzo, are both "improved" brandies.

Some "straight" Greek brandy is made, of course, and a number of brands are imported to the U.S. These are not very highly regarded by experts, but they have been becoming increasingly popular in recent years. The major brand-name is Cambas.

GRENADINE *Grenadine* is French for "pomegranate," and that's the principal flavoring agent in this well known syrup. Grenadine is pinkish-red in color, and very sweet. It is used to add sweetness and/or color to a drink.

Grenadine is usually nonalcoholic, but a few American liqueur firms make a low-proof, usually 25°, grenadine. Ironically, it is because of federal regulations that these firms are forced to make their grenadine alcoholic: the law does not allow a liqueur firm to produce a nonalcoholic beverage.

Alcoholic grenadine—sounds like someone's old spinster aunt—is used in exactly the same way as the nonalcoholic. It sells, of course, for more, but at its lowly price (about $3.25/fifth) it's worth the difference.

GUILD BLUE RIBBON BRANDY Here's a good and trustworthy name in California brandy. It used to be called Winemaster's Guild

Brandy, because that's who makes it: Winemaster's of Lodi, Calif. Lodi, in the Sacramento Valley, could be called the brandy capital of California; a huge amount of brandy is made here. "Lodi Scotch," the natives call it.

It's the Flame Tokay grape that largely accounts for the success of "Lodi Scotch." The grape makes good brandy, and it thrives in Lodi's deep sandy loam soil, blessed by near ideal climate.

Guild Blue Ribbon Brandy comes in two styles: a "regular," selling for around $5, and a 12-year-old, at $8.75 (quart). The "regular"—it doesn't call itself that on the label—is a good, honest potion. The 12-year-old is Guild's pride and joy, and it shows. It has a lovely bouquet, good body, good flavor.

GUILD WINERIES AND DISTILLERIES Guild is a huge California growers' cooperative, headquartered in San Francisco, with seven wineries, plus a half-dozen distilleries. Guild makes wine under a host of different labels (Cresta Blanca, Winemaster's, Tavola, Cribari, to name a few) and ditto with their brandies. Beside their Guild Blue Ribbon, they produce these brandies: Ceremony 5-year-old and 8-year-old, Cresta Blanca, Cribari, Guild Blue Ribbon, Old San Francisco, Roma Director's Choice, and St. Mark. All are independent operations, but all are owned by Guild.

Not all of these brandies are nationally available, however. Roma Director's Choice is found only in California, Wisconsin, Illinois, and the East

Coast. St. Mark Brandy is sold only in Wisconsin, which seems most odd until one realizes that Wisconsin, for some unfathomable reason, consumes more brandy per capita than any other state in the union. More than a hundred brands of brandy are available in the state, and this brandy madness is called the "Wisconsin Mystery."

In a day when bigness is suspect and "conglomerate" a questionable if not a dirty word, one might wonder about Guild with its manifold subsidiaries. But relax, the corporation's not for burning. Guild allows its distilleries (and wineries as well) to do each its own thing. And the overall assessment of their dozen-plus brandies can only be: Well done, son! Some of the brandies, of course, are more successful than others, and for individual evaluations, see under the various brand names.

H

HAIG SCOTCH WHISKY; HAIG & HAIG SCOTCH WHISKY A lot of names associated with Scotch whisky—Ballantine, Grant, Dewar—stretch far back into Scottish history, but none goes back nearly so far as that of Haig. The first Haig came to Scotland with William the Conqueror, in 1066. And they've been there ever since.

As far back as the early 17th century we read of one Robert Haig engaging in a bit of distilling along with his farming—or was it a bit of farming along with his distilling? Through the 18th century, the Haigs were wholly engrossed in the distilling business. In the mid-18th century, of the eleven children of one John Haig, five sons came to own distilleries, and two of the daughters married into families in the whisky business. And the whole Clan of Haig continued to do more of the same through the 19th century.

In 1877 a later John Haig, founder of John Haig & Co., joined with five other distillers to form the **Distillers Company Limited.** In 1923 another distillery by the name of Haig joined the D.C.L. Group—this one, in no way connected with John Haig & Co., was called Haig & Haig. Wherefore D.C.L. today embraces Haig, and Haig & Haig.

The well-known "pinched" bottle was introduced by John Haig & Co. around 1900, and was later picked up by Haig & Haig. Clearly, it has proved a valuable gimmick over the years, and has helped keep Haig, and Haig & Haig among America's most popular Scotch whiskies.

"Plain" Haig—they're all 86° —sells in the U.S. for around $9 (fifth); Haig & Haig 5 Star for about the same; and Haig & Haig "Pinch" for about $12 (fifth).

HAITI — RUMS The only Haitian rum ordinarily found in the U.S. today is **Barbancourt,** coming in both a three-star and five-star version, around $7.50 and $9.50 (fifths) respectively, both 86°. Both are fine, medium-bodied, sipping rums. Haitians consume a lot of their own rum, but they also use it in their voodoo ceremonies, pouring it over the ground for the consumption of the gods. Not heartily recommended at $9.50 per fifth—unless, of course, some big fat fire-belching voodoo monster is hot on your tail.

HANGOVERS AND HANGOVER CURES The Italians call it *stonato*, "out of tune"; the French, *guele de bois*, "mouth full of wood"; the Germans, *Katzenjammer*, "the wailing of cats"; the Swedes, *hont i haret,* "pain in the roots of the hair"—and the ancient Romans simply *crapula,* which sounds about right.

But perhaps the English language puts it best of all: hangover. The name refers, of course, to what hangs over the black infernal precipice on the morning after the night before. Which is to say: all of you, but especially your guts, gizzard, and eyeballs. It all hangs out and over, and you pray fervently to die. But God who sees in secret rewards you (Matthew 6: 4) and He (She?) won't let you die. Not until you learn.

But first one must needs meditate on the blessedness of hangovers. Hangovers, in the final analysis, are the special creation, not of Satan, but of the Almighty. They are the Lord's way of reminding wayward, self-indulgent humankind that all of God's good things—from butterflies and sunsets to alcoholic beverages and Soufflés Grand Marnier—are to be enjoyed in moderation.

Hangovers began the day the first primitive man swallowed the first primitive gourdful of the first primitive fermented brew. And the first hangover cure was invented the following morning.

There have been, by the latest computer calculation, precisely 9,876,025 hangover cures invented since the dawn of fermentation. And they range all the way from boiled cabbage (favored by the Egyptians) to ground birds' beaks (favorite remedy of the Assyrians) to tripe and chili soup (much beloved of the Mex-icans). The British of olden times, when sore oppressed by the malaise, took to slapdash horseback riding. The notion was to jar the poisonous alcoholic vapors out of the liver. And if there were no horses handy, a lusty battle was recommended.

Here in ascending order of effectiveness are the morning-after remedies mostly commonly recommended in our own enlightened land and time:

1. Exercise (jogging, swimming): You need exercise like a moose needs a hatrack—it's precisely overexertion that caused most of your misery.

2. Cold showers: Forget it. They only serve to awaken you and so make you more aware of the ache in your toenails and tailbone.

3. Alka-Seltzer: If you can stand to look at it as it fizzes and hisses at you, you might as well consume it—won't do you any good, won't do you any harm.

4. Fresh air: This is good stuff—if you live in an area that has some. Breathe lots of it deeply.

5. Beef bouillon: Why not? It's nourishment and you need sustenance if you care to survive.

6. Orange juice, cranberry juice: Ditto.

7. Vitamins: They're easy to take—they don't talk back to you, not even when your complexion is green and your liver black—and they may even do you some wee good; especially vitamin B1 (thiamin).

8. Sedatives: Ah, this is probably what the doctor would order. In fact, some do:

Richard S. Shore, M.D., and John M. Luce, M.D., in *To Your Health* (New York: Seabury Press, 1976), recommend "small doses of analgesics with antacids and mild sedatives." A mild sedative such as Valium or Librium just might help soothe those frayed, exposed nerve endings.

But the most ancient, most honored, and most *fallacious* remedy of all is some "hair of the dog that bit you," a modicum of that same cursed beverage that caused this vile distemper to begin with. The expression "hair of the dog" seems to have started with this 17th-century rhyme:

But be sure overnight,
If this dog do you bite,
You may take it henceforth
for a warning;
Soon as out of your bed
To settle your head,
Take a hair of his tail in the
morning.

Below are listed the most popular hair of the dog "remedies." None of them comes with a money-back waranty. Assuredly, they'll all lift your spirits and your saggin' sacroiliac for a trice or longer, but ultimately they are only protracting the inevitable recovery period.

1. Prairie Oyster: This is the most highly regarded of all morning-after cures. It's also the oldest and most shocking, especially since you're supposed to down it in one huge gulp. One authority advises that upon consumption you open your eyes very slowly. Here's how: Mix together:

Some ice cubes, 1 jigger brandy or Cognac, 1 tsp. Worcestershire sauce, 1 tsp. vinegar, dash of Tabasco

On top of this questionable assemblage float one unbroken egg yolk. Sprinkle it with a bit of Cayenne pepper. Down the hatch in one fell swoop without breaking the yolk. It's guaranteed to effect *something*, for good or ill.

Some experts recommend that before the grisly procedure above, you drink a Coke (straight from the bottle) as fast as possible. Not recommended unless you want to suffer from hiccups the remainder of your mortal days.

2. Hair-of-the-Dog Cocktail: Here's a soul-satisfying and gracious kind of drink, whether you're suffering from the malaise or not. If it does nothing else, it provides nutriment. Mix together or shake vigorously, or mix in a blender:

1 jigger Scotch, 1 jigger heavy cream, ½ oz. honey, a few ice cubes

3. **Bloody Mary**
4. **Bullshot**
5. Fernet Branca: This is unquestionably the vilest liquid God has ever allowed to encumber this earth. The reasoning behind this revolting Italian concoction is obviously that anything tasting this bad must do some good to someone somehow and somewhere. And no one on this earthly planet is more in need of having something, anything, done for him than is the hungover one.

No matter how you take Fernet Branca—over ice, with shaved ice, diluted with soda—it still tastes awful. So you might as well brace yourself and take it straight. But watch out for your fillings!

Fernet Branca is said to be made from rhubarb—tastes more like it comes straight from coal tar and raw sewage. It's a respectable 78°, and can be found in just about every country in the world. (Could it be that hangovers are pandemic?) Some people recommend taking Fernet Branca with coffee, but that just ruins the coffee and the Fernet Branca still tastes like the depths of hell. But it just might help. Some drunks swear by it.

Fernet Branca is now made in the U.S., by a branch of the original company, Fratelli Branca; it sells for around $5 (fifth). A kindred bitters—for that's what Fernet Branca is technically—is Underberg from Germany. It's just as vile in taste—and equally effective or ineffective, as you will.

One persistent myth regarding hangovers sorely needs to be laid to rest—forever. But it won't be. Not by this writing nor a thousand to follow. One can only try. It is the almost universal belief that "mixing drinks" causes mammoth hangovers. Balderdash and old wives' tales! Studies have shown over and over again that the amount of hangover is in direct proportion to the total amount of alcohol consumed in a given period of time . . . no more and no less. This, of course, is presuming that all other things are equal—which they rarely, if ever, are. And thereby hangs most of the tale, for it is those "other things" that usually determine the length and breadth and depth of your hangover. You had the beginnings of a cold—you were depressed, fretful—or you were joyous and expansive—you did or did not eat any food—you were very tired. These are the mundane trivia that will mightily influence the size of your malaise.

Of course if one *thinks* that mixing drinks—starting with Scotch, proceeding to Black Russians, and ending with Thunderbird—is going to cause a morning-after horror, then it most certainly will do precisely that. If one is heartily convinced that Tanqueray Gin causes no hangover, but that Rum and Coke causes horrendous ones, then given the same amount of alcoholic intake, it will surely be so.

Let it be noted, however, that the *type* of alcoholic beverage consumed does seem to have some small influence on morning-after distress. The flavoring agents that are carried over after distillation into the finished beverage are called congeners. It is these that give a particular spirit its distinct taste: what makes vodka taste different from gin, and Scotch from bourbon. It is known that different spirits can metabolize in the human body at different rates depending on their congener content. But these are minute differences, and they are not responsible for the mammoth distress you suffered on New Year's Day, 1945. That was caused by mammoth consumption alone, unassisted and unabated.

One authority, Kingsley Amis, in *On Drink* (London: Jonathan Cape, 1972, pp. 95-99), well versed in the subject of hangovers, recommends specific reading and listening for such crapulous times. His recommendations are predicated on the premise that "you must feel worse emotionally before you start to feel better." As for reading, this savant says you should start with *Paradise Lost* (Book XII, lines 606 to end) and conclude with P. G. Wodehouse or Peter De Vries. (All this is presuming you can persuade your eyeballs to focus properly.) As regards listening, you are advised to start with Tchaikovsky's Sixth Symphony, particularly the last movement, which "evokes total despair."

The simple, gruesome truth is that there is no cure for this ancient curse, the hangover. Some of the above "cures" may actually prove helpful, but more for psychological than for physiological reasons.

Hangovers consist mainly of simple fatigue—you stayed up too late, talked too much, clowned too much, exuberated too much, scintillated too much, oh yes, and drank too much. And slept too little. And the remedy for fatigue is rest. The best cure for most hangovers is to sleep for a day and a half. If you cannot do that, go to your "closet" (Matthew 6: 6, King James Version), and pray for deliverance or death—whichever comes first.

(I. W.) HARPER KENTUCKY STRAIGHT BOURBON WHISKEY There never was a person named I. W. Harper. The name seems to be the initials of one of the founders of the business, Isaac Wolfe Bernheim, and the last name of one of the firm's top salesman, Harper.

At all events, the business had its beginning when I. W. Bernheim and his brother, Bernard, began wholesaling whiskey from the back room of a grocery store in Paducah, Ky., around 1870. It wasn't until 25 years later, in 1897, that the Bernheim brothers built their own distillery; by that time they had spread the name of I. W. Harper across the continent.

All I. W. Harper labels display a number of gold medals, and to make sure you get the message, the words "Gold Medal" are also there. It's not all promotion. Truth to tell, I. W. Harper Whiskey received a number of gold medals in the days of its youth: the first, in 1885, at the New Orleans Exposition, followed by similar honors at the Chicago World's Fair, 1893, a Paris award in 1900, and St. Louis in 1904.

I. W. Harper continued to be made on a very limited scale during Prohibition, as a "medicinal spirit." With Repeal, the Bernheim brothers bowed out, and today, I. W. Harper is the property of the mammoth Schenley Industries, Inc.

I. W. Harper is, of course, a classical bourbon. Its gold medals also say something good about it, but not everything, certainly. It is one of the most expensive straights (see the low standing of both the 86° 5-year-old, the 10-year-old, and the bonded, in the list of straights, under bourbon). It is a full-flavored, full-bodied whiskey. Whether it is worth its premium price seems most questionable. But it's your decision, your money. But *taste* and judge—don't drink the label!

HARTLEY BRANDY This is a California brandy made by

United Vintners, the giant California wine organization owned by **Heublein.** Other brands include **Lejon** and **Jacques Bonet.** Hartley is one of its younger, more economical brandies (about $5 a fifth), simple and light, but no great bargain. Experts have detected off flavors in Hartley.

A 100° is also made, about $6 (fifth), a decent price for a bottled-in-bond brandy, but it's not taking any blue ribbons either.

HARVEY WALLBANGER (COCKTAIL)

This drink has a marvelous history—even if it isn't true! The story is that a certain young California surfer by the name of Harvey—surname or given name, it matters not—used to conclude his arduous days of surfing at a tiny, hole-in-the-wall Southern California bar, where he consumed unnumbered "Italian Screwdrivers": orange juice, vodka, and Galliano. By the time Harvey departed, his radar was somewhat askew, and as he exited, he caromed from wall to wall: Harvey the Wallbanger.

This tale was vigorously promoted by the McKesson Liquor Company (New York, N.Y.), sole U.S. importer of Galliano, through the '60s, and the drink became a national favorite, and the sale of Galliano skyrocketed.

The Wallbanger is simply a **Screwdriver** with Galliano. Fill a tall glass with ice, orange juice, a jigger or so of vodka, stir, and then float a half-jigger of Galliano on top.

If the high price of Galliano (around $12 for 23 oz.-bottle) distresses you, use one of the numerous substitutes now being marketed: **Roiano,** Gaetano, Florentino, or Neapolitan. (for details on the latter three, see under **Galliano**).

HAWAII—RUMS

These are the newest rummy arrivals on the American scene, and they're fully in keeping with current American tastes: light in color, body, and proof (80°), similar in price (about $5 a fifth) and quality to **Virgin Island rums.** Leilani is the most popular brand.

HEAVEN HILL KENTUCKY STRAIGHT BOURBON WHISKEY

Heaven Hill is one of the very few independent brands of whiskey left in America today. In fact, the Heaven Hill Distilleries, Inc., is the largest independent distillery in the U.S. in our time. (Heaven Hill also makes **Evan Williams**). Virtually every whiskey brand—and that includes bourbons, Scotches, and Canadians—is in the hands of some conglomerate in these latter days.

And, praise Bacchus, Heaven Hill is good bourbon whiskey—it's from Nelson County, Kentucky, and that fact alone almost guarantees quality. Even the name is real, not a Madison Avenue invention: Heavenhill was the name of the farmer who owned the land where the original distillery was built.

Heaven Hill 100°, bottled in bond, is one of the best buys in that category (see listing under **bourbon**), about $5.50 (750ml, 2 oz. less than a fifth). It also comes in a 4-year-old (nonbonded) version, and a 6-year-old Heaven Hill Old Style, both 86°. The 4-year-old sells for about $4.50 (25.4 oz.), the 6-year-old for about a dollar more. Good values, good bourbon.

HENNESSY COGNAC It's not as Irish as Potsheen or Pattie's pig, but it's purely Gaelic in origin. Hennessy Cognac had its beginning back in the 18th century when a wandering, adventurous young Irishman shipped a couple of barrels of the local brandy of Cognac, France, to some of his old drinking buddies back in County Cork, Ireland. It was an instant success—"marvelous recuperative powers," they said. The lad's name was Richard Hennessy, the year, 1765. Richard's son, James, solidified the business and it's his name that's on the label: Jas. Hennessy & Co.

Hennessy Cognac is a marvelous spirit—all Cognac is wondrous, for that matter, if it's entitled to the name Cognac, by definition, it has a certain excellence and distinction.

Hennessy is one of the three giants of the industry (the other two: Martell and Courvoisier) and is probably the largest of all. Hennessy possesses the largest stock of aged Cognac in the world: some 60 million bottles! ("Bottles-worth" might be more accurate, as the Cognac is stored in casks, where it continues to improve, rather than in bottles, where it would be impervious to further change.)

The Hennessy Company owns the most famous nose in the world—excepting, perhaps, that of Cyrano de Bergerac (which town is just a few miles

down the road), and Jimmy the Schnoz Durante—the renowned nose of the Fillioux family, the chief tasters for Hennessy Cognac for an incredible eight generations. The current chief taster is Maurice Fillioux, and the assistant taster is his son, Yann.

The tasting of Cognac is a refined art, a delicate skill, and it is the human nose that is the sensitive, discerning instrument. Computers here are worthless and chemical analyses tell little. It is the nose alone that can tell which batch of young Cognac will become great with time, which only run of the mill.

The Fillioux family has cultivated delicate noses for more than 200 years. Tradition dictates that Fillioux males marry local Charente girls who have grown up close to the soil and the grapes, and who promise to bear male heirs with talented noses.

And now, heresy of all heresies, Yann Fillioux has up and married a Paris girl. How these alien bloodlines may affect future Fillioux noses, no one nose . . . apologies! Rest assured, however, that Hennessy Cognacs will continue to be of the same nobility.

Hennessy makes six regular grades of Cognac, listed here from the least expensive—one dare not say "cheapest"; how gauche and demeaning—to the most expensive:

Bras Armé: Pronounced *braz armay;* it means "arm of might" and it's pictured on the label—the arm clutching the battle axe. This is the company's standard Cognac—equivalent of three-star—for use in mixed drinks, they say, but at better than $12 (fifth), the peasantry is not advised to squander this beautiful potion in some nameless, formless holiday punch. Sip it—slowly, appreciatively.

VSOP: Only recently become available in the U.S., it's smooth, with a touch of woodiness. Around $16 (fifth).

Bras d'Or: "Arm of Gold"—same arm as the Bras Armé, but of gold, not brass. With quality to match. In blind tastings this Cognac has invariably placed well. It's soft and mellow, less woody than the VSOP. Around, ouch, $18 (fifth).

Bras d'Or Napoleon: Recall that "Napoleon" is sheer hyperbole on a Cognac label. (see under **Cognac**). In fact, this is a new label with Hennessy and the first time the firm has invoked the sacred name. It's an excellent beverage, as well it should be, at about $34 (fifth).

X.O.: The initials mean "Extra Old," and that it is. And X.E. as well: Extra expensive, $37 to $40 (25.4 oz.). Experts say that for the price, X.O. is the best value among Cognacs of this price range. But for the vast majority of humankind, alas, this is like finding a good value in yachts and Lear Jets.

Extra: It's made in limited quantities every year and is not always available. It's a blend of very fine old Cognacs, 50 to 70 years old, and is horrendously expensive: presently around $90 (25.4 oz.). Extra is a wondrous beverage, incredibly suave, elegant, and complex. Sip it very carefully.

So much for the standard Hennessy Cognacs. In 1976, to honor France's historic ties with the U.S., particularly in Colonial times, Hennessy marketed a special bicentennial Cognac. It comes in a special decanter, similar to those of 200 years ago, and is even sealed with cork and wax. It is deliberately blended to resemble 18th-century Cognacs: full-bodied and stout. Cuvée Bicentenaire is similar to Hennessy's Bras d'Or and is similarly priced: about $18 (fifth).

Another special Hennessy Cognac was produced in the spring of 1977 to honor Queen Elizabeth II's Silver Jubilee. And in wholly regal fashion! Sixty bottles of this "royal" Cognac were flown to England by Hennessy Company jet. The precious liquid is about 100 years old, and comes from the Hennessy family's private cellars. It is not a blend (as most Cognacs are) but comes from a single vintage from the Domaine de la Sauzade, in the heart of the Grande Champagne region of Cognac. Each bottle carries a handwritten label, and it sells—are you ready for this—for around $150— that's per each darling 25.6 oz. bottle, of course, not per case. If you use it to toast Her Majesty, restraint is recommended.

HERBSAINT It's not pronounced the way it looks, but after the manner of the French, *airb-sahn*. It's an American successor—born and bred in Louisiana—to that shadowy and potent drink of Europe, especially of London and Paris, at the turn of the century: absinthe. Widely available in the U.S. today is Legendre Herbsaint, 90°, at about $9 (fifth). It's light green in color, with a predominant licorice flavor. When mixed with water, it turns milky.

HEREFORD'S COWS How now brown cow? And green and yellow and strawberry? Time was when cows gave only milk. Today they give booze! Mocha-flavored booze, and chocolate-mint-flavored, and banana- and strawberry- and coconut-. These are the flavors of Heublein's new milk-based cocktails. "Fortified milkshakes," some may sniff condescendingly. But what's wrong with a fortified milkshake? Milkshakes are good —make one big and fat and strong — and with alcohol they're even better; make you human. And at a mere 30°— just 15% alcohol; many wines are more than that—they're merely nutritious, not *intoxicus*. What's more, they're highly recommended in any flavor, for hangovers of any flavor.

In case you're aware that Herefords are poor milk producers, you might prefer the Aberdeen Cows—they come in the same flavors plus walnut, and sell for a mite less: $3.79 vs. $3.99 (fifth).

But best of all, you can make (breed?) your own cows. The basic recipe is simple. In an electric blender combine the flavoring agent (banana, strawberries, walnuts, etc.), the alcohol, milk, lots of ice, a tad of sugar, a dash of flavoring. Here are the approximate proportions for a:

HOMEMADE COW
For two drinks, combine in a blender:

1 cup fresh milk, 2 tsp. pow-dered sugar, 2 jiggers rum or vodka, or 1 jigger Everclear, 2 cups cracked ice, any *one* of these: 2 whole ripe bananas—if this is the flavor you favor, see Banana Cow for the detailed Rx, 1 cup fresh strawberries (or frozen, thawed), ½ cup walnuts, ½ cup chocolate mint candies (or ½ cup chocolate-mint liqueur), 1 cup coconut milk, 2-3 tablespoons mocha

You can add a dash of Angostura Bitters to any of these for added zip, plus a dash of vanilla to any except the strawberry.

HERRADURA   TEQUILA
The name means "Horseshoe" and it's one of Mexico's prestige tequilas. It's definitely expensive, but if you're a true tequila freak, it may be worth the difference. Herradura is incredibly smooth for a Tequila, with a wonderful fresh aroma. If you appreciate your tequila straight, this may be your *copita*.

Herradura comes in three versions: Silver, Reposado ("Tranquil"), and Añejo ("Aged"), all 92°, high for tequila (most are 80°). They are priced (per fifth, in the Western U.S.) in ascending order, according to their age: Silver, around $10; Reposado, around $11; and Añejo, around $14.

The Silver boasts on its label that it is "100% Blue Agave." *A fortiori*, the Reposado and Anejo are the same. By Mexican law, tequila need be only 51% from that honored member of the cactus family—the balance may be sugar-syrup distillate.

Reposado's full name is "Natural Gold Reposado," signifying that the golden color of the tequila is not artificially contrived (usually by the addition of caramel) but comes from the tequila having been aged in oak casks for 8 to 10 months.

Herradura Tequila is imported by the Bing Crosby–Phil Harris Importing Company (Burlingame, Calif.), and other than old Two Fingers himself (see **Two Fingers Tequila** for the story), who would be apt to know more about tequila than these two beloved old drunks?

HEUBLEIN, INC. This is one of the largest spirits and wine conglomerates in the world. Annual sales from all of Heublein's diversified products amount to more than $1.5 billion. In 1977, a disappointing year, net income was down to a mere $41 million (from $73 million in 1976).

Heublein celebrated its 100th anniversary in 1975. The company started most humbly, in 1875, when Gilbert and Louis Heublein opened a modest business on a small side street in Hartford, Conn. Packaging and promotion were in their infancy in those days, and the brothers' idea was to package select food and beverages for home consumption. Their clientele would be the carriage trade. They began with Milshire Gin, A.1 Sauce, and bottled cocktails. Bottled cocktails? Aren't these one of Heubleins' novel promotions of the 1970s, not 1870s? Those handy little canned Wallban-

gers and Manhattans and Tequila Sunrises? Right—and wrong. Incredibly, Heublein introduced bottled cocktails in 1892—and the brand name was "Club" then, just as it is now. In the 1970s, Heublein returned to the scene of its early conquests, with premixed cocktails in handy minicans. The more things change, the more they remain the same.

Today Heublein is a many-splendored bird. Besides its spirits and wine holdings, Heublein now markets many specialty sauces and convenience foods. No. 1, in honor if not in sales, is A.1. Sauce, one of Heublein's earliest acquisitions. In fact it was thanks to A.1. that Heublein was able to survive the desiccated, dispirited days of Prohibition. Heublein today owns and dispenses these principal brands of goodies (among many others): Colonel Sanders' Kentucky Fried Chicken, H. Salt Seafood, Zantingo Mexican-American Foods, A.1. Steak Sauce, Grey Poupon Mustard, Ortega Tacos, Chilis, etc., Snap-E-Tom Tomato Cocktail, Regina Wine Vinegar and Cooking Wines, Escoffier Sauces, and Steak Supreme Sauce.

Heublein's spirits and wine holdings, of course, are its principle asset. These are vast and varied, indeed. Herewith, a *partial* listing of the more important brands:

Spirits: Smirnoff Vodka, **Black Velvet** Canadian Whisky, **Black & White Scotch,** Buchanan's Scotch, Arrow cordials and brandies, **Bahia** Licor de cafe, Heublein Cocktails, The Club Cocktails, Jose **Cuervo Tequila,** Don Q. Rum, **Irish Mist, Lejon Brandy,** Felipe II Spanish Brandy, **Jacques Bonet Brandy**, **Tullamore Dew Irish Whiskey**, **Popov Vodka**, Relska Vodka, McMaster's Scotch and Canadian Whisky, **Matador Tequila**, Malcolm Hereford's Cows, **Yukon Jack** Canadian Liqueur, and **Boggs Cranberry Liqueur**.

California wines: Beaulieu Vineyard, Inglenook Vineyard, Italian Swiss Colony, Petri, Colony, Annie Green Springs, T. J. Swann, Bali Hai, Sangrole, Mission Bell, Santa Fe, H.M.S. Frost, Lejon (Champagne), and Jacques Bonet (Champagne).

Imported wines: Lancers Vin Rose, Vinho Branco, Rubeo, Harvey's Sherries and Ports, Bouchard Père & Fils Burgundy, Egri Bikaver Hungarian Wine, Tokaji Aszu Hungarian Dessert Wine, Vinya Rose, Kiku Masumune Sake, and Taru Sake.

But with all these variagated products, many of them big loud winners in their respective fields, it was a single item that enabled Heublein to achieve its present lofty eminence: **Smirnoff Vodka**. Heublein, with rare insight, coupled with phenomenal good luck, bought that Russian-invented vodka for a pittance in 1939, and nurtured, cajoled, and promoted it into the best-selling spirit in the world! (It is the No. 2 selling spirit in the U.S., behind Seagram's 7 Crown Whiskey.)

If Heublein knows anything, it's brand-building. Look what they accomplished with Smirnoff Vodka: from 2,000 cases per year in 1939 to more than 11 million cases world-wide today. Look at what they are doing today with Black Velvet Canadian Whisky: Introduced to the U.S. market in 1964, it is now the nation's fastest-growing major liquor brand. Look at what they've done with Jose Cuervo Tequila: almost unknown in the U.S. a few years ago, today it's America's best-selling tequila.

Nobody quarrels with success, except when the product is not somehow superior. Which has sometimes been the case with Heublein—as with every other purveyor of spirits in the history of mankind. Some notably unsuperior Heublein products include Yukon Jack, Jacques Bonet Brandy, and Bogg's Cranberry Liqueur. But happily the superior products far outnumber the nonsuperior.

HILL AND HILL KENTUCKY STRAIGHT BOURBON WHISKEY The name seems to have come from two brothers, William and T. C. Hill, who first made this whiskey in western Kentucky around 1880. Today it's owned by the American conglomerate, **National Distillers Products Company**, and is found mainly in the Western U.S. The straight bourbon is available 80°, 86°, and 100°. There is also a Hill and Hill Blend, available at about the same price, about $5.50 (fifth), for the 80°.

HINE COGNAC Don't give the name a spurious French pronunciation, *een-ay*, as it's pure English—rhymes with wine! Thomas Hine was a redoubtable Englishman who married into the **Delamain Cognac** family, and then proceeded to found his own establishment. That was in the early 19th century; today Hine

Cognac is the property of the huge **Distillers Company Limited** of England and Scotland.

Some claim that Hine Cognacs are more distinctive than most—perhaps so, but it would require a highly trained palate and an extremely sensitive proboscis to detect the distinctiveness.

Here, in ascending order of price, are the Hine Cognacs commonly shipped to the U.S.:

Sceptre: This is a three-star Cognac, medium-bodied, with a hint of oakiness. In one blind tasting with California brandies and other Cognacs, it placed dead last. The complaint was of a "bitter, dry taste," and a "soapy nose." Around $13.

V.SO.P. Fine Champagne: Experts have usually given this Cognac high marks. It's light, with a nice touch of woodiness. Around $16.

Triomphe Grande Champagne: Hines' "top of the line," and tops it is. Lovely bouquet, delicious flavor. It is lighter-bodied than other Cognacs in this exclusive price range. Around $46.

HIRAM WALKER CORDIALS

For some reason Hiram Walker still calls its liqueurs cordials—most firms now call them liqueurs (the terms are synonymous). Perhaps it's the Canadian influence, for Hiram Walker is a Canadian-based operation, although the cordials are all American-made.

Hiram Walker cordials are good, not great—standard, not exceptional. They're wholly American, both in consistency and in value. In fact, Hiram Walker cordials are usually a bit cheaper than most of their American competition, and American-made liqueurs are already the most economical of the world's liqueurs. All of which is to say: Hiram Walker cordials are usually excellent values.

HIRAM WALKER CRYSTAL LONDON DRY GIN

This has always been a popular gin—as it deserves to be. It now sells well over 500,000 cases per year. Walker's Gin is priced right—it usually sells for somewhat less than other comparable American gins. Good gin, good value; 80° and 86°.

HIRAM WALKER–GOODERHAM & WORTS LTD.

This Canadian-based holding company is one of the largest liquor companies in the world. Its executive offices are in Walkerville, a suburb of Ontario, Canada; Walkerville owes its existence to Hiram Walker.

Through its various subsidiaries, Hiram Walker–Gooderham & Worts produces and sells all manner of distilled spirits: Canadian whiskies, Scotch whiskies, liqueurs, cognacs, bourbons, gin, rum, and vodka.

Hiram Walker–Gooderham & Worts started out in 1858 as simple Hiram Walker, when an enterprising young Bostonian by that name moved to Canada and began distilling whisky (Canadians call it whisky, not whiskey). At first he called his light, distinctive spirit simply "Club Whisky" to tell the world that it was elegant enough to find welcome in any gentleman's club. Later he added "Canadian" to the name and it sold even better. Hiram

Walker was an astounding business genius, and by 1863 he had formed a partnership, and his company became Hiram Walker & Co. When a son came into the business (1871) it became Hiram Walker & Son, and when another followed a few years later, it became Hiram Walker & Sons.

Hiram Walker & Sons was already a huge and flourishing success when the founder died in 1899. Walker never relinquished his American citizenship, and, in fact, continued to reside in Detroit, commuting daily to Canada to work.

Hiram Walker was succeeded by a man of equal business acumen, Harry C. Hatch. Hatch began in Toronto, Canada, in 1911, with the purchase of a retail liquor store; in 1923 he arranged financing for the purchase of Gooderham & Worts, Canada's oldest distillery. Just three years later he plunked down a cool $14 million for the purchase of Hiram Walker & Sons, Ltd., Walkerville. So was born Hiram Walker–Gooderham & Worts.

Canadian Club Whisky was the backbone of the organization, but Hatch quickly broadened his base, with the purchase of Scotch-whisky blending houses, and in 1936 he acquired the big-selling Ballantine's Scotch. Today, H. Clifford Hatch, son of Harry C., is president of Hiram Walker-Gooderham & Worts.

Hiram Walker–Gooderham & Worts today manufactures and/or sells an unbelievable array of spirits and even some wines: besides its best seller, Canadian Club, and an entire line of Hiram Walker cordials and spirits, here are a few of the familiar names: Peter Heering (cherry liqueur), Kahlúa, Ambassador Scotch, Two Fingers Tequila, Barclay's Bourbon, Skol Vodka, Arandas Tequila, Maraca Rum, Tia Maria, Courvoisier, Sandeman Port, and many, many more.

Oddly enough, the company fell upon bad times in the 1960s, not noting the changing tastes of spirits consumers around the world. Around 1965 the firm toppled from its top position as the world's most profitable liquor company. Today, a resurgence is underway, and Hiram Walker–Gooderham & Worts is slowly regaining some of its lost terrain.

HIRAM WALKER, INC.

This is one of the many subsidiaries of the great liquor firm Hiram Walker–Gooderham & Worts, Ltd., of Walkerville, Ontario, Canada. This part of the sprawling conglomerate is in Detroit, Mich., and produces and/or markets: Canadian Club Whisky, Hiram Walker Brandy, Gin, and Vodka, Hiram Walker cordials, Imperial Blended Whisky, Imperial Gin and Vodka, Lauder's Scotch, Royal Canadian Whisky, Ten High Bourbon, Thorne's Scotch, Two Fingers Tequila, Hiram Walker Special Canadian Whisky, Hiram Walker Private Cellar Bourbon, and William Penn Blended Whisky.

These are the principal brands coming out of the Detroit plant. There are another couple of dozen lesser names.

HOT BUTTERED RUM

Here's one of the world's best warmer-uppers—far superior to and tastier than thermal underwear or electric blankets. Hot Buttered Rum has been an American favorite since Colonial days, and there are as many recipes as there are people who have brewed it from that day to this. Some recipes are too elaborate for common consumption, some too bare-bones. For the perfect Hot Buttered Rum, assemble:

> 1 small cinammon stick— about 1 inch, 2 whole cloves, 2 whole allspice (optional), 1 lump sugar, or one tsp. granulated, 1 pat butter, 1 jigger Jamaican or Demerara rum—preferably; otherwise, any rum, boiling water, ground nutmeg.

Rinse a mug with boiling water (to warm it), put all the ingredients in, fill the mug with boiling water, sprinkle with nutmeg. Be cautioned: don't bolt it down—you won't be able to, it will be too hot. The longer it sits, the better it gets.

HOUSE OF STUART SCOTCH WHISKY This Scotch whisky is marketed by **Barton Brands, Ltd.**, originally of Kentucky, now headquartered in Chicago, a firm that began with Bourbon whiskey, and that is still their forte. House of Stuart is bulk-imported to the U.S. at considerable saving, which should make it a good buy. It's 80° or 86° and economically priced, it's true— about $5 (750 ml: 2 oz. less than a fifth)—but it's still no bargain; like a battered wrestler, it has a flat nose and a hard bite.

Newly introduced in the U.S. is a 12-year-old House of Stuart, only limitedly available at present. Let us hope the additional years will bring distinction upon the ill-famed House of Stuart.

I

IRISH COFFEE It's almost an institution, and it's certainly a liturgy and a celebration, and beyond all question, it's one of the world's best-known and best-loved mixed drinks. Irish Coffee is simply an inspired combination of three substantial but unpretentious ingredients: coffee, whiskey, cream. But such a celestial amalgam!

Nobody knows for sure where or how Irish Coffee originated, but everybody knows why: to bring warmth and comfort to cold bodies and dispirited souls. Shannon Airport, Ireland, and the Buena Vista Café, Fisherman's Wharf, San Francisco, are two prominent contenders for the invention, and there are another two dozen or twenty dozen other claimants around the world.

Here's how:

Heat a stemmed goblet (or mug) by running it under very hot water. Pour in 4 to 6 oz. of hot strong black coffee; add 1 to 1½ teaspoons of sugar and stir well. Add 1 jigger of Irish whiskey. Fill the goblet to about 1 inch from the brim with more of the coffee. Float whipped cream (sweetened to taste) on top. Do not stir after the cream has been added.

And unless you wish to be visited by vengeful Leprechauns all the days of your life, use only *real* whipped cream—none of that ersatz shaving lather. Cream comes from cows, not cans!

Now for some truly festive and *jubilacious* occasion—a grand wedding, perhaps, or a fine funeral—or some high holy day—St. Patrick's, March 17, or St. Bridget's, of Ireland, of course, not Sweden, February 1—you can make a super Irish Coffee, the likes of which neither you nor your guests are likely to encounter this side of heaven itself. It's a flaming spectacular, so do it with verve and bravado. The recipe:

4 strips orange peel, 4 strips lemon peel, 16 whole cloves, 1 stick cinnamon, 2 tsp. superfine sugar, 5 oz. Irish whiskey, 1½ cups strong hot coffee, A dish of superfine or confectioner's sugar, ¼ cup whipped heavy cream, Two 8-oz. stemmed goblets, mugs, or cups.

Stud the strips of orange and lemon peel with 2 cloves each and place them in a skillet or chafing dish with the stick of cinnamon and the two teaspoons of sugar. Set over moderate heat, stirring occasionally with a wooden spoon, until the sugar has melted; pour the Irish whiskey into the pan and light a match to the liquid. Be sure to step back, since the flame will flare up instantly. Shake the pan back and forth slowly until the flame dies out; pour in the hot coffee all at once and let it come to a simmer. Remove from heat.

Rub the cut edge of a strip of lemon peel around the inside of each glass or mug and dip the container into a dish of sugar so that the sugar adheres to the inside rim. Pour in the coffee, trying not to disturb the sugar. Top each serving with a dollop of whipped cream.

Note: From *Foods of the World: Wines and Spirits*. Published by Time-Life Books, Inc.

IRISH DISTILLERS GROUP LIMITED This is a giant spirits-producing conglomerate headquartered in Dublin, Ireland, which makes almost all the Irish whiskey imported into the U.S.A. Americans usually think of whiskey brands, and especially Irish whiskey brands, as competing fiercely—in the manner of the Fighting Irish. Not so here.

Here are a few of the Irish whiskeys produced by this giant, sprawling corporation: **Paddy, Tullamore Dew,** (John) **Jameson, Old Bushmills,** and (John) **Power's.**

These whiskeys, for better or for worse, constitute the vast bulk of Irish whiskey sold in the U.S. of A.

Perhaps even more astounding is the fact that Irish Distillers Group makes such implausible things as Irish gin, Irish vodka, and Irish rum. Most of the world thinks the Irish have never even heard of such outlandish "foreign" beverages as vodka and gin and rum. They not only know them, they make them! Perhaps even drink a wee spot o'

them here and there. Would you believe: Huzzar **Vodka,** made in Ireland? Kiskadee White Rum, Irish-made? Cork Dry Gin? To date none of these are imported to the U.S.—presumably because nobody would believe them.

IRISH MIST Irish Mist is Ireland's answer to Scotland's **Drambuie.** In fact, Irish Mist was created during World War II when another Scotch liqueur, **Glen Mist,** was being made in Ireland because of the scarcity of Scotch whisky. It was a natural. And, truth to tell, it's a most eloquent answer to Drambuie: just as refined, just as complex and suave, just as tasteful—mellifluent is the only word. And, woe, just as expensive.

Like Drambuie and the other Scotch liqueurs, Irish Mist is flavored with honey, herbs and spices. Its base, of course, is not Scotch whisky, but Irish. And the flavor—but not the bite—of the good Irish whiskey comes through most gracefully.

The giant liquor and wine conglomerate of **Heublein** (Hartford, Conn.) is the sole distributor of Irish Mist in the U.S. It's a good liqueur in spite of that. Heublein's promotion of this excellent modern-day liqueur is simply hokey, most of it trying to make Irish Mist into a mysterious, ancient, clandestine beverage. It's none of those things—but it's good. The phony Heublein pitch could ruin one's taste for Irish Mist—well, almost.

Irish Mist is 80° and sells in the U.S. for almost exactly the same as Drambuie, about $12 (23 oz.).

IRISH WHISKEY Legend says that St. Patrick taught the Irish the art of distilling. Perhaps it's the same legend that says he drove the snakes out of Ireland. Or perhaps the two legends are one: St. Patrick drove the snakes out of the land—and into the pot stills that make the Irish whiskey.

At all events, the Irish have known about distilling for at least 800 years, and they've long been noted for their fondness for the fruit thereof. Our very word, "whiskey," is from the Irish: they called it *usquebaugh*, "water of life." (Note that it's Irish *whiskey*, not *whisky*.)

A century ago Irish whiskey was more popular in the U.S. than Scotch. Today it has lower sales than any other major whiskey in America. The American drift toward lighter drinks has made most of the difference. Irish whiskey is simply not to modern American tastes; it's a full-bodied, strong, manly kind of drink, not for the faint of heart. In very recent years, however, a milder blended type of Irish whiskey has been made, but in the meantime Americans seemed to have lost their taste for Gaelic *usquebaugh*.

Irish whiskey is made by virtually the same process as Scotch, with one major difference: It is not exposed to peat smoke; it lacks entirely Scotch's smoky flavor. Lovers of Irish whiskey insist that above all else, it is *smooth*. Like the dentures in *Jaws*! To the uninitiated, at least at first encounter, Irish whiskey comes on as the very antithesis of smoothness. Hearty, hardy, bracing, yes—smooth, nay, laddie.

Experts tell us that it takes at least 7 years for Irish whiskey to age properly, and most of what is imported to the U.S. is at least that old.

Because of its rugged individuality, Irish whiskey does not mix well. And the Irish would be the first to confirm that fact. They insist, to a man, that the only civilized way to drink Irish whiskey is "neat": straight and clean.

Sure and they would make one grand exception, though, in favor of that international favorite, **Irish Coffee**. Other whiskeys are sometimes substituted, but they are interlopers one and all—such "Irish Coffee" is not just fraudulent, it's blasphemous.

G. K. Chesterton, a thoroughbred Englishman if one ever walked the face of the earth, wrote of Irish whiskey:

> If an Angel out of heaven
> Gives you something else to drink
> Thank him for his kind intention
> And pour it down the sink.

Below are listed the most important Irish whiskeys imported to the U.S. Note that the highest-priced brands are almost double the lowest-priced. The difference in price is due mainly to the difference in age. (But notice McCunn's 12-year-old is in third place!) Experts agree that Irish whiskey does improve with age—perhaps more so than any other distilled spirit. Here is a case, therefore, where the cheapest may not be the best value—but, on the other hand, it is difficult to see that one brand could be almost twice as good as another. Notice also that some Irish whiskeys come in varying proofs at the same price. Always buy the higher proof—it is a better value: You simply get more whiskey and less water for your money.

IRISH WHISKIES IN ASCENDING
ORDER OF PRICE

Shannon, 80°, $6.50 (fifth)
Murphy's, 80° and 86°, $7.32 (fifth)
McCunn's, 12 years, 86.8°, $7.39 (fifth)
Kennedy's, 86°, $7.50 (fifth)
Irish Good Neighbor, 80°, $7.63 (fifth)
Dunphy's Original, 80° and 86°, $7.77 (fifth)
Paddy's, 80°, $7.50 (fifth)
Tullamore Dew, 8 years, 86°, $8.16 (25.4 oz.)
Paddy's 80° $7.50 (fifth)
Old Bushmills, 86°, $8.65 (fifth)
John Jameson, 86°, $8.69 (fifth)
Tullamore Dew, 12 years, 86°, $11.35 (fifth)
John Jameson, 12 years, 86°, $11.45 (fifth)

ITALY—BRANDY Only a few years ago you could not buy any Italian brandy—only Italian Cognac! Literally true! But it was a matter of nomenclature, not quality. Thirty years ago Italian brandies *all* called themselves Cognac—you don't call yourself a Tin Lizzie if you can get away with Rolls-Royce. But by international agreement, Italian grape distillates are now called brandy—correctly so.

Thirty years ago Italian "brandies" were a far, far cry from Cognac, but the gap has been steadily closing. Italian brandies still aren't displacing true French Cognac, but today they're clean, savory, tasteful beverages, particularly those imported to the U.S. Their rising sales attest to their rising quality.

The most popular Italian brandy, by 3 country miles, is **Stock.**

IZARRA All of the world's great liqueurs have inevitably been imitated. Izarra—"Star" in Basque, there on the label—is that region's answer to the great and glamorous French liqueur, Chartreuse. Like Chartreuse, it even comes in two colors and two strengths: green, the stronger of the two, at 100°, and yellow, 86°, the sweeter of the two.

Izarra has an **Armagnac** base—the region is nigh—and uses flowers, fruits, and herbs (including mint and anise) from the adjacent Pyrenees for flavoring. It is sweetened with honey.

Perhaps not as elegant and complex as Chartreuse, Izarra is a fine liqueur in its own right, quite similar to Chartreuse, yet subtly different. Yellow Chartreuse, for example, compared to yellow Izarra, is somewhat sweeter; also, the Izarra, besides being slightly higher in proof, is more straightforward, more pungent. Some say Izarra has the taste of sage and lavender.

Though an obvious imitation, Izarra for all that is no Johnny-come-lately. It's been around for almost 300 years, but has been produced commercially only since 1835. It's made by the same folks who make the excellent Clés des

Ducs; see under **Armagnac.**

Izarra deserves to be sipped on its own (slightly chilled), carefully and pensively—or, at most, on the rocks. Some insist on ice with Izarra, and historically they're correct, as in bygone days it was traditionally taken with snow.

Unhappily Izarra is almost as expensive as Chartreuse, though it differs from Chartreuse in that the higher-proof green costs no more than the yellow: almost $11 (23 oz.), in both the Western and Eastern U.S.

J

J&B RARE SCOTCH WHISKY

Justerini & Brooks was originally Justerini & Johnson, of London, purveyors of fine wines and liqueurs. The business had its humble beginning in 1749, when Giacomo Justerini (Just-ter-EÉN-ee) came from Bologna, Italy, and began making liqueurs in his basement. George Johnson later became a partner, and two generations later (1831) his descendants sold out to Alfred Brooks. And so it's been ever since: Justerini & Brooks, J&B.

J&B Scotch is a status whisky in the U.S., and sells more than 2.5 million cases per year; it is, in fact, the best-selling Scotch in the land. J&B's rise in popularity has been due, at least in part, to the fact that it is a light Scotch, and so has been in synch with America's recent drift toward lighter spirits. J&B Scotch is so light-bodied and light-flavored, in fact, that it has sometimes been downgraded in blind tastings as "too bland," even "faded."

But for those not seeking a "Scotchy" Scotch, for the non-cultists, J&B can easily become a favorite. It's well made, it's smooth, it's light. J&B sells for around $9 (fifth) in New York, and some 50¢ less in California.

JACK DANIEL'S TENNESSEE WHISKEY

Jack Daniel is perhaps the most famous single name in the history of American whiskey. Yet Jack Daniel never made a drop of bourbon whiskey—he made only Tennessee whiskey, which is legally a separate entity.

Jack Daniel started in the whiskey business at the ripe, round age of 10 years, around 1860, in Tennessee. By the time he was 13 years old he owned a still, and during the Civil War he sold his whiskey door to door and saloon to saloon.

In 1866 the Jack Daniel's Distillery was registered by the government, making it the oldest registered distillery in the country. By 1890 the Jack Daniel's Distillery was the largest in the state of Tennessee, producing 80 barrels of whiskey per day.

Jack's whiskey was a success from the day he sold the first barrel. The distillery was never able to keep up with the demand. In a day when American whiskey could be a pretty grisly concoction, Jack Daniel took pains to make "the best whiskey in the world." He insisted on using the "Lincoln County process," a method of filtering or "leaching" the whiskey through maple charcoal. (Many whiskeys and other spirits have since adopted the process.) Jack tasted twice every batch of whiskey he made: when it went into the cask and when it came out.

At first Jack called his whiskey "Belle of Lincoln" and "Old Fashioned." In 1887 he began using his own name, and he dubbed his best whiskey "Old Time No. 7." Why 7, no one is quite certain, though theories abound. One legend connects the name with 7 barrels of misplaced whiskey, which were designated as "Old No. 7." Perhaps it was simply the inherent magic of the mystical, the "perfect" number of 7.

Jack Daniel's Old No. 7 received a prestigious gold medal at the World's Fair at St. Louis in 1904, and other medals at subsequent fairs in Liège, Belgium (1905), and Ghent, Belgium (1913). Plus some other awards, as dutifully related on the label.

After the death of Jack Daniel in 1911, a nephew, Lem Motlow, whose name is still on the label, continued the business with as much verve and enterprise as Jack had shown, through a full 50 years.

Today Jack Daniel's Tennessee Whiskey is the property of another great name in the history of American Whiskey, **Brown-Forman**, of Louisville, Ky., makers of **Early Times** and **Old Forester.**

Jack Daniel's Whiskey is certainly one of the most "called for" names in all the world of spirits. It's had a long and illustrious career, and almost everybody agrees that it is fine whiskey. It's been a favorite of such varied notables as Winston Churchill, Lucius Beebe, and William Faulkner. It is one of the best-selling whiskeys in America (over 1.5 million cases in 1977) and it is one of the very few whiskeys that have been increasing sales in recent years.

Jack Daniel's is smooth, rather light-bodied, almost sweet. Whether one could detect it, tasting blindly, from other bourbons and Tennessee whiskeys of the same proof and general price range, is, of course, a wholly different matter.

Jack Daniel's Old No. 7 comes in two styles these days, both 90°, and both "Sour Mash": Black Label, around $8 (25.4 oz.), and Green Label, about a dollar less. The Black Label is aged somewhat longer, but factually, there is no humanly discernible difference between them.

JACQUES BONET BRANDY

Don't let the name fool you. It's as Gallic as hot dogs and pizza! Jacques Bonet Brandy is pure California: produced in the state's Central Valley, bottled in Sonoma County. It's made by the huge United Vintners, and is a younger, more economical version of the company's **Lejon Brandy.** It's 80° and wholly in the California style: sweet and fruity, but also a bit rough. But at $5 (fifth), whadja expect, Martell Cordon Argent ($60 a fifth)?

JÄGERMEISTER

The name means "The Hunter" and it has a picture of a noble stag on the label. Jägermeister, pronounced *YEAH-gur-my-stir*, is a German liqueur, noted for its digestive and tonic properties. It even comes in a tonicky-looking bottle, more medicinal than spirited. When poured,

Jägermeister still looks ominously medicinal: it has the exact prunish, brownish color of a vile cough syrup. It has a deep-down, herbal, bittersweet, heavily aromatic flavor. A little goes a long way. Jägermeister is an uncompromising drink—people will either love it or they will detest it. The Germans love it.

Jägermeister is made with fifty-six different herbs, roots, and fruits. Serve it well chilled, or on the rocks. It is 70° and sells in the U.S. for around $11 (24 oz.).

JAMAICA—RUM Jamaican rums are generally dark, heavy-bodied, full-flavored rums, not particularly in favor in the U.S., at least not at the moment. American tastes these days run almost universally to light spirits. Jamaican rums are the best-known of all the heavy-bodied rums and outsell all the others. They are also said to be the best of them all, principally because British quality-control laws are strictly enforced.

Jamaican rum is much more popular in Britain than in the U.S., and much of it goes to London in bulk to be aged. The severe English weather is said to be beneficial to the aging process. This is called London Dock rum and is often two or more years old. It is an excellent rum, by any standard. The most popular Jamaican rums in the U.S. are Appleton's and Myers's.

Jamaican rum comes in all manner of sizes and flavors, so be reasonable in your choice. The best-known Jamaican rum, with the best values listed

first, according to the price per oz. of alcohol. Listed separately are the "prestige," specially aged Jamaican rums. These are fine bottles of rum, of course, but the subtle differences between these and standard Jamaican rums will indubitably be lost on the uninitiated, and certainly lost on anybody and everybody if they're simply sloshed down in a mixed drink.

BEST VALUES IN JAMAICAN RUMS

White Overproof, 151°, $0.48/oz.

Appleton White, 80°, $0.60/oz.

Appleton Special (Gold), 80°, $0.60/oz.

Appleton Punch, 80°, $0.60/oz.

Appleton Estate, 80°, $0.61/oz.

Trader Vic's Jamaican, 90°, $0.62/oz.

Lemon Hart Special Dark, 86°, $0.63/oz.

Lemon Hart Golden Light, 86°, $0.64/oz.

Lemon Hart Golden Dark, 86°, $0.64/oz.

Myers's Punch Rum, 80°, $0.??/oz.

PRESTIGE AGED JAMAICAN RUMS

Appleton Special Reserve, 12 years, 86°, $7.85 (fifth)

Burrough's White Cross, 12 years, 86°, $7.97 (fifth)

Lemon Hart Jamaican Superb Golden, 15 years, 86°, $10.12 (fifth)

Old Sea Dog, 12 years, 97°, $7.81 (fifth)

(JOHN) JAMESON IRISH WHISKEY This is one of seven

brands of Irish whiskey owned by the giant conglomerate Irish Distillers Group Limited. Jameson has been vigorously promoted in the U.S. for a long time, and it sells well—for an Irish.

The aroma of Jameson is described as "pungent," and it's good Irish whiskey, neither better nor worse than a number of other brands. It sells for around $7.50 (fifth) in the Western U.S., somewhat higher in the East.

There is also a 12-year-old, also 86°, at around $11.50 (fifth); it is highly recommended.

JAPAN—WHISKY

Somehow it sounds totally implausible, but the Japanese have been making whisky from time immemorial. Only in comparatively recent years, however, have they begun to really commercialize it. Suntory is the big name, and 90% of all Japanese whisky bears that label. Suntory is the only brand imported to the U.S.

Japanese whisky is a blend of heavy-bodied malt whiskies and light-bodied grain whiskies. In this respect it resembles Canadian whisky. Anyway we're spelling it "whisky," as does Suntory. But Japanese whisky is still in a category by itself: some say a cross between Irish and Scotch, yet with an individuality and taste all its own. It is not inexpensive (over $10 for Suntory Royal, and about $8 for the "regular"), but it is a smooth, well-made and well-aged spirit. With Japanese whisky, as with most Japanese products these days, you get what you pay for.

JOHNNIE WALKER SCOTCH WHISKY

Johnnie Walker, the man, was born around 1800, in Scotland. Johnnie Walker, the whisky, was born in 1908, in London, when Alexander Walker, grandson of Johnnie Walker (the man), commissioned the artist Tom Browne to do a portrait of his grandfather for use in advertising the Scotch whisky which he had inherited from his grandfather.

John Walker had started selling scotch whisky around 1820, in Kilmarnock, Scotland. For almost 100 years the whisky was called "Walker's Kilmarnock Whisky"—until that dashing dandy, Johnnie Walker, strode vigorously onto the scene in 1908.

The portrait is known around the world, and today Johnnie Walker Red Label is the largest-selling Scotch whisky in the world. It travels around the globe in 800 different bottle shapes and labels.

Johnnie Walker, like many another whisky, has lost some ground in the U.S. market in recent years, but its international sales have remained steady, and even increased in some areas. Johnnie Walker Red is almost a staple in France, and it is said that every French household contains at least one bottle of it, even if it is reserved for guests.

John Walker & Sons, Ltd., is now a member of that giant spirits conglomerate, Distillers Company Limited.

Is Johnnie Walker as good as its reputation? Remarkably, the answer is probably Yes. Beyond question, this is high-quality Scotch. The whisky connoisseur who has not sung the praises of Johnnie Walker Scotch has not existed. In blind tastings Johnnie Walker has often been selected for its superior aroma and taste. Most casual drinkers, however, would probably not be able to detect any superiority whatever. The Black Label is 12 years old and sells for considerably more—about $12 vs. $8.50 (fifth)—though some experts say they prefer the Red. Both are 86.8°. Johnnie Walker is a blend of more than forty malt and grain whiskies.

In an ironic turn of events, Johnnie Walker Red Label will soon be unobtainable in England. Heretofore Red Label has sold for almost twice as much on the Continent as it did in Britain. This led to a reprimand from the European Common Market, and since it was not fiscally possible for Distillers to lower the price of the exported whisky—they would have lost more than 30 million pounds—Johnnie Walker Red Label is simply being withdrawn from the British Market, so that no discrepancy in price will exist.

JORDAN BLEND (COCKTAIL) This highly caloric, totally decadent after-dinner drink is a specialty of Don Fox, purveyor of good spirits at the National Hotel, Jackson, Calif., in the heart of the Mother Lode. The drink seems to have wande~~~ Sierra foothi~~~ cisco, probably named after some shadowy bartender in some disreputable waterfront bar.

In a blender, combine:

1 oz. Kahlúa (or other coffee liqueur), 1 oz. amaretto, 2 oz. light cream, Ice cubes.

Blend at high speed, strain into a cocktail glass.

K

KAHLÚA If it wasn't the Kahlúa people who invented the **Black Russian** cocktail, it should have been. It was that felicitous combination of two unlikely bedmates, Russian vodka and Mexican Kahlúa, that brought about the spectacular rise in popularity of Kahlúa over the past several decades.

Kahlúa is a coffee-flavored liqueur, produced in Mexico. (Today, under special license, Kahlúa is also produced in several other countries, including Denmark.) It has a good roasted-coffee-bean flavor, and is smooth and very sweet. Kahlúa is one of the most expensive of the coffee liqueurs (around $10 for 23 oz.), and truth to tell, it is not all that superior. It is a fine beverage, certainly, but there are better coffee-flavored liqueurs sold in the U.S., some of which sell for less (see listing under **coffee liqueur**).

KENTUCKY GENTLEMAN KENTUCKY STRAIGHT BOURBON WHISKEY Although bourbon whiskey does not have to be made in the state of Kentucky, it helps, or so it is said. It is true that the best bourbon generally comes from that state, and the very finest is said to emanate from Nelson County, not Bourbon County. Ironically there's nary a distillery today in the length and breadth of Bourbon County—well, at least not a legal one. **Barton Brands,** which makes this whiskey, is located in the heart of Nelson County, in the town of Bardstown. And it's good, reliable straight bourbon, 80° and 86°, with a touch of sweetness. It sells for around $5.25 (fifth) for the 80°; to see how that price compares with other bourbons of the same type, see under **bourbon.** For an 8-year-old straight, Kentucky Gentleman is wondrously low-priced.

KESSLER AMERICAN BLENDED WHISKEY This is another property of that supergiant of the spirits industry, **Seagram.** It's made by **Four Roses,** a subsidiary of Seagram. Kessler is one of the best-selling whiskeys in America, almost 2 million cases in 1977, and is, in fact, the second-best-selling blend in the land, ranking only behind that best best seller of all spirits, **Seagram's 7 Crown.**

It's named after Julius Kessler, a prominent pre-Prohibition distiller—his picture is on the label. At one time Kessler operated some fifty different distilleries. He later sold out to Seagram's Sam Bronfman.

Kessler's is a good blended American whiskey—some recommend it as a substitute for its more expensive cousin,

Seagram's 7 Crown. It is medium-priced, and truth to tell, no better and no worse—at least the difference isn't humanly discernible—than other blended whiskeys. Kessler's 80° sells for something over $5 (fifth); it's also available in 86°.

KING GEORGE IV SCOTCH WHISKY George IV (1762–1830) wasn't much of a king, but this is pretty good Scotch, and when you consider the price, it's very good. It sells for around $5.50 (fifth) in the U.S., thanks to its being shipped here in bulk and then bottled in the U.S. The same bottle would cost you around $8 in London.

KING JAMES SCOTCH This Scotch whisky, produced in Scotland but bottled in the U.S. (at a considerable saving in taxes and shipping costs), is a new offering of American Distilling Company.

Some time ago the firm ran some ads calling it "The King James Version." The ruckus that ensued rivaled the upheavals of the Reformation, or, as Jimmy Durante would say, "All Bethlehem broke loose." Fundamentalist preachers called for God's judgment to fall upon the perpetrators of this abominable desecration. But the truth of the matter is that the whisky is better named than is that 1611 version of the Scriptures. King James didn't write a word of that English translation—he merely appointed a commission to do so. In no sense was it "his Bible." He probably never even read it, for James was not a devout, nor even a good, man. He was a tryant, bigot, coward, and sodomite. It is much more fitting that a whisky be named after King James than that a version of the Scriptures should be.

King James Scotch is a bonny —not bony—Scotch: smooth, with good flavor, and an excellent value. The 80° brings about $5 (fifth) and the 86° about $5.50.

KING'S GINGER LIQUEUR This is an elegant ginger-flavored liqueur, fit for a king. Which is precisely how and why it was created: for King Edward VII of Britain (1814–1910). It was first made by one Henry Berry, of Berry Bros. & Rudd Ltd., 3 St. James's Street, London, and is still marketed by that prestigious firm. It was first prepared at the request of the king's physician, to be administered to His Majesty for purposes of internal fortification, before he set out to brave the elements in the royal "horseless carriage." It seems to have worked admirably well, for it became the king's favorite potion.

King's Ginger Liqueur is, indeed, an admirable and tasty beverage: golden in color, dry and crisp, with a wonderful gingery pervasiveness. But the bad news is that it's rarely imported to the U.S.—it used to be, long decades ago, in small quantities—and, in fact, is available practically only in London, on St. James's Street. It is still made according to the original formula, on a Cognac base. These days it is prepared in Holland for Berry Bros. & Rudd, but only in very limited quantity—total production is a mere 500 cases per year. If you espy it, buy it, try it. It sells for about six pounds, is 72° (as the British measure things) and 88° in U.S. terms.

KIRSCHWASSER (or KIRSCH) The name means "cherrywater," and oh that all the world's cherries would produce such water! Kirsch is the best known and the most popular of all the world's fruit brandies. And probably the best. It is distilled from cherries with their pits. It is pure white in color.

Imported kirsches are of three different nationalities, coming from these principal areas:

Switzerland: Especially from the Basel region—these are usually labeled Basler Kirschwasser. The biggest name is Dettling.

Germany's Black Forest: It's the Schwarzwald in German, and the kirsches from here are called Schwarzwalder. These are probably the best kirschwassers in the world. The most important brand is Kammer.

Alsace (and the surrounding area to the west): Lighter and more delicate than the kirsches of Switzerland and Germany. Some say that these, not Germany's, are the best of all kirsches.

All imported kirsch is expensive, but happily, most major American liqueur producers also make respectable kirschwassers, not the equal of their European counterparts, but decent, honest citizens in their own right, and at their own price, usually half or less than of the imports. A comparison:

AMERICAN

Arrow Kirsch, 90°, $6.80 (24 oz.)

Jacquin Kirsch, 90°, $6.98 (24 oz)

De Kuyper Kirschwasser Cherry Brandy, 90°, $7.45 (fifth)

Garnier Kirsch Cherry Liqueur, 96°, $7.60 (24 oz.)

Leroux Kirschwasser, 90°, $7.75 (24 oz.)

IMPORTED (Fifths)

Basler Kirschwasser, 90°, $13.37

Black Forest D.E.S. Kirschwasser, $14.65

Marie Brizard Kirsch, 100°, $17.90

Kirsch D'Alsace, 86°, $15.85

Black Forest Kammer Kirschwasser, 100°, $18.29

Kirsch De Zoug, 90°, $19.15

Dopff Kirsch, 90°, $19.91

Dettling Kirschwasser, 92°, $19.98

Dettling Reserve Exceptionelle, 12 years, 86°, $25.98

KORBEL BRANDY This California brandy has many devotees, and it's often compared to Christian Brothers Brandy, which it does, in fact, resemble. Both are very popular. The Korbel product is a mite less sweet, and it is equally clean, grapy, soft. In several blind tastings Korbel Brandy has led the field of California brandies. It's 80° and just a trifle more expensive than the majority of California brandies: about $5.75 to $6.00 (fifth). Good brandy, decent price.

KÜMMEL The name means "caraway" (in German and

Dutch) because that's the principal flavoring of this northern European liqueur. You can pronounce it either *kim-ell* or *kee-mell*, depending on the degree of your list toward Germanic pronunciation, the *kee-mell* being closer to the authentic German.

Kümmels vary greatly in sweetness, and the dry versions are really more gins than they are liqueurs. German kümmel is such; Berliner kümmel is the driest of all. A famous brand of Berliner kümmel is Gilka, an excellent beverage with a long history. It sells in the U.S. for around $9 (fifth). Ironically, Berliner kümmel is now made in Hamburg, Germany, not Berlin. French kümmels are generally sweet and so are taken after dinner. Allasch kümmel (sometimes: Allash) from Holland is also sweet; it is an old and respected name. Sugar is sometimes allowed to crystallize in the bottle, and then it will be labeled "Kümmel Crystallizé."

Kümmel has been around for a long time, more than 200 years. It was "invented" in Amsterdam in 1575 by Lucas Bols, still a familiar name in the world of cordials, for today **Bols liqueurs** are found around the world. And Bols-kümmel is still one of the finest to be had.

Kümmel is usually colorless. Besides the essential flavoring agent of caraway seeds, other common agents include cumin, coriander, and aniseed, and when the last is used, the beverage has a distinct licorice flavor.

The base for kümmel is usually neutral grain spirits. In proof, it is rather high for a liqueur: 70° to 100°, though some American kümmels descend to around 50°.

Authentic, historic kümmel comes, almost by definition, from northern Europe, especially the Baltic countries, including Russia. But many American liqueur producers market a respectable kümmel. It's not the distinguished, complex, sometimes austere beverage of northern Europe, but it's a gracious and tasty after-dinner libation, moderately priced ($5 to $6 a fifth), with notable sweetness.

Aquavit from Norway and Sweden is very similar to kümmel, though much drier. Another kissin' kin is **goldwasser**, which has many of the same flavoring agents (caraway, anise) plus some suspended gold flakes to aid the digestion.

Another wonderful old kümmel is Wolfschmidt, originally made in Riga (then Latvia, today Russia), but now being produced in Holland. Great kümmel, if you can find it.

Drink your kümmel either straight—sippingly—or "over" (rocks).

L

LAIRD O' LOGAN SCOTCH WHISKY It's also called Logan Deluxe—that's on the label too—and it's the property of **White Horse** Distillers Ltd., Glasgow. It's White Horse's top-of-the-line whisky, 12 years old, selling for about $12 per fifth (slightly more in the Western U.S.).

"Laird" is an old Scots title similar to "Lord," but "Logan" has no particular significance— it just sounded nice with "Laird."

Sir Peter Jeffrey Mackie, founder of White Horse Distillers, was an inventive, unpredictable, crusty old Scotsman who died in 1924; he left the formula for this deluxe blend of Scotch whisky. About thirty of Scotland's finest whiskies (says the company) go into the blend. Many of the whiskies are more than 12 years old.

This is fine premium 86° Scotch with fine premium price tag to match.

LAPHROAIG MALT SCOTCH WHISKY The three greatest names in Scotch malt whisky are probably The Glenlivet, Glenfiddich, and Laphroaig (pronounced *la-froig*). All three are very distinctive whiskies—that's almost a definition of a malt—but Laphroaig is the most distinctive of the three. Laphroaig may well be the most distinctive whisky in the world.

That's because it comes from the Island of Islay (pronounced *I lay*), that rugged, storm-tossed island off the North Channel between Scotland and Ireland. Whiskies from the Island have always been noted for their individuality—they are heavily pungent, highly aromatic. Islay malts are actually one of four types of **malt whisky,** according to where they are produced. Each area produces a distinct type and flavor of whisky. The other three: Highland, Lowland, and Campbeltown.

Laphroaig Whisky is named after the area near Port Ellen on the Isle of Islay where the whisky was first made. That was around 1815, when Donald and Alexander Johnston started farming in the area, and built a small distillery there. In 1836 Donald bought out his brother, Alexander, and became sole owner. Laphroaig is still made by D. Johnston & Co. Ltd.

Laphroaig is owned today by the same people who make Long John Scotch: Long John International, which, in turn, is a division of **Schenley.**

Laphroaig is certainly not to everyone's taste. Some non-Scotch-lover once described its flavor as a "mixture of seaweed and tarry rope." Perhaps it takes a true-blue Scotsman— his blue color is thanks to the frigid climate, not the whisky—to really appreciate Laphroaig. It has a pungent, very peaty flavor. But perhaps every serious drinker of Scotch whisky—and there are obviously millions of those around—owes it to himself to taste, at least once, a big, unblended single malt such as Laphroaig.

Laphroaig 10-year-old is 91.4° and sells in the U.S. for $10 to $11 (fifth).

LARRESSINGLE RESERVE TRESOR ARMAGNAC This good 10-year-old Armagnac brandy, though not well known in the U.S., has one of the most venerable names in all of Armagnac. Larressingle Armagnac has been around for more than 700 years: since 1250. It is named after the 13th-century Chateau de Larressingle, whose fortified walls still stand. Larressingle is 86° and sells in the U.S. for around $12 (fifth).

LAUDER'S SCOTCH WHIS-KY This is one of the myriad spirits marketed by the huge Canadian conglomerate of Hiram Walker. It's made by the same people who make Ballantine's Scotch, one of Scotland's truly premium whiskies, and some people recommend it as an economical substitute for Ballantine's. Lauder's is shipped to the U.S. in bulk at high proof, in 5,000-gallon stainless-steel tanks, and then bottled in the U.S., at substantial savings. This American bottling in no way denotes an inferior Scotch. It only denotes a more economical one. Lauder's sells for around $6 (fifth), a decent price for a quality 86°. Lauder's Scotch is light in body, slightly sweetish.

LA VIEILLE CURE Offhand, the name sounds like "The Old Curé," "The Old Priest," surely a most fitting name for a venerable old herbal French liqueur. But there's no accent here on "Cure": it means the home of the curé (priest): the manse, the vicarage, the parsonage, the rectory, presbytery—all the same. Neither does it mean "The Old Cure (Remedy)" as recommended to *cure* one's arthritis or hangover. It's pronounced *la vee-yay kewr*—more or less.

But it's still a good name, for this good aromatic liqueur was created by the monks of the Abbey of Cenon, in the village of the same name. Today it's made by a secular firm (Intermarque, a subsidiary of Bols), in the same Bordeaux suburb of Cenon.

Vieille Cure, like the Basque liqueur Izarra, is very similar to that great classical French liqueur, Chartreuse, and even comes (as does Izarra) in the two identical colors, green and yellow. Vieille Cure was almost certainly made in direct imitation of Chartreuse—monkish copy-cats are not unknown. But Vieille Cure, or any other liqueur, should be judged on its own merits, not in comparison with anything else. And so judged, Vieille Cure is a fine liqueur.

It's quite sweet, highly aromatic, with overtones of anise. Many find it similar to that other illustrious monkish liqueur, Benedictine, though not as sweet. Some fifty different flavoring ingredients go into the making of Vieille Cure.

The yellow and green versions of Vieille Cure are made

according to the same formula, and both come to the U.S. at 86° and sell at the same price, around $13 (20 oz.). This is even more expensive, ounce for ounce, than green Chartreuse! All of which nets this simple conclusion: fine French aromatic liqueur, but overpriced.

LEJON BRANDY Lejon is one of America's best-known brand names. It belongs to United Vintners, California's second-largest (after E. & J. Gallo) wine producer.

Lejon Brandy is rather sweet, medium-bodied, 80°, with decent, not notable flavors. In its medium price range, about $5.50 (fifth), there are better California brandies around (see under United States—brandy), and there are certainly worse.

Lejon Brandy in the simplest of terms is average California brandy at an average price.

LEMON HART RUM Lemon Hart & Sons is an English firm, founded in 1804. The company specializes in Jamaican and Demerara rums, and today it is the largest shipper and blender of these rums in the world. The rums, of course, come from their designated land of origin: Jamaican from Jamaica, and Demerara from the island of Guyana—Demerara is the name of a river there. They are then shipped to London, where they are blended and matured in the famous "London Dock" warehouses. Lemon Hart is the largest-selling brand of rum in England.

The principal Lemon Hart rums imported to the U.S. are these: Golden Jamaica, 80° and 86°, about $7 (25.4 oz.); Dark Jamaica, same; Demer-

ara White, 80°, about $6 (fifth); Demerara, 86°, about $7 (fifth); and Demerara 151°, about $11 (fifth). These are all fine rums. The 151° is too strong for sipping; it's used for flaming and seasoning.

LEROUX BRANDY Leroux & Co., Inc., headquartered in Philadelphia, Pa., is a division of that sprawling giant, **Seagram,** the world's largest distiller.

Leroux makes a formidable array of liqueurs and brandies, from absinthe and blue Curaçao to kirschwasser, and all manner of flavored brandies in between—would you believe Leroux Polish Blackberry Brandy and Ginger Brandy? They *even* make some "straight" brandies: Leroux Deluxe and Leroux 5-Star. Both are rather typical California brandies: somewhat sweet, soft, grapy. The Leroux Deluxe is 80° and sells for around $5 per fifth (somewhat more, Eastern U.S.). It can only be described as *adequate.* The 5-Star is 84° and is said to be a blend of domestic and imported brandies. At only 50¢ more per fifth, it is definitely the better buy.

LEROUX LIQUEURS Today the name Leroux on a bottle of liqueurs connotes American-made: Leroux liqueurs are everywhere available, they are economical, they are dependable—and all that adds up to American. Yet oddly enough, Leroux liqueurs had their beginning, around 1840, in Brussels, Belgium. The name is pronounced after the manner of the Belgians: *leh-roo.*

Leroux liqueurs migrated to

the U.S. after the repeal of
Prohibition, and the name is
now owned by General Wine &
Spirits Company of New York,
a division of Joseph E. Seagram & Sons, Inc.

Today Leroux has come full
circle, and the firm has recently added five European-
made imports to their already
formidable array of American-
made liqueurs: from Austria,
Fraise de Bois; from Denmark,
Cherry Karise; from Italy,
Amaretto di Torino; from
France, Cognac with Orange.
Leroux's latest import (1976)
is a sambuca from Italy.

At latest count Leroux was
producing no less than fifty-
two different liqueurs, all the
way from a 25° grenadine to a
formidable absisante, a latter-
day absinthe, at 100°. They
range in sweetness from the
very sweet Crème de cassis
(35°) to the dry kirschwasser
(90°).

Leroux is the third-largest
producer of domestic liqueurs
in the U.S. (behind Hiram
Walker and Arrow), now marketing almost 1 million cases
of liqueurs and brandies per
year.

Leroux makes good, reliable
liqueurs and they are almost
always good values. A few are
exceptional: the Jezynowka
Blackberry Brandy (the strange
name is Polish for "blackberry"), the Peppermint Schnapps,
and the Cognac with Orange,
an import. Leroux is eminently
safe. You are well advised:
When in doubt, buy Leroux.

LIQUEURS Liqueurs are a
big wide wonderful world.
Bigger and wider and wonder-
fuller, probably, than any other
spirituous realm. And often un-

explored and unappreciated.
Bourbon lovers, beer freaks,
wine snobs rarely venture here,
and they are the poorer and
drier for it.

The word "liqueur" is not to
be confused with liquor, which
means simply a distilled spirit,
and frequently has some rather
unsavory connotations. Liqueurs have all good vibes.

A liqueur or cordial—they
are synonymous—is simply a
very flavorful, sweet, distilled
spirit. "Flavorful": the flavor
comes from herbs, fruits,
plants, flowers, seeds, roots,
barks—not simply from the
spirit that forms the base.
"Sweet": Sweetness varies greatly, but U.S. law requires that
a liqueur must have more than
2½% sugar content by weight.
Otherwise, whatever it is—perhaps a fruit brandy—it's not a
liqueur. "Distilled spirit": If it's
base is not a spirit (distilled) it's
not a liqueur—it may well be
a flavored wine, a pop wine,
or a fruit wine.

Since liqueurs are spirits, not
wines, their proof is considerably higher than that of wines,
even sweet wines (which can
get up to 20°, and even higher
on occasion). The majority of
liqueurs run between 40° and
80° (20% to 40% by volume),
but a few (crème de cassis, Egg
Nog) will reach as low as 30°
and some few (Southern Comfort, Yukon Jack) as high as
100° or 110°.

Most liqueurs have neutral,
tasteless, odorless, high-proof
alcohol as their base. The flavor of the finished product
comes wholly from the flavoring agents, none of it from the
spirit base. Some liqueurs, however—usually the very finest,
and mostly those made in Eu-

rope—use a brandy (perhaps even a Cognac or Armagnac), or a whiskey, rum, or Scotch. In this case, the base will contribute significantly to the taste of the bottled liqueur. **Grand Marnier** is a good example: the Fine Champagne Cognac base comes through loud and clear.

There are different processes for making liqueurs—distillation, maceration (or infusion), percolation—but most liqueurs, and all the best ones, use a combination of techniques, and in most cases the makers-and-shapers are not about to tell the world how they do it. These are trade secrets.

Simple, cheap liqueurs may be made from a single flavoring agent—blackberries, let us say—but most of the time a number of agents are used. Or a multitude of them, as with **Chartreuse**, for example. And the identity of the agents—"botanicals" is the trade term —and their proportions are carefully guarded secrets.

In typical plastic American fashion, most made-in-the-U.S. liqueurs are not produced from fresh or dried fruit at all, but from natural fruit concentrates. These extracts are often purchased by the liqueur producers from firms specializing in such production. If these concentrates are synthetic—not usually the case—the word "artificial" or "imitation" must appear on the label.

Thousands upon thousands of liqueurs are manufactured around the world today—virtually every country has a few of its own. The best and most readily available are individually treated in this book.

Color in liqueurs is not always for real; in fact, it is more often artificial than not. Some fruit liqueurs derive all their color from the fruit from which they are made, but color is often added to boost salability, and all plant liqueurs are normally colorless or nearly so, and color is usually added. Americans are convinced that if an alcoholic beverage is colorless in pigmentation, it is therefore also the same in character.

Two liqueur-like beverages need mention: **fruit brandy** and **fruit-flavored brandy.** Fruit brandies are not liqueurs—they lack the necessary sweetness.

"Fruit-flavored brandy" is an American-invented term. It is used in order to distinguish it from true fruit brandy. True fruit brandies are made wholly from the fruit in question. Fruit-flavored brandies are not. They merely have fruit added for flavoring to a brandy base, and they are highly sugared. True fruit brandies are difficult and expensive to make; they are relatively dry. Fruit-flavored brandies are inexpensive to make and are very sweet.

It was in Europe that the confusion began—and it is there that it remains, mostly. In Europe there is no difference between an apricot brandy and an apricot liqueur.

Liqueurs should ordinarily be served chilled or over ice—if it's shaved ice you forthwith have a frappé. The dilution with icewater is helpful to many liqueurs, cutting the intense sweetness, and protracting and prolonging the richness. Some of the drier and more elegant liqueurs, however, are better appreciated straight up.

Serve liqueurs in glasses

large enough for the beverage to breathe in. Not in thimblefuls. No need, though, for pretentious balloon snifters, but the glass should be large enough to hold at least twice the amount of liqueur to be served. The glass should be clear, so that the brilliant color of the liqueur may be duly savored. Elegant crystal is splendid, and somehow, the thinner the glass, the better the liqueur tastes—Henriques's Law.

Store liqueurs upright, not on their side as one does with fine wine. In this way the cork will not deteriorate.

Once opened, liqueurs keep well—for several years at least—but not unto all eternity. In the course of years any opened liqueur will slowly deteriorate, and eventually it will simply disappear, not by way of stealth and pilf, perhaps, but by way of evaporation.

There are many ways to divide liqueurs—according to their flavoring agent (fruit or herb, etc.), or according to their base (whiskey, brandy, neutral spirit, etc.)—but the most practical way is to divide them into generic and proprietary names.

Generic liqueurs are named simply by their flavor: apricot, crème de menthe, chocolate, etc.

Proprietary liqueurs are known by their invented brand names, and made by just one producer: Benedictine, Kalhúa, Chartreuse, Tia Maria, Strega. All the common generic liqueurs are listed in this book (in their proper alphabetical location): rock & rye, maraschino liqueur, cherry liqueur, crème de menthe, etc. Below, in alphabetical order, are listed

the world's most famous and best proprietary liqueurs. All are listed in this book.

Aurum
Bahia
Bailey's Original Irish Cream
Benedictine
Chartreuse
Cheri-Suisse
Ciao Liquore
Cointreau
Cordial Medoc
Curaçao
Damiana
Drambuie
Forbidden Fruit
Freezomint
Galacafe
Galliano
Glayva
Glen Mist
Grand Marnier
Irish Mist
Izarra
Jägermeister
Kahlúa
King's Ginger Liqueur
La Vieille Cure
Lochan Ora
Love, Cafe de
Peanut Lolita
Pistasha
Ricard
Roiano
Royal Chocolate liqueurs
Royal Mint-Chocolate
    Liqueur
Sabra
Sabroso
Sciarada
Southern Comfort
Strega
Tia Maria
Trappistine
Tuaca
Van der Hum
Vandermint

LIQUEURS, HOMEMADE

Most of the world's greatest liqueurs—Chartreuse, Benedictine, Drambuie—can never be remotely, vaguely duplicated in your kitchen. But many of the simpler ones can.

Liqueurs, praise God, are eminently simple concoctions: a distilled spirit that's been flavored and sweetened. To make one at home, therefore, only three simple ingredients are required: neutral distilled spirit (vodka will do), flavorings (usually fruits and spices), and sugar.

The process used in the home will almost always be the simple, foolproof one of maceration: The flavoring ingredients are steeped in the spirit base for a given period of time. The sweetener—sugar, honey, syrup—is usually added at the same time. After the maceration period, the liqueur is filtered and set aside for a "marrying period" during which the flavors harmoniously cohabit and smoothly blend together.

One excellent book on the subject is *Liqueurs for All Seasons*, by Emilio Cocconi (Wilton, Conn.: Lyceum Books, 1975). It contains more than a hundred liqueur recipes, from absinthe to "Jujubes in Liqueur." The recipes are lucid and simple, and the end product deliciously heartwarming.

Liqueur extracts, mostly from abroad, are also available, and the technique for making liqueurs from these is equally simple, or even more so. One such that is widely distributed is Noirot's Extracts from France. "Flavors" run from amaretto to verbeine, and include some highly implausible flavors such as imitation Benedictine, called "Reverendine," and two imitation "Chartreuses," called "Green Con-

vent" and "Yellow Convent" (as Chartreuse comes in these two colors). The taste of "Reverendine" and "Convent" (in whatever color) is as outlandish and phony as are the names. The general quality of the extracts, however, is excellent. But the finished liqueurs are not as good as those made with real fruit and berries and barks and leaves and nuts and flowers and roots and peels— and not nearly as much fun to make.

LIQUOR The word "liquor" often has rather malodorous connotations, and perhaps that's as it should be, as liquor—alcoholic beverages—has so often been so poorly used and so well overused. It's a perfectly decent word, however, derived from the Latin *liquidus*, meaning simply a liquid. Somehow "liquor" over the course of centuries has come to denote only alcoholic liquids, much as the word "drink" often means an alcoholic drink, no other.

In very recent years, the word has come more and more to denote distilled spirits, as distinguished from wine and beer and drinks of lesser proof and potency.

The Biblical term is "strong drink": *shekar* in Hebrew and *sikera* in Greek. Even modern translations have stayed with the good honest term "strong drink." The word occurs some twenty times in the Old Testament, mostly in a cautionary framework. Proverbs 20:1 (New English Bible) is typical: "Wine is an insolent fellow, and strong drink makes an uproar." There is only one use of the word "strong drink" in the entire New Testament, but at least it's of heavenly origin. The "angel of the Lord" admonishes Zechariah that his son, John the Baptizer, must "never touch wine or strong drink" (Luke 1:15).

LOCHAN ORA If imitation is the sincerest form of flattery, then the Scottish liqueur **Drambuie** has had its fair quota of flattery over the years. Lochan Ora is the latest Scotch-whisky-based liqueur to do the flattering. Others in recent years include **Glen Mist** and **Glayva**. All of these liqueurs are obvious imitations of Drambuie, and all of them have been successful, and all of them are good beverages.

Lochan Ora, like the others, is sweetened with heather honey, and flavored with various herbs and spices. Its base is 12-year-old Scotch malt and grain whiskies. It's made by Chivas Bros., Ltd., the makers of the prestigious Scotch whisky **Chivas Regal**. It was introduced in 1968. The name means "Golden Loch (Lake)," pictured on the label.

Lochan Ora, though only 70°—the other Scotch liqueurs are all 80°—is the most expensive of them all, including Drambuie, though only slightly so. Lochan Ora sells in the U.S. for about $13 (fifth). Sip it slowly, pensively, gratefully, straight up or on the rocks.

LORD CALVERT CANADIAN WHISKY It's a Seagram product, though that name is no longer on the label. Now the name "Canadian" is what's big on the label; in fact, according to the label, its name is now Canadian Lord Calvert. Many experts agree that Lord Cal-

vert is superior Canadian whisky, and a good value. It is 80° and sells for around $6 (25.4 oz.), which is rather middle-of-the-road (**Canadian Ltd.**, for example, is about $5 a fifth and **Canadian Club** and Seagram's **V.O.** are about $8 a fifth).

LOVE, CAFE DE The name, in bastardized Spanish or Mexicanized English (depending on your point of view), means "Coffee of Love," and it's a coffee-flavored liqueur from Mexico. It's a newcomer to the American liqueur scene, but a welcome one, even though the land is awash these days with coffee liqueurs. Despite the hokey name, this is a marvelous liqueur. It has a wonderful roasted-coffee aroma and flavor, not found in any other coffee liqueur, domestic or imported. (See the comparative standings under **coffee liqueur**, and note that Cafe de Love heads the list.) Cafe de Love is 53° and sells for around $8 (fifth, i.e., 25.6 oz.)— compare that with **Kahlúa** at around $10 for only 23 oz.

LUXARDO MARASCHINO This is one of the world's best-known—and best—cherry liqueurs. It doesn't call itself that—the label says simply "Maraschino." Maraschino here is not to be confused with those highly processed cherries which Americans sprinkle over their cocktails and desserts—this is maraschino in its root sense: the liqueur made from marasca cherries.

Marasca cherries are a special breed: they're a wild cherry, small and bitter, and make for terrible eating but glorious drinking. Marascas' homeland is Yugoslavia, and that is where Luxardo Maraschino was created: in the town of Zara (today, Zadar), then Dalmatia, under Austrian rule (today, Yugoslavia), in 1821. Girolamo Luxardo, a Genoese by birth, was a diplomat and had evidently developed a taste for good ratafia. Over a period of years he developed his maraschino liqueur, using a new method of double distillation—today, Luxardo Maraschino is triple-distilled—and long aging in ash barrels. Luxardo Maraschino was a success the moment it was put on the market.

Two world wars virtually annihilated Luxardo—the distillery was totally demolished in World War II—and after the war, Giorgio Luxardo decided not to await World War III on Yugoslavian soil. In 1947 the firm relocated in Torreglia, near Padua (Padova, in Italian) at the foot of the Euganean Hills. A vast cherry plantation—something like 100,000 trees, one of the largest in the world—now graces the rolling Torreglia plain.

Since the very day of its creation, Luxardo Maraschino has come in green, rather squarish bottles, plaited with straw (against breakage). An imitation maraschino, made by Maraska of Zadar, comes in almost the identical bottle with a look-alike label. Maraska Maraschino has been banned in Italy by court decree, but is still imported to the U.S. Even if it were a legitimate imitation, it ought to be shunned. It is a decidedly inferior beverage.

Luxardo also makes a "super" maraschino, Perla Dry, 80°, unfortunately not presently available in the U.S. It's aged five years in ashwood, and is drier than the "regular" maraschino.

Luxardo likewise produces a fine cherry liqueur, made from the same marasca cherries, but lower in proof (60° vs. 80°) and produced by infusion, not distillation. It is just a whisper sweeter than the maraschino, but lacks some of the latter's elegance. Its proper, given name is Sangue Morlacco, "Morlacchi Blood," a name given it by the Italian poet Gabriel D'Annuzio, who served it nightly at his dinner table. The Morlacchi were a race of fierce and fearless warriors of Latin stock who saved Venice from the Turks in the 17th century. Because of the drink's deep-red color, D'Annunzio gave it the name.

Though none of them are available in the U.S., Luxardo today makes an array of other spirits, including a sambuca, a Curaçao, and even a gin and vodka.

Luxardo Maraschino sells in the U.S. for $11 to $12 (25.4 oz.).

M

MACADAMIA NUT LIQUEUR It comes from Hawaii—presumably—and it's a noble experiment—probably—and it tastes like almost nothing—indubitably. It's not unpleasant to the taste, but it scarcely tastes. In fact, if there is any identifiable flavor here, it's of coffee as much as it's of any breed of nut. Macadamia Nut Liqueur is made by Hawaiian Distillers and sells . . . well, poorly, undoubtedly.

MACNAUGHTON CANADIAN WHISKY This whisky is one of the many owned by that huge American spirits conglomerate, Schenley Industries, Inc. That is neither pro nor con. Most major brands today are in the hands of conglomerates.

MacNaughton's is popular, regularly placing among the fifty top-selling spirits in the nation. In 1977 it was in forty-second place. It is good, standard Canadian whisky. It is 80° and medium-priced, about $5.50 (fifth).

MAI-TAI (COCKTAIL) Trader Vic says he invented this busy drink back in 1944. He tells how he set out one afternoon to concoct the "world's finest rum drink." Humility not being Vic's strong suit, he was immediately convinced that he had succeeded, and he proceeded to call his noble invention a Mai Tai-Roa Ae—in Tahitian, "Out of This World—the Best." The Trader (Victor J. Bergeron) used a 17-year-old Jamaican rum, no longer available, because, he says, within a short time he had used up all the 17-year-old Jamaican rum in the world. Here is the original recipe:

2 oz. 17-year-old J. Wray Nephew Jamaican Rum, ½ oz. French Garnier Orgeat, ½ oz. Holland De Kuyper Orange Curaçao, ¼ oz. rock-candy syrup, Juice from 1 fresh lime.

Today, however in these plastic times, the Trader recommends that you cease your worldwide search for the 17-year-old rum, and *simply* substitute the following: "Some high-ester-flavored Rum from Jamaica; Pungent Rums from Martinique; A little Puerto Rican, to give some other taste and lightness." (From "Rum" by Victor J. Bergeron, *House Beautiful*, August 1972).

On a more practical note, to make one fine Mai-Tai, assemble:

1 jigger rum—any kind (some experts call for Jamaican, others insist on a light-bodied rum, others recommend half of each), 1 oz. Curaçao or triple sec, ½

tsp. powdered sugar, 1 tbsp. Orgeat (or any almond-flavored syrup, or a tsp. of an apricot liqueur), 1 tbsp. grenadine, 1 tbsp. lime juice.

Some would add 3 tablespoons (1½ oz.) of both lemon juice and orange juice (both fresh) but this is strictly optional.

Shake well with cracked ice—strain into a cocktail glass (chilled), or serve on the rocks. Garnish with any or all of these: lime slice, maraschino cherry, mint sprig, hunk of (fresh) pineapple.

MALT WHISKY To the true-blue Scot this is the only true Scotch whisky. This is the original Scotch whisky, the whisky which, even to this day, is the determining factor in the Scotch blends which Americans favor. This is Scotchiness at its apex.

Only a handful of malt whiskies are shipped to the U.S., but the number is increasing. Flying in the face of today's trend toward lighter drinks, suddenly and with deliberate pace, malts have been increasing in popularity across this land. And this despite their out-of-sight price tags. Malts are rather "in"—in limited, affluent, Scotch-digging circles.

What makes malt whisky so different from the Scotch blends consumed in the U.S. is the fact that it is made entirely from malted or sprouted barley, and is not blended with any light whiskies made simply from grains. Further, it is distilled in old-fashioned pot stills, which produce a very robust and *flavorful* brew though you may not favor the

flavor. Few Americans do.

But if you really do like the flavor of blended, "Americanized" Scotch, you will probably *love* these malts. If you mildly dislike the smoky Scotch flavor, you will probably *hate* these brews.

Sometimes the label says "single whisky." This means simply that this is a single whisky from a single distillery: it's unblended. Some malt whiskies are blended with other malt whiskies—these are still *straight* malts, of course—and the label will read: "vatted whisky."

There are four types of Scotch malt whisky, and the particular type will often be designated on the label:

Highland malt: The best and most expensive.

Islay malt: From the Island of the same name; it's pronounced *I lay*, as in "now me down to sleep." It's the most pungent and aromatic.

Campbeltown: The strongest-flavored.

Lowland malt: The lightest, mildest, and cheapest.

Here are the principal malt whiskies imported to the U.S., listed in alphabetical order. The more important of these will be found in their proper alphabetical place in this book, with more detailed information.

Capercaillie, 86°, $15.31 (fifth)

Cardhu Highland, 86.8°, 12 years, $12.42 (fifth)

Glendronach Single Malt, 86°, 12 years, $12.89 (fifth)

Glendullan Single Malt, 94°, 12 years, $12.47 (fifth)

Glenfarclas-Glenlivet, 104°, 12 years, $13.19 (fifth)

Glenfiddich (Grant's) Single, 86°, 10 years, $12.31 (fifth)

Glen Grant Glenlivet, 86°, 10 years, $11.13 (fifth)

The Glenlivet, 86°, 12 years, $13.18 (25.4 oz.)

The Glenlivet, 91°, $12.49 (fifth)

Glenmorangie, 86°, 10 years, $10.95 (fifth)

Keith, 86°, $11.37 (fifth)

Laphroaig, 91.4°, 10 years, $10.09 (fifth)

Littlemill, 86°, 5 years, $5.99 (fifth)

Macallau-Glenlivet, 86°, 12 years, $12.76 (fifth)

Mortlach Highland Single Malt, 86°, 12 years, $13.11 (fifth)

MANDARINE, CRÈME DE

Or mandarin, or mandarines, or mandarinette, or Mandarine Napoleon. All same. A mandarin is a Chinese potentate, resplendent in regal silken robes, but it is also a simple tangerine, and that's what this is, a tangerine-flavored liqueur. This is a true liqueur, usually 80°, not an aperitif wine of the same name, Mandarin, a wine from—logically enough—China.

The most commonly available mandarin-flavored liqueur in the U.S. is Mandarine Napoleon, made in Brussels. It's moderately sweet, soft, a lovely copper-orange color (probably synthetic), and, above all, redolent of tangerines. The tangerines are steeped in a brandy base, to which aged Cognac is added before bottling. It sells for around $11 or $12 (23 oz.).

MANHATTAN (COCKTAIL)

It is said that this famous cocktail was invented by a certain Herman A. Miller, a well-known bartender, at the Delmonico Restaurant, New York City, in 1897. The original recipe, according to the theory, was simply two parts of bourbon to one part Italian (sweet) vermouth. Period. No ice, no garnish, no nothing. And at least one purist—George Leonard Herter, *Bull Cook and Authentic Historical Recipes and Practices* (Waseca, Minn.: Herter's, 1969)—insists that that is still the only legitimate and civilized way to make a Manhattan.

But everything has become complicated in these last days, and now there are numerous versions of the once-simple Manhattan. The original, classical Manhattan is made thus:

2 oz. bourbon or blend, 1 oz. sweet vermouth, Dash Angostura Bitters, 2 or 3 ice cubes.

Mix or stir or shake. Strain into a chilled cocktail glass. Add a maraschino cherry and/or a strip of orange peel—but know that purists may wax violent if they learn of these addenda!

For a Dry Manhattan simply substitute dry vermouth for the sweet.

For a Sweet Manhattan, just add a little cherry juice or grenadine.

For a Perfect Manhattan, use ½ oz. sweet vermouth and ½ oz. dry vermouth.

If you substitute Scotch for bourbon, you have a Rob Roy.

MARASCHINO LIQUEUR

Here's a bet Americans have been missing out on. Maraschino liqueurs, at least the European ones, are distinctive and delectable. They deserve to be sipped and savored. The American imitations—Bols, Leroux, Garnier, Dubochett, Jacquin—are trustworthy in their own right, but fit mostly for mixing, cooking, and flaming.

Authentic maraschino is made, not from maraschino cherries, those highly processed, resplendently rose-colored cherries Americans float on top of their Old Fashioneds, but from the wild sour cherry, marasca. Marascas are grown almost solely in Yugoslavia and Italy. And the only authentic maraschino liqueur comes from precisely those two countries.

The biggest, oldest, and best producer of maraschino is Luxardo, formerly of Zara (today, Zadar), Yugoslavia (formerly Dalmatia). The liqueur is made by a complicated and costly process, with three distillations and at least 3 years of aging. **Luxardo Maraschino,** 80°, sells in the U.S. (New York) for around $12 (25.4 oz.).

Another old and important name is Drioli (Venice, Italy), though the liqueur is difficult to find in the U.S. Drioli Maraschino has been around for more than 200 years, and is still sold in the old four-sided, straw-covered bottles. It is an excellent beverage.

A third brand of European maraschino available in the U.S. is Marasca, from Yugoslavia. It's also straw-covered and sells for around $10, but is not worth the price. Look for Luxardo, or go to an American maraschino at half the price.

Quasi-maraschinos—though they call themselves simply maraschino, of course—are made in the U.S. and they are quite adequate for most purposes, though they all lack the intense cherry flavor of the European originals. The best are Bols, Leroux, and Garnier, all selling for around $6 (24 oz.).

Maraschino is water-white, and has a wonderful concentrated cherry aroma and flavor. It is an inspired addition to desserts, fruit salads, sorbets, even coffee (a few drops only). Maraschino liqueur: good to eat and good to drink.

MARC It's pronounced *mar* —with the French the "r" is almost silent, so it becomes more like *ma*—and it's made from garbage. Well, practically. It's inexpensive French brandy made from wine pomace, the stems and pips and skins and mess that is left after the grapes are pressed to make wine. In the U.S. pomace is often used for cattle feed. It's proper name is eau de vie ("water of life") de marc. Many districts have their own marc, and the best-known, and probably the best, is Marc de Bourgogne. The firm of Louis Jadot imports one to the U.S., A la Mascotte (86°), but by now it's far removed from the true marc economy class, selling for around $15 (fifth).

Marc has a strong, distinctive, grapy—some say earthy —taste, which some connoisseurs seem to appreciate. The very same beverage, coming from Italy, is called **grappa.** For how to drink marc, see under **brandy.**

MARGARITA (COCKTAIL) Nobody knows where it was invented, by whom, or how— but everybody knows why: to give **tequila** respectability and the perfect entourage.

Along with enchiladas and chili con carne, the Margarita cocktail is surely one of Mexico's most notable contributions to the advancement of civilization. (Whether the Margarita was actually invented in Mexico is a moot question. Juarez, Puebla, Taxco, and Acapulco have claimed the honor; others say it was the creation of some inventive monks in Guadalajara. But a second school of thought insists that the Margarita was an American inspiration. Los Angeles' Tail o' the Cock restaurant is one important claimant.)

It is this delicate little cocktail with the soft feminine name that has accounted in large measure for the incredible rise in popularity of that once-contemned, often-condemned, now commended Mexican spirit, tequila.

Somebody out there has good taste; the Margarita is one of the happiest combinations of flavors either side of the Rio Grande. Everybody has his or her favorite Margarita recipe, and there are a host of prepared Margarita mixes, but here's one that's simple, *puro Mexicano*, and *delicioso*:

Prepare your glasses (preferably the stemmed cocktail variety) by rubbing a lime around the edge and then dipping the glass in salt (coarse or kosher salt is best). In a blender put equal parts of tequila, orange liqueur (there are many: **triple sec, Cointreau, Curaçao**, or Mexico's own, Controy), and freshly squeezed lime juice. Fresh lime juice—not canned, not frozen—is of the essence. Add a goodly portion of ice, so that the finished drink, after blending at high speed, will be icy-thick and slurpy. *Salud*!

But if you're a perfectionist or an incurable Margarita-freak, read on. Over the past few years, certain intrepid, self-sacrificing souls have gone forth into the hazy demimonde of cocktail lounges and bars in search of that golden grail, the Perfect Margarita. Some, it is said, have never returned. Most of those who have returned have duly filed their reports (not always readily decipherable). The results have been a mixed bag: for the Perfect Margarita, some demand a slushy consistency, while others say it must be served either straight up or on the rocks; some demand the addition of egg white; others, rock-candy syrup; a few require pineapple juice.

One who returned in rare good spirits was a certain Blake Green of the San Francisco *Chronicle*. In the name of duty and the advancement of science, Green visited scores of bars in the San Francisco area, painfully and dutifully sipping Margaritas. Here is Blake Green's favorite, the Perfect Margarita (Or Nearly So), from Henry Africa's Cocktail Lounge, San Francisco.

1½ oz. Jose Cuervo Especial, ½ oz. triple sec, ½ oz. lemon juice, ¼ oz. sweet-and-sour mix, Juice of ½ lime.

A very similar Perfect Margarita comes from Verita Thompson's La Cantina restaurant, Century City, California:

1 jigger tequila, ¼ jigger triple sec, 1 jigger sweet-

and-sour mix, Juice of ¼ lime, ½ tsp. egg white, 1 scoop ice.

Put into blender and blend to a froth. Serve in a shallow champagne glass.

(Note: The research in this case was done by Jefferson Morgan, and was reported in *Bon Appetit* magazine, August 1977.)

In the name of completeness and fairness, a final Margarita formula must be added. Some purists insist that unless you've had a Margarita in Mexico, you haven't had a Margarita. The essential difference lies in the lime juice. The Mexican lime—*limon*, in Spanish—is a different variety from that generally found in the U.S. And, truth to tell, it does make a superior Margarita. Here's the authentic Mexican formula:

"Take a chilled, stemmed cocktail glass and deftly brush the rim with dry salt. The thin jacket of frost on the glass should hold the salt.

"Next, scoop chipped ice into a metal shaker, add at least the necessary 1½ ounces of tequila, ½ ounce of triple sec, and 1 ounce of freshly squeezed *limon* juice.

"Now take the final step—a gentle shaking to blend the mixture. No whirling electric gadgets to blend it and bruise it. Just a gentle, polite shaking." (Reprinted from *The Tequila Book*. Copyright © 1976 by Marion Gorman and Felipe P. de Alba.

MARIE BRIZARD LIQUEURS Marie Brizard is one of the grand old names, and she is one of the grand old dames of the world of liqueurs. It's pronounced *bree-zahr*. Madame Brizard started making an anisette liqueur more than 250 years ago—around 1750, in Bordeaux, France. Her name has been on 100 million bottles of French liqueur since that time, and it's still there today.

The full name of the firm, however, is Marie Brizard and Roger. Roger was an in-law taken into the business at the very beginning. The Roger family still runs the enterprise. Marie had little yen for business—she spent most of her time doing charitable work among the poor and sick. In fact it was while she was caring for a West Indian native during an epidemic that he, in gratitude, gave Marie the secret formula for an elixir of anise that, he said, would cure many ills.

Marie Brizard Anisette is still the mainstay of the firm, although some thirty other liqueurs are produced today.

Marie Brizard has always made and still makes fine liqueurs. They are distinctly more expensive than their American-made counterparts, but they are usually considerably superior. When you seek the very best—especially for genteel sipping purposes (as distinguished from mixing, or cooking or flaming)—you will do well to start with Marie Brizard.

All Marie Brizard liqueurs sell in the U.S. in the $10 range (usually 23.6 oz.), with the kirsch (100°, fifth), being an exception, around $17, a breathtaking price, but a wondrous beverage. The most famous, and among the best of

their respective breeds, are anisette, apry (apricot liqueur),
and crème de cacao.

MARMOT CHOCOLAT SUISSE LIQUEUR Marmot
is the name of the company,
Chocolat is the way it's on the
label, because the Swiss don't
spell too good. Suisse is Swiss
for Swiss. And Liqueur is
American and Swiss and every
other language for liqueur.

This is an absolutely luscious
liqueur made from ground
chocolate—remember, the Swiss
are famous for their chocolate—
with small pieces of Swiss chocolate suspended amidships. You
can drink it or eat it.

The bad news, however, is
that it retails in the U.S. for
around $13 (24 oz.). It's 48°.

Marmot also produces a
chocolate-coffee liqueur called
Marmot Cafe (48°), and it
also contains bits of suspended
chocolate. It is equally fine—
and equally extravagant.

Both of these liqueurs will
provide a wondrous spur-of-
the-moment dessert if simply
poured over vanilla ice cream.

MARTELL COGNAC Things
are not always what they seem.
For example, sherry, that most
Spanish of all wines, bears
many British labels: Sandeman,
Harveys, Wisdom & Warter.
Cognac, the aristocratic quintessence of all French brandies,
bears some distinctly non-Gal-
lic labels: Hine (rhymes with
"wine"), Hennessy, and, here,
Martell.

Jean Martell came to Co-
gnac, France, in 1715 from
Britain's Channel Islands to
found the firm that bears his
name. By the time he died, in

1753, the business was flourishing.

Martell is not only one of
the oldest of Cognac firms—a
full, round 250 years of age—it
is also the largest. It presently
has 40% of the Cognac market
(followed by Courvoisier and
Hennessy), and it is France's
top-selling Cognac, the ultimate accolade.

Martell is a huge operation:
daily output of Cognac alone is
200,000 bottles. Many big-
name Cognac firms are, in effect, merely "blenders" and
"agers." They buy Cognac, usually young, from various distillers and blend and age the
Cognac to their own taste and
specifications. Martell does it
all: they own vast vineyards
(though they also buy grapes
from some 2,700 growers),
they own and control several
dozen distilleries, and they
even have their own cooper
shop and their own coopers,
some now unto the seventh and
eighth generations.

Today Martell also produces
Noilly Prat Vermouth and Jan-
neau Armagnac; it distributes
Black & White Scotch Whisky,
Jack Daniel's and Old Forester
whiskeys, and Sandeman wines.
But even with all these multi-
farious distractions, Martell
continues to make fine Cognacs.

Martell Cognacs are noted
for their fruitiness (as distinct
from "woodiness"), and they
are mostly light-bodied.

Here is the formidable array,
from least expensive to out-
rageously so:

V.S.P.: It's a three-star Cognac, and a fine one. V.S.P.
has a pleasant sweetness and
good flavor. Average age is
over 5 years. It sells for

around $13 (fifth)—some bad whiskeys cost that much.

Medallion V.S.O.P.: At $4 more than the V.S.P., it is also recommended. It has more body than the V.S.P.; it's tasty and well-balanced. Average age is 15 years.

Cordon Bleu. The name means "Blue Band," as pictured on the label. An excellent 30-year-old Cognac, around $27 (fifth).

Cordon Argent: It means "Silver Band," and there's one on the label. This is highly respected Cognac, 35 to 40 years of age, with wonderful flavor. Experts place it among the best of Cognacs in this exclusive, high-priced company: around $60 (fifth).

Extra: That it is: extra good, extra old (50 to 60 years), and extra expensive (around $75 per fifth). One critic says the bouquet jumps out of the glass at you.

(PAUL) MASSON BRANDY The Paul Masson Vineyards are owned by the sprawling Seagram Corporation; the brandy (as also the wine) is marketed by the giant Browne Vintners. Masson Brandy is a child of conglomerates. But that is not necessarily bad: Paul Masson Brandy is, in fact, a good, consistent, standard California brandy. It's definitely on the sweet side, smooth, with nice flavor. At $5.75 or $6 (fifth) for the "regular" it's neither better nor worse than a host of other reliable California brandies, and it's a good value—just as the others are.

Masson also markets a "super" brandy, in a blue apothecary jar which is changed every few years. It's their top

of the line, and it's fuller in flavor, more Cognac-like than the regular. However, only a true brandy aficionado might agree that it's $5 (fifth) better than the regular.

MASTIKA It can be spelled masticha, or mastiha, or mastikha, or mastic plus various other ways. The name comes from mastic, a resin. Not raisin. In most countries resins are used to make varnish, but in Greece they make wines and brandies from them! Specifically, mastika is a Greek brandy flavored with mastic. Though the resin flavor is not as all-pervasive as it is with Greek wines, mastika is still pretty much an acquired taste.

Cambas makes one, called Mastiha, 92°, selling for around $8 (fifth). Metaxa calls its Mastica (92°); it sells for around $9 (fifth).

MARTINIQUE—RUM Rums from the islands of Martinique and Guadeloupe are scarcely to be found in the U.S.A., and that's a pity, for they can be splendid beverages. Martinique and Guadeloupe are Islands of the French West Indies, and understandably you're more likely to encounter these rums in Paris than in New York. These are full-bodied rums, almost black in color, ideal for the kitchen, whether to flame Babas au Rhum or to flavor a gateau or a holiday fruit cake. St. James Rhum, 94°, is the best-known and deservedly so; it is a fine rum. It comes in a tall squarish bottle, sells for around $9 (fifth).

MATADOR TEQUILA Along with Jose Cuervo Tequila,

Matador is the property of that giant of the liquor and wine industry, **Heublein, Inc.** of Hartford, Conn. It's not as expensive as Cuervo—about a dollar less—but it's not among the "best buys" in tequila either. Matador is standard tequila—almost all 250 brands imported to the U.S. are that—and there is precious little difference between them. If your tequila is going into Margaritas and Sunrises and Sours, be sagaciously advised to soberly buy the most economical (see listing under **tequila**). Matador Tequila comes in both White and Gold, both 80°, sells for around $6 (fifth) in the Eastern U.S., and somewhat less in the West.

MENTHE, CRÈME DE For Americans this is probably the best-known and most appreciated of all the world's liqueurs. The name also happens to be the most mispronounced in all the world of spirits—or perhaps in all the world, period. It's French, of course, and the only proper pronunciation is *krem deh mahnt*. Let us not Americanize and thus bastardize this classical name.

Crème de menthe is a comparatively simple liqueur to produce, and this is why it is relatively inexpensive. This does not detract from its excellence, and at the right time and place, crème de menthe can be one of the world's most satisfying liqueurs.

It is made from several varieties of mint, but chiefly from peppermint. The mints are usually separately distilled and then blended. Crème de menthe comes primarily in two colors, green and white, but nowadays also in pink and gold. There is no difference whatever between these variously hued beverages, for the coloring is simply a tasteless (and harmless) vegetable dye.

Almost every American liqueur firm makes a crème de menthe, and generally speaking, these are fully as good as their European counterparts. The American products are all reliable, tasty, and of approximately equal merit. Buy the most economical.

There are two principal "prestige" mint liqueurs shipped to the U.S. from France: Cusenier's **Freezomint** and Get **Pippermint**. They are a mite more elegant and more minty than American crèmes de menthe, and are worth trying, as they cost only about $1 more.

Crème de menthe is the best-known of all after-dinner drinks, and with good reason, for mint is an excellent digestive, and the clean, cool freshness of menthol and mint is a fitting conclusion to any meal. The simplest and best way to serve crème de menthe is frappé, that is, over shaved or cracked ice. That way, it's even cooler, and it lasts longer.

Virtually all American crèmes de menthe are 60°, and sell for around $5; European crèmes de menthe, for some reason, are frightfully overpriced. Most are 24 oz. but a few are 23 oz. Both **Marie Brizard** and Garnier are right around $10. If you have a large money tree in your backyard and no good sense, buy them.

There are a host of mixed drinks made with crème de menthe, green and white—one book lists a neat 181 of them!

—and some of them may be absolutely, unconditionally inspired—but the truly classical ones are precisely two: **Grasshopper** and **Stinger.**

METAXA This is the brand name of America's favorite Greek brandy. But Metaxa is not a simple, "straight" brandy. It's a brandy with a difference, the difference being its added sweetening and special flavorings. It is a distinctive and most beguiling beverage.

Metaxa comes in three grades, depending on the age of the brandy base. The flavoring, however, is so pervasive that differences in age are wholly unappreciated. The 5-Star is far and away your best buy: 5-Star, $10.75 (fifth); 7-Star, $12 (fifth); Grande Fine, $17.50 (fifth).

MEXICO—BRANDY As totally illogical, impossible, and insane as it sounds, Mexico produces and consumes more brandy than it does tequila. *Verdad!* There are more than fifty brandy-producing distilleries in Mexico.

The quality of Mexican brandy is quite good—it's not Cognac, but neither is it execrable. The best brands are Pedro Domecq and Casa Madero. Domecq's Presidente (80°) sells for around $7.50 in the U.S. and many find it a better brandy than Domecq's **Fundador** from Spain. Casa Madero's Reserva de la Casa is 75% pot-stilled—that's good! —and it is highly esteemed.

MEXICO—RUM Rum is becoming increasingly popular in Mexico, just as in the U.S. Mexican rums are generally light-bodied, with no flavoring ingredients added. **Bacardi** makes rum in Mexico, as does **Ronrico** and others. But more typically Mexican are such brands as Ron Cortes and Ron Castillo. "Ron" is not a proper name—it simply means "rum" in Spanish.

MEZCAL (OR MESCAL) Mezcal is **tequila** that can't call itself that. It is virtually the same beverage, made by the same process, from the same maguey plant, a kind of cactus. (Strictly speaking, mezcal can be made from a number of different agave species, whereas tequila is required by government regulation to be distilled principally from the blue agave.) It can only be called tequila if it is made in the area of the town of that name, in the Mexican province of Jalisco. Mezcal is distilled from **pulque,** just as brandy is distilled from wine. It contains a small amount of mescaline, a hallucinogenic, and this may have led to its use in Indian ceremonies. It is not aged and can be pretty raw stuff.

The most famous—or infamous—thing about mezcal is its worm: It usually comes with a bona fide worm, but a rather dead one, in the bottle. The worm lives in the agave plant and he's clean and harmless, even if eaten. (Gulpppp . . . he is said to be very tasty.) There's really no good reason for him to be in the mezcal, but then there's really no good reason for him to be in the agave plant in the first place. But Mexicans swear that the worm adds to the flavor of the mezcal.

Very little mezcal finds its

way to the U.S., and perhaps that's just as well. One brand sometimes available is Monte Alban, imported by **Barton Brands.** It's proudly labeled Mezcal con Gusano: "Mezcal with a Worm."

MINT JULEP (COCKTAIL)

The best way to start a fight in a bar, at least in Kentucky, is to tell the bloke next to you how to make a *true* Mint Julep. Reams have been written on the subject, and there are as many *original* recipes as there are horseplayers in Louisville on Derby Day. Somebody said that Mint Juleps are as much a state of mind as they are a drink. They're an aura, an era, a mystique. And they are surely one of the most refreshing, not to mention insidious, of all summer drinks. Perhaps they are also the most American.

Kentucky colonels and Mint Julep freaks insist on elaborate recipes and precise rituals for the proper construction and consumption of Mint Juleps. Modern-day barguides rush to the other extreme and oversimplify. The following recipe falls between Scylla and Charybdis.

Use a silver or pewter mug, if you want to be authentic. Non-Kentuckians and other peasant types are allowed to use a tall highball glass (12 oz.). Into the container place 1½ tsp. sugar, 3 or 4 sprigs fresh mint, 2 or 3 dashes Angostura Bitters, and 2 tsp. water. Use a muddler (or spoon) to bruise the mint slightly and dissolve the sugar. Fill the mug (glass) almost to the top with crushed ice, and pack it down. Add 2½ to 3 oz. bourbon and stir until the mug (glass) is well frosted. Garnish with slices of lemon, orange, sprigs of mint.

For a more authentic Mint Julep, and if you can prepare it in advance, after you have added the bourbon, wipe the mug (glass) dry and place it in the refrigerator for about an hour (or the freezer for half an hour). The ice in the mug should be almost solid and the outside of the container well frosted. Handle the drink in gingerly fashion so as not to remove the frost. Mint Julep lovers are sorely divided between Mint Bruisers and Non Mint Bruisers. The version above follows the former school; this will give the drink a distinctively minty flavor.

True Mint Julep purists would use the above recipe only in case of the most dire emergency. They would insist upon the following additional stipulations:

1. The container must be very tall, at least 14 oz., and preferably of silver, and certainly with a handle (insulated, of course).

2. Absolutely fresh mint must be used, and only the small, tender leaves at the tip of the sprig.

3. Use only bonded straight Kentucky bourbon. Never rye. Irwin S. Cobb, himself a good ol' Kentucky boy, said that a man who would use rye instead of bourbon in a Mint Julep was capable of putting a scorpion in a baby's crib.

4. Use only sugar syrup, never dry sugar.

5. The mint sprigs used for garnish must first be rinsed in cold water, patted dry with a paper towel, dipped in powdered sugar, then immersed in the drink.

MIRABELLE A fruit brandy made from a yellow plum of the same name. Mirabelle comes primarily from France, though it is also made in Germany and Switzerland. Unlike most fruit brandies, it is matured in glass 1 to 4 years, and is considered distinctly superior to quetsch, which it resembles. It is rarely imported to the U.S.

MOËT—HENNESSY Moët stands for wine, as in Möet & Chandon Champagne, one of the world's greatest, and Hennessy stands for Cognac, as in **Hennessy Cognac.** Moët-Hennessy is the name of the prestigious Paris-based parent company which owns those two luxury items, plus a few others, such as Mercier Champagne, Ruinart Champagne, and Christian Dior Perfumes. And now the company also owns a Napa Valley (California) wine name: Domaine Chandon, a brand-new sparkling wine already receiving rave notices, though it's been on the market scarcely a year. Notice: *sparkling wine,* not Champagne. The French parent company is very careful not to call their new bubbly California wine by that hallowed name, Champagne—Champagne comes only from France.

MONNET REGAL COGNAC Here's an excellent buy in Cognac: about $9, compared to at least $12 for most three-star Cognacs, which this is. (It sells as Regal only in the U.S., as 3-Star elsewhere.) Regal is a trifle on the sweet side, which makes it all the more acceptable to most American palates.

MONTEZUMA TEQUILA This good, clean, tasty tequila received an award recently as one of the top liquor values of the year. *Verdad,* it is a tasteful spirit and a good value, particularly in the Western U.S. It's 80°, and comes in the standard White and Gold versions. (They are precisely the same bottle of tequila. The difference is purely in the coloring, not in the aging. The Gold simply has coloring—usually caramel—added.) Montezuma sells in New York State for around $6 (fifth). In the West, you can get a full quart for the same price. *Olé* to Montezuma!

(A.R.) MORROW BRANDY Presuming that California brandies are female in gender—and what else, considering their beguiling smoothness and allure?—this is the sister brandy of **Aristocrat Brandy.** It's a little less expensive than Aristocrat (about $4.75 vs. $5.50 a fifth), a trifle younger and somewhat rougher. It's slightly sweet, rather severe overall. Adequate is the word.

Better is A. R. Morrow Bottled-in-Bond (100°). It's a full 6 years old, and some find it rather bourbonish. It's got noticeable woodiness, and is remarkably smooth for a 100° beverage. For a bottle-in-bond spirit, it's a good value at about $6.25 (fifth).

MORTLACH SINGLE MALT SCOTCH WHISKY Mortlach is an old name in Scotch whisky, dating back to at least 1823. The distillery is in the quaint old village of Dufftown, in the dell named Mortlach. Mortlach Scotch is 12 years old, and has only recently become available in the U.S. It is imported by the Kobrand Corporation. It is a typical, good, peaty, full-flavored single-malt; it is 86.8° and sells in the U.S. for about $13 (fifth).

MOSCOW MULE (COCKTAIL)

This drink is one of the reasons for the success of **Smirnoff Vodka**. Just before the outbreak of World War II, Smirnoff sales were going nowhere—the name had been purchased by **Heublein**, the spirits conglomerate of Hartford, Conn., only a couple of years before. By his own telling, George G. Martin, then president of Heublein, invented the Moscow Mule at the Cock 'n Bull Restaurant in Hollywood, when he met there one sunshiny day with Jack Morgan, owner of that famous watering and feeding hole. Martin had vodka which he could not sell; Morgan had an oversupply of ginger beer which he could not sell; Morgan had a friend with a stockpile of copper mugs which he could not sell. They put the three items together, and *voilà*, the Moscow Mule!

Here's how: Into a copper mug—well, a tall glass in case of emergency—pour 1 jigger vodka and juice of ½ lime. Fill with some ice cubes and ginger beer.

MOUNT GAY BARBADOS RUM

Rums from the island of Barbados (British West Indies) are "in-betweeners": in heaviness and body, they stand between the light-bodied rums of Puerto Rico (**Bacardi**, for example) and the heavy-bodied ones of Jamaica and Demerara (e.g., **Lemon Hart**). Mount Gay is the best-known and probably the best of the Barbados rums. It dates back to at least 1809. The origin of the name is unknown, but happily it is not a favorite of homosexuals! Two versions are commonly seen in the U.S.: Refined Eclipse, the lighter of the two, and Reserve Sugar Cane, made in the more traditional style. Both sell for around $7 (fifth).

MR. BOSTON and OLD MR. BOSTON

They seem to be one and the same person, Mr. Boston and Old Mr. Boston. For no good (or bad) reason, the company calls some of its products Mr. Boston, and some of them Old Mr. Boston. Same guy, same booze.

Mr. Boston/Old Mr. Boston is now, since 1968, the property of the **Glenmore Distilleries Company.**, of Louisville, Kentucky. Glenmore also produces and/or markets such well-known items as **Yellowstone Bourbon**, Kentucky Tavern Bourbon, and Amaretto di Saronno, plus a gaggle of others. But the Mr. Boston line represents the vast bulk of Glenmore's total sales.

And a formidable array it is: the largest, longest line of liqueurs in the world. There are now, incredibly, more than 100 products bearing the Mr. Boston (or Old Mr. Boston) label. This is not to mention the other brand-names marketed by Glenmore, such as:

Old Thompson American Whiskey

Yellowstone Kentucky
Straight Bourbon
Desmond & Duff Scotch
Old St. Croix Rum
Gavilan Tequila
Amaretto di Saronno

Mr. Boston not only produces just about every liqueur and spirit known to man, it also produces a host of mixed drinks, both in the standard 24 oz. size and in the new miniature "Cocktails for Two" size, 200 ml., somewhat less than the old half-pint size (6.8 oz. as compared to 8 oz.).

Mr. Boston ready-mixed drinks have only recently been introduced, and, in fact, are still on somewhat of a trial basis. They range in potency from 25° to 40°. They come with a built-in cup and practically all the classical cocktails are offered: Piña Colada, Screwdriver, Daiquiri, etc., and even a Cappuccino and an Apricot Sour.

One of the major reasons for the popularity and success of the Mr. Boston line has been the wide acceptance of the familiar, red-covered Mr. Boston Bartender's Guide. Indeed, it has become an accepted standard among barguides. And with good reason, for it is precise, concise, thorough. There is no better all-around barguide available in this or any land. More than 7 million hardcover copies have been sold since it came out more than 40 years ago. It is now in its 60th printing.

How good are the Mr. Boston spirits, liqueurs, and cocktails? Quite. None of them are posing a threat to Grand Marnier or Chartreuse, but they are wholly satisfactory, decently priced, American-type spirits. Which is precisely what their name, Mr. Boston, connotes: purely American.

MYERS'S RUM Jamaican rums are *puro macho*: lusty, full-bodied, rich. And the most *macho* of them all is Myers's. Fred L. Myers & Son has been making rum in Kingston, Jamaica, for some 75 years now, and doing it well.

Sadly, only one Myers's rum is seen in the U.S. these days: "Planters' Punch." It's the most expensive of the Jamaican rums commonly imported (see listing under Jamaican Rums), but may be worth the difference, at least on occasion, such as for use in Planters' Punch.

Before World War II one could sometimes find Myers's "Mona" Rum, a luscious 30-year-old beverage, which more than one connoisseur has hailed as the world's finest rum. Alas, it seems to have departed from the scene, and we are the poorer—and the richer—for it.

Myers's "Planters' Punch" Rum, 80°, sells for around $8 (750 ml.).

N

NATIONAL DISTILLERS PRODUCTS COMPANY

This sprawling American spirits conglomerate had its beginnings in 1924, under the leadership of Seton Porter, who died in 1953. From that day to this, National has wheeled and dealed in spirits and whiskeys, brands and labels, distilleries and distributorships.

National Distillers is actually only the liquor division of National Distillers and Chemical Corporation, one of the Big Four, and it embraces (besides spirits) chemicals, metals, plastics, and fertilizers.

National Distillers managed to survive Prohibition—just barely—because it was allowed, in 1929 and 1931, to produce "medicinal" whiskey. Only five other distilleries were so licensed.

Today National Distillers has distilleries in Cincinnati, Ohio, Frankfort and Louisville, Ky., and Canada. Headquarters are Louisville. It owns the huge wine enterprise Italian Swiss Colony, which is said to account for a full 25% of all the wines sold in the U.S. It also owns Almadén Vineyards (California) and it produces and/or markets these international brands: Gilbey's Gin and Vodka, DeKuyper liqueurs, Merito Rum, and Monnet Cognac. Here are National Distiller's principal brands of whiskey: Bellows Bourbon, Bond & Lillard Bourbon, Bourbon de Luxe, Century Club Bourbon, Dominion Ten Canadian, Hill and Hill Bourbon, King George IV Scotch, Mount Vernon Blend and Rye, Old Crow Bourbon, Old Grand-Dad Bourbon, Old Hermitage Bourbon, Old Overholt Rye, Sunny Brook Blend, Old Taylor Bourbon, and PM Blend.

National has recently fallen on lean times, especially regarding its whiskeys. Whiskey sales in the U.S. have fallen off generally for the past 5 years. Domestic whiskeys have suffered the most; blended whiskeys have dropped almost 30%, and bourbons about 16%. National's whiskeys have been particularly hard hit: Old Crow has plummeted almost 15% since 1974; Old Taylor is off almost as much; also down are Old Grand-Dad and Sunny Brook.

NEGRONI (COCKTAIL)

This drink is purely Italian in origin, but it's rapidly getting Americanized. First, the classic, unadulterated version. Into a cocktail glass, put:

> 1 oz. Campari, 1 oz. gin, 1 oz. sweet vermouth, 1 or 2 ice cubes, Twist lemon (optional)

Some add a splash of club soda. Stir, drink.

If you use dry vermouth instead of the sweet, it becomes a Cardinal.

This is a somewhat austere, Continental type of cocktail, and most American palates will not suffer it gladly. A modified, Americanized—some would say bastardized—version adds: ¼ cup orange juice and 1 oz. Orgeat syrup.

NEW ENGLAND–RUM This is the only authentic American rum. It's beloved of New Englanders, has been made by them since Colonial days. (Some New England rum used to be made in Kentucky, but American law—logically enough—now specifies that it can be made only in New England.) In fact, most New England rum is consumed right there in New England. It's native-born, bred, and consumed in everything except the molasses from which it is made: That still comes, as it has for the past 400 years, from the West Indies. New England rum is heavy-bodied, dark-colored, pungent, and hearty. It is of good quality, yet economical. It even comes in a bonded version, at 100°.

It is said, evidently with good authority, that Paul Revere's famous ride was a success thanks only to some stout New England rum. On the 18th of April of '75, the good man was riding madly through Middlesex—and we thought those times were so "straight"!—with the news of the imminent arrival of the British, but Paul was keeping it all to himself. Evidently the strong, silent type, he galloped through the night in silence un-

til he reached the home of one Isaac Hall, a rum distiller. After a couple of shots of Isaac's hearty rum, Paul rode on shouting and bellowing that the British were coming, the British were coming!

NOYAU (or NOYAUX), CRÈME DE The word *noyau* (plural *noyaux*—both pronounced *noy-oh*) means the pits or stones of fruit, and that's exactly what this is: a liqueur with a bitter-almond flavor, made from the pits of various fruits, mainly apricot, peach, and cherry.

Crème de Noyau comes in two colors: water white, and pink. The almond flavor is not generally as pronounced as it is in most amarettos, and noyau, as the name crème indicates, is almost always sweeter than amaretto. Noyau rarely, if ever, has the finesse of the finer amarettos.

Crème de noyau originated in France and Holland, but practically none is imported to the U.S. today, as it seems to have fallen from favor. And it's really no great loss, for it has been supplanted by amaretto, generally a superior beverage.

A few American firms still make a crème de noyau: Both Hiram Walker and Bols have a crème de noyaux (Hiram Walker, 56°; Bols 50° and 60°), around $5.25 (28 oz.); Old Mr. Boston's is 54°, Leroux, with spelling the French wouldn't recognize, markets a Crème de Noya (54° and 60°), also around $5.25 (28 oz.).

Other American companies produce what is probably exactly the same liqueur, made by precisely the same process, only they call it by an Americanized name, creme de almond(s). Like noyau, it's usually pink in color, 50° to 60°, and quite sweet. At least one brand, **De Kuyper**, taking no chances, has both names on the bottle. **Garnier** calls its crème d'amande (60°), around $5.50 (24 oz.). **De Kuyper's** crème de almond (56°) is perhaps the best of the lot. It has a good, nutty flavor, and—prodigy of prodigies—even uses some real almonds in its production. It sells for about the same as the others, $5.50 (24 oz.).

Only one noteworthy drink is made with crème de noyau (or creme de almond, as you will), the **Pink Squirrel**.

O

OJEN This is an anise-flavored liqueur, made in Spain, pronounced *OH-hen*. Technically it's a rum, and is the Spanish equivalent of the Greek ouzo. Ojen comes in both a sweet and dry version. It is not ordinarily available in the U.S.

OLD BUSHMILLS IRISH WHISKEY (86°) This is a venerable name. The Old Bushmills Distillery is the world's oldest, first licensed in 1608. It's in the little village of Bushmills, in County Antrim, at Ireland's northernmost tip. That, of course, is Protestant Ireland, very very distant from the Republic of Ireland, the southern part, which is 99% Catholic.

This good Irish whiskey is by no means a favorite of the Catholics of southern Ireland, but at least they allow it in the land.

The distillery prides itself on the fact that for more than three centuries, it has drawn its water from a particular stream, St. Columb's Rill, which rises among the heather some 5 miles away, and comes to the distillery laden with the flavor of peat and heather.

Old Bushmills is one of Ireland's finest whiskeys—in blind tastings it is consistently a front-runner. In the U.S. it outsells all other brands of Irish whiskey. Some believe this is because it is more "Scotch" in taste than are the other leading brands. But Irish is still Irish: assertive and heavy-bodied, though today's trend is definitely towards lighter whiskeys. And if Irish is your kind of whiskey—and sometimes it is the *only* kind of whiskey, e.g., for Irish Coffee—there is no finer to be found in all of the Ould Sod than Ould Bushmills.

OLD CROW KENTUCKY STRAIGHT BOURBON WHISKEY Old Crow Whiskey is not named after a bird—though his portrait, the bird's, is right there on the label. It's named after a man, one Dr. James Crow, a Scottish physician and chemist.

Dr. Crow came to Kentucky in the early 1820s, and in 1835 built his own distillery and began producing bourbon whiskey which became known as "Crow" or "Old Crow." James Crow is an important figure in the history of bourbon whiskey, for he was one of the first to use scientific instruments and controls in his whiskey making. He seems to have invented the sour-mash method of distillation, and he was always careful and painstaking in his work.

Scientific care was something

whiskey makers of the day sorely needed to learn. Whiskey distillation in the early 19th century was a haphazard and carefree procedure. One newspaper account describes it: "Distilling was not accomplished by any regularly defined rules, but rather after the old formula for bread-making; by taking a "passel of meal, a passel of salt and about so much water, biled down until it was done" (New York Times, Sept. 9, 1897).

Old Crow Whiskey was an immediate success. At one time it was the largest-selling bourbon in the world. Probably no other American whiskey has been acclaimed by so many famous people: Andrew Jackson, William Henry Harrison, Henry Clay, Daniel Webster (he said it was "the finest whiskey in the world"), Mark Twain, Jack London, O. Henry. But the most illustrious incident of all featured Abraham Lincoln. After hearing numerous complaints about the whiskey-drinking habits of General Ulysses S. Grant, Lincoln mused, "I wish I knew what whiskey General Grant drinks, I would send it to my other generals." Someone told him Old Crow, and even if he didn't send all the Union generals a case of Old Crow, he did send a case to General Grant, in appreciation of the fact that he fought and he won—two things Lincoln's other generals steadfastly refused to do.

Old Crow is still fine bourbon whiskey, but it's heavy-bodied and full-flavored, and those qualities are out of fashion these days; Old Crow has slipped drastically in sales over the past several years. The more's the pity, for the whiskey is as good as it ever was, and more reasonably priced than the other premium bourbons—about $5.50 (fifth) for the 80°. The 100° bonded is also relatively cheap: $6.50 to $7 (fifth). There is also a **Crow Light.**

OLD FASHIONED (COCKTAIL)

Like many another fine invention, the origin of the Old Fashioned is controverted. Some say it was created by Jenny Jerome, the mother of Winston Churchill, when she served it for the first time at a reception in New York in the 1870s. Others insist that it was invented by one Thomas Louis Witcomb, a respected bartender, at the Pendennis Club in Louisville, Ky., in 1889. Some friends requested Witcomb to make them a good, simple, "old-fashioned" drink, with undiluted whiskey, and not "a damn loused-up fancy mixture."

Today there are almost as many Old Fashioned recipes as there are brands of bourbon whiskey. Here's a composite recipe with the best features of them all. Into an old-fashioned glass put:

½ to 1 lump sugar (depending on your taste for sweetness), dash Angostura Bitters, few drops cold water

Muddle to dissolve the sugar. Add:

1 jigger bourbon or rye, 2 or 3 ice cubes

Stir. Add twist lemon. Some would add as garnish a slice of orange and/or a maraschino cherry, but purists frown upon such additional "garbage." A few "authorities" insist that the original Old Fashioned was made with brown sugar, and should still be so made (about ½ tsp.).

OLD FITZGERALD KENTUCKY STRAIGHT BOURBON WHISKEY

There really was an Old Fitzgerald—he was John E. Fitzgerald, who made quality bourbon in Kentucky a hundred years ago. John E.'s bourbon was appreciated from the start, and he sold it to an elite clientele: to steamship lines, private clubs, and railroads.

Today Old Fitzgerald is made by Stitzel & Weller Distillery, Louisville, Kentucky. And they were real people also. Stitzel was the brothers Phillip and Frederick Stitzel, who built a small distillery in Louisville in 1872. Weller was William Larue Weller, who by the time of the Civil War was selling "honest whiskey at an honest price." The Stitzels and the Wellers merged their operations, a piece at a time, during the 1920s. Stitzel and Weller was one of the few distilleries allowed to produce "medicinal" whiskey during Prohibition.

Old Fitzgerald started tiny, but today it's engulfed by bigness. Stitzel & Weller is now owned by Somerset Importers, Ltd., a huge operation, and the nation's largest importer of Scotch whiskies. It imports Johnnie Walker Scotch, Tanqueray gin, and Hine Cognac,

to mention a few. Somerset, in turn, is the biggest single marketer of the products of Distillers Company Limited, the giant British distilled spirits conglomerate.

Old Fitzgerald was a prestige whiskey almost from the day of its birth, and it still is. Bourbon fanciers down the years have been fervent in their praise of it. Today it comes in several versions, all of them Kentucky straight bourbon: Old Ftizgerald Bonded, 6 years, 100°, $8 (fifth); Old Fitzgerald 1849, 8 years, 90°, $8.50 (fifth) (the same in a Wheaton Crystal decanter: $7, pint); Old Fitzgerald Prime, 6 years, 86°, $7 (fifth).

The other products of Stitzel & Weller include: Cabin Still Kentucky Straight Bourbon, 5 years, 86°, $5 (fifth); Cabin Still Kentucky Straight Bourbon, 6 years, 80°, $5.50 (fifth); W. L. Weller Special Reserve Blend, 7 years, 90°, $8 (fifth). (There is also a 107° version—arrgh, proceed with caution—at $11.50 a fifth.)

OLD FORESTER KENTUCKY STRAIGHT BOURBON WHISKY

This is one of the best-known bourbons in the world, with annual sales of almost 1 million cases. It launched the great spirits firm of Brown-Forman of Louisville, Ky.

There are at least four explanations of the origin of the name. One says that it was named after General Nathan Forrest, the dashing Confederate cavalryman. Others say simply that the name was derived from the lumber industry, which was flourishing in the area at that time. More probably, the name was purely imaginative, springing full-blown, without cause or antecedent, from the creative mind of George Garvin Brown, the founder of the business.

In 1970, Old Forester celebrated its 100th anniversary. It was originally conceived as an honest "medicinal" whiskey—and it is ironic that during Prohibition it was sold as exactly that. In those early days, Old Forester was 90°, a blend of straight bourbon whiskeys. When Prohibition struck, it continued to be made, under government supervision, for "medicinal purposes," but only as a straight bonded bourbon, 100°. When Repeal came, Old Forester simply remained a 100° straight bonded bourbon. It was not until 1959 that an 86° was introduced.

Is Old Forester Whisky as good as its reputation? A bold, unequivocal yes and no! Yes, it is a good, medium-bodied, slightly sweet, full-flavored Kentucky straight bourbon. No, it is not so outstanding that you could select it, tasting blindly, from other bourbons of the same type. Old Forester 86° sells for around $6.50 (25.4 oz., 2 oz. less than a fifth), and the 100° bonded for around $8.

Note that it's Old Forester *Whisky*, not *Whiskey*. The company, for no discernible reason, insists on the Scotch and Canadian spelling.

OLD GRAND-DAD KENTUCKY STRAIGHT BOURBON WHISKEY This is one of the most historic and prestigious names in bourbon whiskey. It also has a most prestigious price tag affixed, about $7 (fifth), making it one of the most expensive of America's premium bourbons.

The brand name goes back to 1882, but the whiskey goes back almost a century further. The Hayden family who "invented" Old Grand-Dad was making whiskey in Kentucky as far back as 1796. It was Colonel R. B. Hayden who named the whiskey after his grandfather. Like almost all the other premium bourbons, Old Grand-Dad was first made only as a 100° bonded whiskey. The 86° was introduced only in 1958.

Nobody disputes the excellence of this straight bourbon whiskey, although the 100° bonded was judged only "acceptable" in one well-known tasting. Realizing how slight are the differences between bourbon whiskeys of the same type, it is a question of whether the difference justifies the higher price. Unto each his own.

OLD OVERHOLT STRAIGHT RYE WHISKEY Through most of the 19th century, rye whiskey far outsold bourbon in America. Things began to change around 1880, and over the course of the ensuing century, bourbon has pulled further and further ahead of its sister (brother?) spirit. And now, a century later, bourbon has begun to decline in sales, and for the first time in our history, vodka is the No. 1 spirit in the land.

One of the few ryes that have survived all these vicissitudes is Old Overholt, established, as the label loudly proclaims, over 150 years ago. It was in the early part of the 19th century that Abraham Overholt, whose grandfather had come from Germany in 1730, began making rye whiskey for his family and friends. Everybody agreed that it was great stuff—and Old Overholt, at first nameless, was born.

This is good rye whiskey— perhaps the best you will find in the land. Because it's often the only rye to be found in the land. (Other nationally distributed ryes include Hiram Walker Meadowbrook, Rittenhouse Rye, and Wild Turkey Rye.) Still the fact remains that this is a fine tot of whiskey, and if you're a bourbon lover, you'll probably adore Old Overholt. It is 86° and sells for about $6.50 (fifth), reasonable enough, especially when compared with Wild Turkey's 101° Rye, at $10 (New York) or $11 (California) a fifth.

OLD SAN FRANCISCO BRANDY It's well named, is this hearty, heady, 8-year-old California brandy: after the rollicking, roistering city of San Francisco of 1847. Embossed into the back of the bottle are the words: "To San Francisco—her tradition, promise, and enduring elegance."

Old San Francisco has to be the only brandy in the world that comes with three different labels. One label shows the original ferry house; another, General Ulysses S. Grant being feted in S. Francisco after the Civil War; and a third, the Grand Court Palace Hotel, for three decades "lavish host to the nobility and notoriety of San Francisco society" (so saith the back label).

But enough of the trappings . . . what's within? Full-bodied, lusty California brandy, that's what. Perhaps too lusty for today's tastes and tasters; some have downgraded this brandy as being too forthright, too heavy-handed.

OLD TAYLOR KENTUCKY STRAIGHT BOURBON WHISKEY The name derives from a Colonel Edmund H. Taylor, a Civil War veteran, who began making bourbon whiskey in Bourbon County, Ky., in 1887. His distillery was in the shape of a castle—you can still see it on the label, along with a portrait of the colonel himself—to tell the public that his bourbon was of the highest nobility, having been born in a proper castle.

Today Old Taylor, like every other major brand of whiskey, is no longer sufficient unto itself; it's now owned by a conglomerate—in this case, National Distillers Corporation.

Many experts agree that Old Taylor is exceptional whiskey, even among the premium bourbons. It seems to get just a mite extra TLC along the way. The 86° sells for around $6.50 (fifth) and the bonded 100° for around $8.50. There is also an 80°.

OLÉ TEQUILA With the overnight proliferation of tequila brands in the U.S. over the past decade, it was inevitable that sooner or later a brand would be named simply Olé, as one might name an American bourbon simply

Rah!—not Raw—Bourbon. Schenley dood it.

Olé is one of the few tequilas found in the U.S. in a 100° version. There is also an 80°, and both come in the regular Gold and White colorations. And it's quite decently priced: about $5.75 for the 80° and $6.50 for the 100° (both fifths); somewhat more in the Eastern U.S. Olé is standard reliable tequila, wholly adequate for mixed drinks, and for the matter of that, for straight sipping too.

OLMECA TEQUILA This and El Charro Tequila are marketed in the U.S. by that giant American conglomerate, **Seagram**. (The tequila itself, by law, is a product of Mexico. There is no such thing as an American-made tequila.) Both Olmeca and El Charro are medium-priced, well-made, standard tequilas, no better and happily no worse than a multitude of others. Both come in both a Gold version (with a slightly golden tinge) and a White (untinted), both 80°, and both selling for around $6.50 (fifth).

ORANGE- AND CITRUS-FLAVORED LIQUEURS Orange- or citrus-flavored liqueurs are the world's favorites. They come from more countries, in more guises, under more brand names, than any other liqueurs of this earth. Here is a partial listing: **Aurum, Cointreau, crème de mandarine, Curaçao, Forbidden Fruit, Grand Marnier, Parfait Amour** (it's violet-scented and colored but it's basically a citrus liqueur), **rock & rye, triple sec,** and **Van der**

Hum. All of these are available in the U.S.

When face to face with an orange or grapefruit, most people eat the fruit and throw away the peeling. Not so the liqueur industry; they use the peels and throw away the fruit. The deep, somewhat bitter citrus flavor, together with the essential oils of the rind, are what is sought, not the soft sweet flavor of the fruit.

Further, liqueurs are made predominantly from the bitter orange, *Citrus aurantium*, not the sweet eating orange (*Citrus sinensis*), such as navel, that Americans are familiar with. The bitter (or sour) orange does best in the Antilles, Curaçao, and Haiti. The modern liqueur industry usually dries the peel, which is then shipped to the distillery, where it is reconstituted with water and alcohol.

By general consensus, the world's finest orange liqueurs are Cointreau, Curaçao (and triple sec, which is simply white Curaçao), and Grand Marnier.

OTARD V.S. COGNAC The final "d" is silent: *oh-tar*. This is good, reliable Cognac, French by birth (as all true Cognacs are), with slight sweetness, and light-bodied. It's especially designed for the American market. Around $12 (fifth).

OUZO It's got just two syllables—*oo-zoh*—and it's Greece's national liqueur. It's often called a brandy, and indeed it does have a brandy base, but it's more liqueur than brandy. Ouzo's sweet fragrant flavor comes from anise, licorice, and other herbs. Drink your ouzo in a tall glass—three to five parts of water to one of ouzo—with lots of ice. It will turn milky upon mixing.

Here are some of the most popular Ouzos imported to the U.S., in ascending order of price. Buy the most economical you can find: Achaia Clauss, 92°, $7.65 (fifth); **Cambas**, 90°, $7.85 (fifth); **Metaxa**, 90°, $8.20 (fifth); Keo Extra Fine, 98°, $9.45 (fifth).

P

PADDY'S BLENDED IRISH WHISKEY Oliver St. John Gogarty, the celebrated Irish wit and author, once said that the Irish prefer drink to food because it interferes less with conversation. Aye, lad. And one of the most-loved drinks of the Irish is, of course, Irish whiskey. Aye, Irish, a darlin' drink, is the way the sons of Eire put it.

Paddy's is the most loved, most esteemed, most consumed of all Irish whiskeys by the Irish themselves—at least by the citizens of the Republic of Ireland, the Catholic part of the land, which is three-fourths of the whole.

Paddy's is made by the giant Midleton Distillery, County Cork—and that makes it "Catholic" whiskey! And truth to tell, Paddy's is a fine whiskey, deserving of its good repute. It is 86° and sells for about $8.50 (fifth). Paddy's also comes in 80° at about $7.50.

PANCHO VILLA TEQUILA Too bad this good Mexican tequila is available only in the Western U.S. It's a fine bottle, and an excellent value. It comes in the standard White and Gold, both 80°, at around $5.25 (fifth), which is just about $2 less than Jose Cuervo, and it's just as good. Should anyone doubt that, taste them *blindly* (labels hidden), side by side.

PARFAIT AMOUR One critic said of this purple-hued liqueur that it looks poisonous and tastes like melted jelly beans. It's a rather questionable potion, all right, but it's strictly nonpoisonous and it doesn't taste *precisely*, strictly like jelly beans. Tastes more like violets, from which it happens to be made. But which is preferable, jelly beans or violets?

Parfait Amour is very sweet, with a totally nondescript taste. And small wonder: Besides all those violets, it's flavored with rose petals, citrus peel, coriander, vanilla, and citron—for starters.

Actually, Parfait Amour is made in several different styles—one tends to be more flowery, another more citrusy—but they all have two things in common: They're very sweet and have a nauseous purple color.

Parfait Amour comes from France and Holland mostly; Garnier (24 oz.) and Marie Brizard (23.6 oz.) each have one (60°) at around $10. And Bols has an American-made one at half the price (25 oz.).

Crème de violette and crème Yvette are precisely the same beverage; both are in effect American-made versions of Parfait Amour. Crème Yvette is said to be popular in Europe—why is beyond all human understanding.

Parfait Amour means "perfect love," and that sentiment, it seems, was more popular in the 1920s than it is today. Perhaps that also explains why these violet-hued beverages were at their height 50 years ago, and so little known or appreciated today.

PASSIONFRUIT LIQUEUR
The name does not suggest that this beverage is some kind of an aphrodisiac: that it arouses sexual passion. In fact, the name has a religious significance; the passionfruit was so named because its flower resembled the crown of thorns that Christ wore during his sacred Passion.

Passionfruit liqueur originated in Australia, but today it comes from Hawaii as well. It is golden in color, sweet in taste. In flavor, it's delicate, elusive, "almost orgiastic," says one authority. It has a faint citrus flavor. But it's not about to replace Grand Marnier.

PASTIS; PASTIS DE MARSEILLES
This is a generic name, originally slang, used mainly in southern France, especially the Marseille region and the Riviera, to denote any of the many popular anise-flavored liqueurs. The best-known are Ricard and Pernod.

PEACH LIQUEUR
America produces most of the world's peach liqueurs, none of them outstanding. A few European imports do find their way to these shores, but none of these are very remarkable either, even though some of them are twice the price of their American counterparts. The simple truth of the matter is that peaches may make for good eating, but they do not make for very good drinking: they are not as distinctive and assertive in flavor as are apricots, for example. And so it is that apricot liqueurs, overall, are far superior to peach liqueurs.

Most of America's peach liqueurs call themselves peach-flavored brandy or peach liqueur and brandy, not peach liqueur. Hiram Walker has a peach cordial. Most of these are 70° and sell between $5 and $6 (24 oz.).

In imports, Marie Brizard has a peach cordial, 80°, at around $10 (23.6 oz.), but it's not much better than the domestics. Cusenier has a peach liqueur 64°, at around $6 (24 oz.).

And as a last resort you can always make your own peach liqueur. Like so:

2 lbs. fresh peaches, peeled, pitted, cut into small pieces

1 fifth 80 or 90° Vodka or 1 tenth 190° Everclear

Sliced peel of ½ lemon

1 cup sugar syrup (1 cup sugar boiled with ½ cup water)

Combine the peaches, vodka, and lemon peel in an airtight jar and allow to marinate for about a week. Shake the jar vigorously every day or two. Strain the goop, add the sugar syrup.

And if things are really tough, and you don't have any peaches, only peach leaves, despair not: Substitute a mess of peach leaves —75 or so—for the peaches. Since peach leaves aren't quite as tasty as peaches, your brew will need longer to macerate: give it at least six weeks. And if you want a truly gourmet liqueur, add a bottle (24 oz. or so) of semisweet white wine.

And if you're still not satisfied, perhaps you will appreciate **Southern Comfort**, America's illustrious peach-flavored, whiskey-based cordial. And if that doesn't please you, quit drinking.

PEANUT LOLITA If .you can get past the name, it's not a half bad beverage! Surely Peanut Lolita is the most outlandish, most ungainly, most ill-advised name for a liqueur in the history of mankind. All of this is from an aesthetic point of view, of course, not a commercial one. Commercially, Peanut Lolita is probably already a huge success, thanks to good distribution and extensive promotion. Peanut Lolita is the brainchild of Publicker Distillers Products of Philadelphia, and it's been on the market only since 1976. (There are two other "Lolita" products—unfortunately—Caffe Lolita and Amaretto Lolita.)

The fact that Jimmy Carter happened to be in the peanut business before his present employment is not unconnected to the appearance of Peanut Lolita. In fact, brother Billy was present at a gala Peanut Lolita inaugural in New York City when the beverage was launched. (Billy would undoubtedly have preferred a can of Billy Beer, or even some other, inferior brand, but sister Ruth may have advised him to the effect that not on beer alone. . .)

If the notion of a peanut-flavored liqueur tends to rend your soul, allay your fears. Peanut Lolita is, indeed, redolent of peanuts, but somehow, this is a rather civilized and satisfying potion—in small doses.

It's a bit too goopy-sweet to be taken straight, but on the rocks, Peanut Lolita can warm the soul and settle the belly. Peanut Lolita (and the other two Lolitas as well) sells for about $6.50 (750 ml, or 28 oz.).

PEPE LOPEZ TEQUILA Tequila is pretty much tequila—at least as it is imported to the U.S. It would take a true aficionado with an abundance of divine guidance to distinguish between most of them. Pepe Lopez is standard, trustworthy tequila, not a hairsbreadth different from a warehouse full of others. It differs only in this, that it's well priced: around $6 (per 25.4 oz.) for both the White and Gold (both 80°) in the Eastern U.S., and about $1 less in the West. A good value in good tequila.

PEPPERMINT SCHNAPPS The name sounds very Germanic—and, in fact, peppermint schnapps is of German origin, but today there's a lot more made in the U.S. than in Germany, or, for that matter, in all of Europe. Virtually every major U.S. liqueur firm makes a peppermint schnapps.

In taste it's very similar to crème de menthe (and may be substituted for it), and it even looks like the white version, for they're both water-clear. Peppermint schnapps is usually a trifle less sweet and lighter in body than crème de menthe, and for that reason it makes for better straight-up sipping than does the syrupy-sweet crème de menthe. It's usually 60° (but J. W. Dant and Old Mr. Boston are a lowly 42°), and the domestic ones sell for $5.50 to $6 (24 oz.). Stock's imported version sells for about the same.

A few American firms also make a mint-flavored gin, which is precisely what the name says: true gin, flavored with mint. It's much, much drier than either crème de menthe or peppermint schnapps, usually around 70°. If you like gin more than you do mint—or if you like mint but not sugar—mint-flavored gin may be for you.

PERNOD Pernod—pronounced *payr-no*—is the direct legal successor to illegal absinthe. When absinthe was outlawed by the French government in 1915, the firm of Henri Louis Pernod was the major producer of the worm-wood-laced liqueur. It was the supposedly harmful and habit-forming wormwood which had caused the legal prohibition, so Pernod simply dropped the wormwood and added to the amount of anise. Today's beverage is labeled "liqueur d'anis."

Other legal descendants of absinthe include **Ricard, Herbsaint,** and **Ojen.**

The Pernod commonly found in the U.S., Pernod Anis, sells for around $8 (fifth). A more authentic successor to the classical absinthe, with wormwood and all, was made by Pernod S.A. in Tarragona, Spain, until 1937, when it too was outlawed.

Old-time absinthe was a very powerful (150°), greenish, very bitter beverage. It was probably the high alcoholic content that should have been banned, not the wormwood. Today's Pernod is a much gentler drink: soft, with notable sweetness, and a predominant licorice flavor.

The classic manner of drinking Pernod is to employ the "Absinthe Drip": Slowly pour icewater over a lump of sugar held in a slotted spoon into a glass containing Pernod. The yellowish Pernod will turn milky. Sip it nostalgically, toasting the memory of the Bohemian poets and artists who sipped their fiery absinthe a century ago in the salons and cafés of London and Paris.

PERU—BRANDY This unlikely little South American country makes one of the world's most renowned—or notorious—brandies, Pisco. Pisco is made from Muscat and Mission grapes, and it's a zestful beverage, tasteful as well, though perhaps a trifle rough, by *gringo* standards. Pisco is distinctive, true—but not an abomination, as some would have us believe. Beverage snobs have a tendency to condemn Pisco *because* it is different.

As shipped to the U.S., Pisco is only 90°, but it is noted for its insidious ways. *Con mucho cuidado!* Pisco is briefly aged in beeswax amphorae and great care is taken to make sure it retains some of the odor and taste of the beeswax.

There is only one notable drink made with Pisco: the Pisco Sour. Here's a swashbuckling potion with a lurid past: It was standard fare along San Francisco's notorious Barbary Coast in the Gold Rush days. And it is favored to this day by the city's cognoscenti. Here's the Rx, guaranteed to make you yearn for that city by the Bay:

1 jigger Pisco, 1 oz. lemon or lime juice, 1 tbsp. powdered sugar, 1 egg white, 3 or 4 ice cubes

Combine all the ingredients and shake well; strain into a cocktail glass (preferably pre-chilled). Add a dash or two of Angostura Bitters. In Peru they sprinkle a bit of nutmeg on the top.

PEYCHAUD'S BITTERS

Bitters are just what the name says, and Peychaud's Bitters are perhaps the bitterest of all bitters. Peychaud's is made in New Orleans, as it has been for many decades. It is considered absolutely essential to the constuction of that grand old drink of New Orleans, the Sazerac. Peychaud's sells for around $3 for 10 oz.

PIMM'S CUP

More than a century ago, Pimm's Oyster Bar in London created a lemon-flavored, gin-based drink that became very popular over the years. It was the first Gin Sling: lemon juice, gin, sweetener, and a bit of water. And that is basically what Pimm's Cup is today (it was first bottled in the 1870s).

Or, more exactly, that's what Pimm's Cup No. 1 is today, for originally there were six Pimm's Cups. No. 1 was based on gin, No. 2 on whiskey, No. 3 on brandy, No. 4 on rum, No. 5 on rye, and No. 6 on vodka. No. 1, however, has always been the most popular—though the Canadians of bygone days, for some mysterious reason, favored No. 2—and in recent years, No. 1 has been the only one made. And now, even the No. 1 has been taken from the label.

As it comes from the bottle, Pimm's Cup is amber-colored, viscous, bittersweet—and you won't turn green if you drink it straight, but its best use is as the base for a tall refreshing drink with ice and soda. The back label tells all: Use 8 oz. glass, 2 oz. of Pimm's over ice, fill with soda or tonic, add a slice of lemon, stir well. A slice of cucumber or a sprig of mint makes it look—and taste—even cooler.

Pimm's Cup is simply, unadornedly, one of the world's most inspired drinks! Be cautioned: Pimm's Cup can be deceptive. It seems to be virtually nonalcoholic, yet it's a respectable 67°. It sells for around $6.50 (fifth).

PIÑA COLADA (COCKTAIL)

The name means "strained pineapple," not *overextended* pineapple, but *sieved* pineapple. It's a drink that's become popular only over the past decades, and a very tasty potion it is. Somebody should have invented it sooner. The heart of the Piña Colada is coconut milk, or cream, which you can obtain in several ways: You can purchase it in a gourmet or specialty store, or you can simply drain the milk from a fresh coconut, or you can boil some coconut "meat" and then strain out the "milk."

Here's the recipe for two drinks. In a blender put:

2 jiggers light-bodied rum (Puerto Rico, Mexico, Virgin Islands), 2 tbsp. coconut milk, 3 tbsp. crushed pineapple—fresh or canned, 2 cups cracked ice

Blend at high speed until smooth. Not only delicious—nourishing too.

PINEAPPLE LIQUEURS
There's one from Hawaii, called, logically enough, Hawaiian Pineapple Liqueur. It's made by the same people (Hawaiian Distillers) who proudly (?) bring us **Macadamia Nut Liqueur** (yuk).

Hawaiian Pineapple Liqueur is as close to zero as anything you're going to encounter among alcoholic beverages. But in all honesty, it's not a complete, total, absolute zero, zilch—would that it were. Better zero than to taste of moldy coconut and seaweed. Back to the drawing boards, Hawaiian Distillers.

An excellent pineapple liqueur, however, is made by the English firm of Lamb & Watt, called by its French name, crème de ananas. But you'll have to go to Britain to obtain it, as it's not imported to the U.S.

PINK GIN (COCKTAIL)
Pink Gin is so called because it's vaguely that color. More to the point, it's also called Gin & Bitters, because that's what it is: Gin and Angostura Bitters. That's it, that's all: a jigger or two of gin, and a dash or two of Angostura Bitters.

You can just swirl them around in a glass, no ice. That's the traditional British way, for this cocktail is an old British favorite, especially beloved of the Royal Navy, who call it "Pinkers." And if you want to be ultra-British, you don't drink the bitters at all: you simply swirl them around in the glass, then toss them out, and pour in the gin. Tally-ho! Ice-happy Americans, however, are allowed to dilute their Pinkers with water or a couple of ice cubes. Purists insist that this tasty, potent, simple cocktail can be made only with Plymouth gin. Simple, peasant-type drinking folks say, any gin.

PINK SQUIRREL (COCKTAIL)
This is the only noteworthy cocktail made with **crème de noyau**, or, as you will—for they're exactly the same thing, under different labels—creme de almond.

For one drink, mix 1 oz. crème de noyau (almond), ½ oz. white crème de cacao, and 1 oz. light cream. Shake together with ice, then strain. Some mixologists call for equal parts of all three ingredients, but it's better to halve the crème de cacao, lest it overpower the delicate almond flavor.

Heublein markets a ready-mixed Pink Squirrel, 30°, at around $4.50 (24 oz.), but you'll have a better and more economical Squirrel by constructing it yourself.

PIPPERMINT
Pippermint is not a typographical error—it's just the way some crazy Frenchmen choose to spell "peppermint." It's the name of the crème de menthe of the French liqueur firm Get Frères (pronounced *zhay*), Revel, France.

Along with Cusenier's **Freezomint**, Pippermint is one of the best-known, most widely exported, and best mint liqueurs in the world. It comes in a uniquely shaped bottle, patterned after an old oil lamp, and unchanged for some 200 years.

It is made from five different mints—all mint liqueurs use various mints—imported from various countries. The green-colored Pippermint, (60°), is the most popular but it also comes in a white, which is a trifle stronger.

Pippermint sells in the U.S. at about $7.50 (24 oz.) and deserves to be tried.

PISCO LLAMA It comes in what looks like a handsome decanter-type bottle, but on closer inspection, it turns out to be just a plain old booze bottle, wrapped in a decorative plastic wrap. It doesn't even have a llama on it. The bottle is said to glow in the dark—after imbibing freely of Pisco Llama, the consumer may well do so, but the bottle, never.

Pisco Llama has only recently been imported to the U.S., by Browne Vintners, the giant wine and spirits marketing firm of San Francisco. It's logical enough, as San Francisco is the city that made Pisco famous in the U.S. in the first place. That was via its famous Pisco Punch of Gold Rush fame (see under **South America—brandy**).

Pisco Llama is a typical Pisco brandy: colorless, fiery, interesting. It comes from Chile—"The Great Spirit of the Andes," says the label—and is guaranteed to warm one's extremities, whether on Andean heights or subterranean depths.

Whether Pisco Llama is worth its $7.50 (fifth) price tag, however, is quite another matter. In its birthplace, Pisco

is an economical, peasant-type beverage, but that's before tariffs, freight, and importers' markups have taken their toll. Dollar for dollar you do much better with a California brandy.

PISCO SOUR (COCKTAIL)
Pisco is South America's colorless *macho* brandy—it often needs taming, at least for *gringo* American tastes. The Pisco Sour contains the perfect element for subduing this wild spirit:

> 1 oz. Pisco, juice of ½ lime (lemon, in emergencies), 1 tsp. powdered sugar (or dash of sugar syrup), 1 egg white (If you're making 2 or 3 sours at one time, one egg white will suffice), 2 or 3 dashes Angostura Bitters

Combine all the ingredients except the bitters and shake vigorously with ice. Strain into a cocktail glass, and shake the bitters on top.

If using an electric blender, cut down on the egg white if you're making just one sour. For each sour use two ice cubes. You can blend at high speed so that you get a slushy sour, or at low speed so that some of the ice chunks remain. Either way it makes a pleasant, frothy drink.

PISTASHA There are a minuscule number of liqueurs made from pistachio nuts, or supposedly so made—this is America's contribution. Some contribution. This **Regnier** product may see some pistachio nuts during production, but it's accomplished furtively and fleetingly. This greenish-hued liqueur (the color is artificially derived) tastes almost exactly like any of a dozen American crèmes de noyau, which are literally liqueurs from the pits! They're made from the pits of various fruits, mainly apricots, which impart an almond flavor. If you delight in crème de noyau, but green's your favorite color, not pink, Pistasha is precisely your snifter of liqueur. It is 48° and is one of Regnier's most expensive liqueurs, almost $8 (24 oz.).

PLANTER'S PUNCH (COCKTAIL) A refreshing summertime drink which, like most good cocktails, is simplicity itself. In this case, essentially rum and lime (just as the Daiquiri). Here's how. In a tall (Collins) glass put:

Juice of 1 or 2 limes (or 1 lime and 1 lemon), 2 tsp. powdered sugar, 2 oz. carbonated water

Fill the glass with ice and stir well. Then add:

2 dashes bitters, 1 jigger Jamaican rum (it is important that the rum be a heavy-bodied one; Myers's, a Jamaican rum, boldly proclaims "Planter's Punch brand" right on the label)

Stir. Enjoy.
If you dig the frills, garnish with a slice of lime, a maraschino cherry, a sprig of mint.
P.S.: This is essentially the same drink as the Rum Swizzle.
P.P.S.: If you have them on hand you may substitute a dash each of grenadine and rock-candy syrup for the sugar, as Trader Vic does, and he says

he has sold at least a jillion of these Planter's Punches in his day.

PLYMOUTH GIN Plymouth gin is gin made in Plymouth, England, just as London gin is gin made in London. Or was. Both names are now generic terms, specifying a type of gin rather than their place of origin. London-type gin is now made around the globe, but oddly enough, Plymouth gin is still made in only one place in the world: Plymouth, England. In fact, there is only one brand of Plymouth gin still made on earth today: Coates.

Time was when Plymouth gin was something quite different from London gin. Historically it was midway between London Dry gin, which is only lightly flavored, principally with juniper berries, and Dutch (Holland) gin, which is comparatively heavily flavored. The distinction today is almost wholly blurred. In blind tastings, even professional tasters have often been unable to distinguish between London and Plymouth gin. Let it be said, however, that Plymouth gin devotees still lurk here and there, and they stoutly maintain that there *is* a difference, and that Plymouth gin is the only gin, repeat sole and only gin, fit for a "Pink Gin."

POIRE WILLIAMS (or PEAR WILLIAM) It's absolutely delicious, is this exquisite fruit brandy. The name means simply Williams or Bartlett Pear. It comes, as do most fruit brandies, from France, Germany, and Switzerland. Poire Williams is sometimes aged a year or two, but this is not essential, nor is it required.

A most unusual type of Pear William is sometimes seen—with an elegant price tag affixed, about $25—the bottle contains a for-real, full-grown pear. This is a trick of the Swiss: They hang a bottle from a tree, draping it over a small starting pear, and the fruit ripens inside the bottle. This is, of course, a very expensive procedure, but all the expense is lavished on the silly pear, not on the brandy. Net result: $22 worth of pear, $3 worth of brandy. These pear-in-the-bottle brandies may make for good conversation, but they are not good values, nor good brandy.

If you're looking for a name, Kammer (Germany) makes an excellent Pear William, as does 3-Tannen (Germany). In Swiss brand names there's Rathaus (about $20) and Dettling (about $21), both 25.4 oz., and then there's Meirhof, which makes a pear-in-the-bottle extravaganza (about $25 a fifth).

POPOV VODKA This and Relska Vodka are Heublein's "economy" vodkas, as contrasted with **Smirnoff**, the firm's premium brand. Both Popov and Relska come in both 80° and 100°, and they sell for roughly $1.50 less than their Smirnoff counterparts.

Both brands are well publicized by Heublein, and it shows: Both are among the nation's top-selling spirits. Popov in particular has had spectacular sales growth, up almost 20%, 1976 to 1977. It is now selling almost 2 million cases per year. Relska's sales leveled off in 1977, but it is still clipping along at almost 1 million cases per year.

These two vodkas are made by a less laborious process than is Smirnoff. They do not go through the same protracted, laborious charcoal-filtering process that Smirnoff is subjected to. Some of their purification is accomplished by means of centrifuging.

Nonetheless it is extremely difficult to detect the difference between the three brands of Heublein vodkas. If you remain skeptical, simply taste them blindly.

These are good, standard American vodkas, medium-priced, wholly reliable. The 80° of both brands sells for around $4 (fifth), the 100° for about $5 (fifth).

PORTUGAL–BRANDY Rather surprisingly, Portuguese brandy outsells Spanish brandy in the U.S. It all began back in World War II when French and Spanish brandies were simply unavailable.

And Portuguese brandy is a good and wholesome spirit. Indeed, it is made from much the same grapes as Porto, one of the world's truly great wines. It is rather similar to Spanish brandy, though a tad less sweet. It's got a wonderful deep-down flavor and a heady bouquet.

Look for these names: Napolitan Brandy, 100°; and Primavera Aguardiente, 100°.

PORTUGUESE (or PORTUGEE) COFFEE This luscious, nutritious after-dinner drink is really not Portuguese in origin, at least not directly so. It's just that it was invented by a Californian of Portuguese extraction, a sometime bartender, sometime clergyman, one E. Frank Henriques, *qui supra*, cf. title page, who labels any successful experimental recipe, whether food or beverage, "Portuguese."

This is a spontaneous kind of drink: Ingredients can vary vastly, depending on what's on hand—and it's a very flexible drink, for portions can vary greatly without noxious effects. All quantities are *very* approximate.

Into a blender, put:

1 part strong coffee—the vile, leftover kind is best—or just toss in some instant coffee, or a decaffeinated version, 1 part brandy—or Cognac (ideal, but who can afford it?)—or gin, or vodka, or bourbon, or rum (rum goes great!), ½ part crème de cacao, white or dark—or coffee-flavored brandy—or Kahlúa, or other coffee liqueur, ½ part white crème de menthe—or peppermint schnapps—or coffee-menthe liqueur, ½ part light cream or milk (whole or low fat)—or powdered milk, a blob or a glob, A whole bunch of ice cubes. For extra richness you can toss in an egg or two (whole, raw)

One or the other ingredient may be omitted—except, of course, the coffee, because then you'd have a coffeeless coffee. And you need the cream too—to make it soothing (and caloric). Blend at high speed. Serve, enjoy, relax.

POTCHEEN It's also called poteen, potheen, potsheen, or potyeen, and it's preferably pronounced *pot-sheen.* But no matter how you spell it or say it, it's the same thing: illicit Irish spirits.

Potcheen is usually referred to as illegal Irish *whiskey*, but this is not quite accurate, because potcheen may be (and is) distilled from a number of different materials. If malted barley is used, as it usually is, you have a true whiskey. But if unrefined sugar, for example, is used as a base, as it sometimes is, you have rum, not whiskey.

The name means "little pot," a reference to the small movable, hideable, disguisable pot stills used in Ireland to make this clandestine Irish moonshine.

Potcheen is still made in the Emerald Isle, but on a much diminished scale, as compared with the deluge produced only a few decades ago. And, most odd to relate, today there is legal potcheen—a clear contradiction in terms, something like a chaste prostitute. It is even available in the U.S., labeled simply Potcheen, at around $8 (fifth). (At that price, small wonder that the illegal stuff still flourishes.)

Potcheen is not necessarily the crude and fiery spirit that most people imagine. Its lack of age, of course, can leave it a bit untamed, but when properly matured potcheen can be a quite decent brew—no Cognac, to be sure, but rather civilized and entirely respectable. But at $8, sure and it will only be true Sons of Eire who'll be after buying it.

(JOHN) POWER'S IRISH WHISKEY It is often thought that different brands of whiskey are in fierce competition with each other, particularly Irish whiskeys, because the Irish are such a fightin' clan. But most of the Irish whiskey sold in the U.S. is the property of a single huge consortium, **Irish Distillers Group**. Power's Irish Whiskey is one of the seven brands made by that body.

This is not to say that the whiskey is the poorer because of such conglomerate ownership. In fact, the opposite may be true, for in this case the energy and resources go into the product, not into futile competition, wrangling, and promotion.

Power's is standard Irish whiskey, though it has received low marks in a few blind tastings. In others, however, it has scored well. It is 86° and sells for around $8 (fifth). The Gold Label (80°), "Three Swallow"—those are birds, not belts of whiskey; they're pictured on the neck label—goes for about the same. Stick with the "plain" Power's Irish Whiskey: same whiskey, higher proof.

PRESBYTERIAN (COCKTAIL) You don't meet many Presbyterians anymore, and that's a pity, for this is a good middle-of-the-road, main-line drink, not too sweet, not too dry, most refreshing. Where it got its name is an ecclesiastical (but not supernatural) mystery.

Into a tall glass, put:

2 to 3 oz. bourbon, 2 oz. ginger ale (chilled), 2 oz. club soda (chilled), 3 or 4 ice cubes, twist lemon peel.

Stir, drink. Praise God for Presbyterians.

PROOF As most tipplers fully understand, proof is simply the percentage (by volume) of alcohol in a distilled beverage. In the American system the proof is twice the percentage of alcohol: 100° = 50% alcohol; 200° (possible only in the laboratory) = 100% alcohol. The British have a different system, totally incomprehensible except to professional mathematicians—and the British.

Proof is lowered or increased simply by the subtraction or addition of distilled water. Obviously, the higher the proof, the more of that particular spirit, and the less water is contained in a given volume. If you have two bourbons of equal quality and selling for the same price, one at 80° and one at 86°, you should buy the higher-proof beverage, for it contains 7½% more whiskey. And if you—wisely—prefer to take your whiskey at a lower proof, you can lower the proof yourself simply by adding water. That's not stretching your whiskey—that's lowering your proof, maintaining your sobriety, saving your money and lengthening your days, all while enjoying your whiskey!

PRUNELLA (or PRUNELLE, or CRÈME DE PRUNELLE) It sounds like the name of one of the ugly witches of Cucamonga or somewhere, but it's the name of the European version of our American sloe gin. Most prunella is tastier, drier, and more elegant than our rather pedestrian sloe gin, but the principal flavoring ingredient is the same: the sloe berry, which happens to be a wild plum, not a berry.

Prunella is strictly a liqueur —sweet, dark in color—not to be confused with true plum brandies such as slivovitz or mirabelle.

A few prunellas are imported to the U.S., most of them selling for around $10, all 60°, though Stock's is a best buy at around $6 (fifth).

PUERTO RICO—RUMS A lot of these come to the U.S., and they're well received here, for Puerto Rico rums are mostly light-colored and light-bodied, in accordance with current American tastes. An astounding 84% of the rum consumed by Americans is from Puerto Rico. It's good rum, usually a trifle more expensive than its sister type of rum from the Virgin Islands (see Virgin Islands—rums). The Puerto Rico government, noting Americans' present fondness for light drinks, has recently been pushing its white rum, especially in magazine ads.

PULQUE *Gringos* who don't know how to pronounce it— *POOL-kay*—are advised not to drink it. Mexican *descamisados* (shirtless ones: the poor) love it; they've been drinking it since the days of the Aztecs. It's actually "cactus beer": the fermented juice of the maguey (agave), a type of cactus. It's milky white in color, 4% to 7% alcohol—higher than beer, less than wine—and has a sweet, sour-milk taste. In Mexico it's more common than beer—which is everywhere and of excellent quality—and cheaper. The Mexicans prize it as a cure for stomach ailments, but according to most translations, it was wine, not pulque, that St. Paul recommended to Timothy, for his "stomach's sake and often infirmities" (1 Timothy 5:23).

Q

QUETSCH A fruit brandy made from a dark-blue plum of the same name. Quetsch is produced in France, Germany, and Switzerland, but mainly in Alsace. It is rarely imported to the U.S. **Mirabelle** is quite similar.

R

RAGNAUD COGNAC Ragnaud Cognacs, from the most economical to the "top of the line," are consistently among the very best values to be found in Cognacs. They are in short supply and always difficult to find in the U.S.; they deserve special mention not because of their scarcity, but because of their excellence.

Ragnaud V.E. Grande Fine Champagne is the least expensive, around $15 (fifth), and experts declare it one of the finest of V.S.O.P. Cognacs. The V.S.E.P., at not much more money, is perhaps even better.

Also excellent is Ragnaud Reserve Speciale Grande Fine, with an average age of 20 years, at around $18 (fifth).

Ragnaud's Heritage Madame Paul Ragnaud Grande Champagne, around $100 (fifth) is the prestige label, but a much better value is the Grande Reserve Fontveille Grand Champagne, around $25 (fifth), about 35 years of age.

RAKI (or RAKA, or RAKIA) It's pronounced *rocky*, and that pretty well describes this Middle Eastern spirit. It can be made from dates, grapes, grain, palm toddy (sap), or rice; it's flavored with aniseed and coriander. Even diluted with water, raki is a rough, rustic drink, not designed for export. The name is a variation of arak.

RAMOS GIN FIZZ (COCKTAIL) If Strawberry Cream Waffles and Eggs Benedict are beginning to pall for breakfast, you might consider a Ramos Fizz or two as a temporary—prithee, not permanent—alternative. This famous and inspired invention from New Orleans is one of the best waker-uppers—*the* best?—ever devised by bumbling humankind.

And it actually is nutritious, and rather caloric, sorry, but on that special festive occasion when you indulge yourself in New Orleans fashion, you can skip the bacon and eggs. (It is quite legal, even if unkosher, to drink Ramos Fizzes other than in the A.M., but it's clear that the ingredients simply work better together, unto good, in the morning hours.)

The classical Rx for this New Orleans classic says to shake the drink for a full five minutes, no more and no less. So much for orthodoxy. A blender does a better job in five seconds. Here's how.

Put the following in your blender:

1 to 2 oz. gin, 1 egg white, 1 jigger cream, juice of ½ a lemon, juice of ½ lime, 1 to 2 tsp. powdered sugar, several

173

dashes Orange Flower Water, 1 cup crushed ice

Blend at high speed for a few seconds. Pour into a tall, chilled glass. Add enough club soda to fill the glass. A perfectionist would tell you to coat the rim of the glass first with lemon and then with powdered sugar.

For nonperfectionists, nonfizz-freaks, and slobs in general, there's a simplified, unclassical recipe for the Ramos Fizz which fills the bill admirably in unsophisticated, slobbish circles. Perhaps it should be called simply a Gin Fizz; delete the Ramos. At all events it's a quickie, wondrous facsimile to the real thing:

Put in a blender:

1 can (6 oz.) frozen lemonade, same can filled with gin, same can filled with milk (or half-and-half), same can filled with club soda, 1 white of egg (or even whole egg, if you wish—some would then call it a Golden Fizz), a few dashes of Orange Flower Water, 1 to 2 cups cracked ice

Blend at high speed for several seconds, and you have a breakfast that sure beats scrambled eggs.

RASPBERRY LIQUEUR
Raspberry liqueur is hard to find and somewhat expensive —evidently because raspberries are likewise. A few American liqueur firms make a raspberry liqueur, usually labeled "Raspberry Flavored Brandy." Leroux has one with the highsounding name of Malinowy Raspberry Liqueur, 50°, around $5.50 (fifth). *Malinowy* is Polish for "raspberry," but the beverage is as American as raspberry pie or violence. J. W. Dant's entry is called Raspberry Liqueur & Brandy.

Note that none of these are true raspberry brandies— they're merely flavored with raspberries, not distilled from raspberries. No true raspberry brandies are made in the U.S. Europe has several, all expensive: **framboise** from France, and himbeergeist—the "spirit" of raspberry—from Germany and Switzerland. The French firm of **Dolfi** makes a true raspberry brandy, framboise, expensive and elegant, as well as a hybrid beverage which they aptly call Framberry, seeking to capture the best of both worlds. And it is well named, for it is somewhere between a true raspberry brandy and a liqueur.

RATAFIA
Back in the 16th century, ratafia—accent on the penultimate, *rah-tah-FEE-ah*— meant any liqueur. The name seems to come from the fact that liqueurs were drunk whenever a treaty or agreement was *ratafied*.

Today ratafia means a liqueur made by steeping, as contrasted with distilling, the flavoring materials in an alcohol base. This is the way all homemade liqueurs are made, and so the name often refers to a homemade liqueur, usually very sweet, and often with a high alcoholic content.

Ratafia de Champagne comes from France's illustrious Champagne region, and is made with grape juice laced with high-proof neutral spirits and then sweetened and flavored.

Drink your ratafia chilled, but not diluted with ice.

RÉMY MARTIN V.S.O.P. FINE CHAMPAGNE CO-GNAC Most of the great Cognac houses produce an array of Cognacs, ranging from a three-star, their most economical (around $12 a fifth), to their ancient and grand aristocrats, at $100 (fifth) and more. Rémy Martin is the exception: it produces virtually only one Cognac, the V.S.O.P.

The concentration seems to work. Rémy Martin V.S.O.P. is an excellent Cognac, smooth and elegant, with a lovely grapy flavor. It is the best-selling of all "prestige" Cognacs of this price range, about $17 (fifth).

But if Rémy Martin V.S.O.P. is too "pedestrian" for your sophisticated palate, you may be able to find their 250th Anniversary bottle (Cuvée Speciale 250 Grande Champagne) at $280.49—that's per 25.6 oz., of course, not per case.

The "Champagne" in the title of the V.S.O.P. has no reference to the bubbly, "celebracious" wine of France, but to the top-quality area—"field" or "area" is the original meaning of the word—from which the grapes come.

A full 92% of Rémy Martin Cognacs are exported. They are especially popular in Germany, Switzerland, and Hong Kong—No. 1 import in all three countries. And now, add Japan. The Japanese in recent years have been busy acquiring some very expensive tastes, es-

pecially in fine wines and spirits. The consumption of V.S.O.P. Cognac in Japan has increased dramatically over the past decade, and Rémy Martin leads the parade.

RICARD This is first of all an anise-flavored liqueur made by a firm of the same name, in Marseilles, France. But before Ricard became the name of a firm and a liqueur, it was the surname of a man, the "Emperor" Paul Ricard, an evanescent Frenchman whose face no one ever saw. Ricard founded his firm in Marseilles some 40 years ago. About 5 years ago he disappeared even more totally from the scene, by resigning from the business. Nobody has seen him since.

Ricard is a **pastis**, a legal type of **absinthe**, which was outlawed in France in 1915. Essentially Ricard is absinthe without the supposedly harmful wormwood which caused it to be banned. Like absinthe, it is licorice-flavored, made with anise.

Ricard (like other anise-flavored drinks) is regarded principally in the U.S. as an aperitif; in Europe, primarily as a digestif (after-dinner drink). Ricard is not as popular in the U.S. as **Pernod**, its kissin' cousin, but the opposite is true in Europe. It sells for around $9 (23.6 oz.).

RICKEY (COCKTAIL) Perhaps the term "rickey" once had a very precise meaning, but no longer. A rickey is now simply a tall drink, usually with lemon (or lime) juice, and soda (carbonated) water. It's akin to a Collins, but originally was made without any sweetening.

(The recipe below has been modernized, not bastardized, and the use of sugar is permitted.) A purist would claim, probably correctly, that a true rickey is made only with limes, never with lemons. The best-known rickeys are the Gin Rickey and the Sloe Gin Rickey.

Here's the basic formula, and by changing the spirit you can make any kind of rickey in the world. Into a highball glass, put:

1 jigger liquor: gin, applejack, bourbon, apricot brandy, Irish whiskey, rum, Southern Comfort, vodka . . . whatever, juice of ½ lime (or lemon), 1 tsp. powdered sugar if using a dry spirit (bourbon, Scotch, vodka); if using a liqueur, the sugar probably won't be necessary

Fill with club soda.

ROB ROY (COCKTAIL)

This is nothing more nor less than a Manhattan made with Scotch instead of bourbon. To wit:

1 jigger (1½ oz.) Scotch, ½ jigger (¾ oz.) sweet vermouth, dash Angostura Bitters, 2 or 3 ice cubes

Stir, strain into cocktail glass. Garnish: maraschino cherry and/or orange-peel strip.

ROCK & RYE

The "rock" is rock sugar candy and the "rye" is rye whiskey. Originally the rocks (crystallized rock candy) were always there in the bottle, clinging to the sides.

Today the rocks are often dissolved: rock-candy syrup is used. But at least it's the same rye whiskey as of old.

Rock & rye comes in two styles these days. Old-fashioned rock & rye has the crystallized sugar, but usually no fruit flavorings. A newer version is made with rock-candy syrup and fruit juices. Some brands even include fruit slices in the bottle. Leroux, for one, makes both types: the old fashioned type is called Irish Moss Rock and Rye, 70°—Irish moss is a kind of seaweed used in the flavoring—and the fruit-flavored version (with fruit slices) is called simply Rock and Rye, 60°.

Almost all American liqueur firms make a rock & rye, usually 60°, and selling for $5 to $6 (fifth).

And of course you can always make your own rock & rye by simply plunking a hunk of rock candy into some rye whiskey. Add a little lemon juice to make it professional.

Rock & rye began as a winter comforter, and that perhaps it where it still fits best. Slip it into a Hot Toddy in place of bourbon. Or even simpler: Fill a hot whiskey glass with hot water, stir in a teaspoon or so of sugar and the juice of ¼ lemon, and stir. Add about a jigger of rock & rye.

Rock & rye also makes an unusual but very palatable after-dinner drink, straight up or on the rocks: It's medium-sweet, with nice whiskey undertones.

ROIANO

Its full name is Liquore Roiano, and it's made by the huge Italian firm, Stock, of Torino (Turin). Roiano is made in obvious imitation of another Italian liqueur, the eminently successful **Galliano.** Like Galliano, Roiano has a beautiful golden color and a silken texture on the tongue. It has an aromatic vanilla and anise flavor, with the anise predominating. It does not, perhaps, have the elegance and suavity of Galliano, but it is a well-made, well-balanced, very tasty liqueur. It is considerably cheaper than Galliano—$9 vs. $12 (fifth)—and most folks tasting the two of them blindly would not be able to detect the original from the imitation.

RONRICO RUM The name means "Rich Rum," so when you say Ronrico Rum, you're saying Rum Rich Rum. It's from Puerto Rico, and dates back to at least 1855. The distillery was allowed to continue in operation during Prohibition, producing industrial alcohol. Ronrico came to the U.S. in 1935.

Ronrico is typical Puerto Rico rum: light-colored, light-bodied, eminently mixable. It is the second-best-selling rum in the U.S. (after **Bacardi**), selling some 600,000 cases per year.

Ronrico comes in the predictable Gold and White, both 4-year-old, both 80°, both selling for about $5.50 (fifth). There is also a 151° Diablo Azul—"Blue Devil" (Purple Label)—at about $8 (fifth).

Ronrico is good, standard Puerto Rican Rum.

ROYAL CHOCOLATE LIQUEURS There are seven different Royal Chocolate liqueurs, all elegant, all made by the illustrious British firm, the House of Hallgarten. Further, they were all invented by Peter A. Hallgarten, who is still running the operation. Now, however, the liqueurs are actually made, according to the Hallgarten formula, in France.

Hallgarten's first creation and probably still the best of the lot is the **Royal Mint-Chocolate,** invented in a north London kitchen in 1966. This was followed, in 1969, by Royal Orange Chocolate, and subsequently by Royal Banana Chocolate (developed especially as a mixer for long rum drinks), Royal Raspberry Chocolate, and the latest creation, Royal Lemon Chocolate, introduced in 1977 to celebrate Her Majesty Queen Elizabeth's Silver Jubilee, 1952–1977.

These chocolate lovelies are among the world's finest chocolate-flavored liqueurs. Heretofore they've been available primarily in Britain, but it appears that they will be available in the U.S. in the forseeable future. Watch and pray . . . Royal Chocolate liqueurs are expected to sell for $10 to $12.

ROYAL HOST BRANDY This California brandy comes in two versions: a blended one, and a 6-year-old, both 80°. The blend sells for around $5 (fifth), and the 6-year-old for about 50¢ more. These are surely reasonable prices, and the brandies are adequate enough. In fact, they have taken several medals at the Los Angeles County Fair (Pomona). But both are rather heavy-handed beverages, more for mixing than for sipping. They are made by the East-Side Winery of Lodi, California.

ROYAL MINT-CHOCOLATE LIQUEUR

Chocolate-*cum*-mint is one of the world's happiest marriage unions. Witness the popularity of after-dinner chocolate mints. Witness the popularity of that favorite postprandial cocktail, the Grasshopper. And there are many chocolate-mint liqueurs made around the world. Royal Mint-Chocolate is one of the finest—perhaps the finest of all. It's made in France for the English firm the House of Hallgarten. Many flavoring ingredients go into its production, and it took two full years of experimentation to perfect it. Royal Mint-Chocolate is only one, but it is the first of seven different chocolate liqueurs made by the House of Hallgarten. (For more, see **Royal Chocolate liqueurs.**) Royal Mint-Chocolate is not presently available in the U.S.; in London it sells for about 4.20 British pounds per 17 oz.

RUM

Rum is the most romantic of all the world's great spirits. It smacks of swashbuckling pirates and buried treasures, of lithe, undulating women. But rum is also the *demon rum*, the bane of the American laboring man. "Away, away, with rum, by gum . . . the song of the Temperance Union."

No other beverage, alcoholic or otherwise, has had such a checkered and colorful past. Rum may date as far back as the 2nd century to China—that would make it mankind's oldest spirit. Rum for long decades was the keystone of the American-African slave trade. It became an institution with the British Navy in the 18th century—the swabs got their daily tot of grog (rum and water), and the practice was only recently discontinued. (Small wonder that Britannia no longer rules the waves.)

Rum first fell into ill repute, and with good reason, in the 1600s when it was the keystone of the infamous "New England Triangle": rum was shipped from New England to Africa to buy slaves; the slaves were shipped to the West Indies and traded for molasses; molasses went from the Indies to New England to make rum. A "hot, hellish, and terrible liquor," said one writer of the time. "Rattleskull" was its common sobriquet. But rum reached its absolute nadir only in 19th-century America, when the Prohibitionist movement damned it as "demon rum." It became synonymous with all dastardly and sinful booze, and all drunkards were "rummies."

Rum is made from sugar cane and wherever sugar cane is grown—all over the world, even in Russia. Sugar cane is a grass, and it used to be said that this grass has given more enjoyment to more of mankind than any other. Now with the advent of a new "grass" in these latter days, the statement may need modifying.

Rum is distilled at less than 190° (otherwise it would be tasteless, like vodka) and reduced to not less than 80° before bottling.

Rums, for some arcane reason, are inclined, no matter what the country of origin, to come in a 151° version—not 150° and not 152°. This is a high and mighty potion, the strongest of any of the world's common spirits, and it is not ordinarily for drinking—it's for flavoring and flaming.

Many rums, especially those sold in the U.S., are aged little (a year or so) or not at all. But it takes about three years of aging in wooden casks to make a good smooth rum, and it will continue to improve for up to 20 years. Actually almost all rum sold in the U.S. is a blend of rums of different ages. Rum comes in every shade of color, from almost colorless (which it is when first distilled) to near black. The color means very little, however—it is no indicator of either flavor or quality. The color of rum, in fact, is usually added artificially, by the simple addition of caramel.

The light-colored rums usually call themselves white or silver label; the dark-colored, gold or amber label. Sometimes these darker rums will be a trifle more flavorful and sweeter—but don't bet on it.

Another caution: don't let the word "Ron" on the label throw you—it's simply Spanish for "rum." *Ron blanco*, white rum; *ron oro*, golden rum. In recent years the rum industry has been pushing white rum, especially via magazine ads.

Most of the rum consumed in the U.S. comes from the myriad islands of the Caribbean. It is said that there are as many rums as there are islands. It is certainly true that rum is made differently and

tastes differently depending on its place of origin.

Except for **brandy,** there is no other spirit that comes in such a wide assortment of colors, flavors, types, and brands. Besides all the Carribbean rums, there are rums from the U.S., Hawaii, the French West Indies, Martinique, the Philippine Islands, Mexico, Malaysia, even Russia.

There are however, only two principal types of rum: lightbodied and heavy-bodied. Almost all of the world's rums may be classed as one or the other. Some would made a third classification—pungent and aromatic rums, such as those from Java—but these are rarely found in the U.S. In the U.S. almost our entire concern is with light-bodied rums, for they constitute 95% of the rum we consume.

Almost all of this rum comes from Puerto Rico and the Virgin Islands. Cuba used to supply a lot of it, but nowadays Fidel's lost his taste for bourbon, and we for Cuban rum.

Light-bodied rums are generally distilled at higher proofs (160° to 180°) than their darkskinned counterparts (140° to 160°).

One might quite logically conclude that light-colored rums are light-bodied, and dark-colored ones heavy-bodied. But rums are rarely logical, and ordinarily the difference in color is precisely and only that, a difference in color. The same brand of rum will often offer a White Label and a Gold, both tasting exactly the same.

In the U.S. a bottle of rum must state on its label whence it comes. Further, it may not claim to be a specific type of rum, as, for example, an American rum may not claim to be a Jamaica type of rum. If it is made in the U.S. it must so state.

The principal types of rum found on American shelves are from Barbados (and Trinidad), Haiti, Hawaii, Jamaica, Java, Martinique (and Guadeloupe), New England, Puerto Rico, and the Virgin Islands. There are also Demerara rums and Batavia arak.

Rum is one of the worlds' greatest mixers—many would say simply *the* greatest. Gin and vodka are extremely popular mixers because they are virtually tasteless, and so do not distract from the taste of the mixing elements. With rum the opposite is true: It is a popular mixer precisely because it adds something, but not too much, to the taste of the finished product. In a Cuba Libre you taste that good aromatic rum. In a Screwdriver, you taste only the orange juice (plus, of course, naked alcohol).

Rum has a special predilection for fruit juices. Hence all those wild tropical creations—from the Potted Parrot and the Loose Goose to the Zombie and the Hurricane. They may not be better, but they're taller, wider, wilder—and more expensive.

Rum stills holds only a small portion (3.8%) of the American spirits market, but its percentage of the action has steadily increased over the past two decades. Sales have nearly quadrupled in 20 years.

Rums vary from brand to brand more than many other distilled spirits, but even so, the differences are so minute that the ordinary drinker will rarely, if ever, be able to detect any difference. Moreover, 99% of all rum consumed in the U.S. slides down the American gullet in the form of a mixed drink—though real rum lovers always take it neat—and it takes a rare rum freak to distinguish one rum from another in diluted form. The only sane and sober course of action in buying rum, therefore, is to buy the most economical. Unless you're entertaining a bevy of professional rum tasters or distillers, Virgin Islands rum will usually be your best bet and best buy, for the simple reason that rum from there is shipped to the U.S. in bulk at considerable saving. By their own law, Puerto Rican rums must be bottled in Puerto Rico.

Rum has an honored place in the kitchen, as well as the bar. It finds more employment as a flavoring or flaming agent than any other spirit, for it harmonizes with just about everything from raw meat to ice cream. In fact, it is one of the best of all meat flavorings, and is particularly recommended with wild game. You can marinate the meat in a rum-and-olive-oil-vinegar combination (spices added: peppercorns, garlic, parsley, thyme, etc.) or you can toss in a few jiggers of rum while the meat is cooking. And it's an inspired addition to dessert sauces, ice creams, candies, cookies. Literally from raw meat to ice cream, and just about everything in between.

Rum has no peer as a mixer, and it would require an entire book to list all the possible, or even probable, rum drinks—not to mention the improbable ones: all those exotic local inventions. Listed here are the most famous and most durable of that mighty host of rum concoctions: **Bacardi, Cuba Libre, Daiquiri, El Presidente, Mai-Tai, Planter's Punch,** and **Rum Cooler.**

In a very true sense, rum is the most natural of all spirits, for it is made directly from sugar. It simply skips that initial process of converting starch (grain, potatoes, etc.) into sugar. It is subjected to less chemistry than any other spirit. It retains more of the flavor of the original elements—sugar cane, in this case—than do other distilled spirits. Rum is indeed a *natural*, and that's why Lord Byron could commend it so highly:

There's nought . . . so much the spirit calms

As rum and true religion. Amen to that!

RUM COOLER In a tall glass dissolve ½ tsp. powdered sugar in 2 or 3 ounces of carbonated water. Fill the glass with cracked ice, add 1 jigger of rum. Add carbonated water or ginger ale, depending on your inclination toward sweetness. Garnish—time and mood allowing—with a lemon and/or orange spiral.

And if this doesn't cool your fevered brow, you're beyond saving.

A Rum Ginger Cooler is the identical drink, only fill the glass with ginger beer instead of carbonated water or ginger ale.

RUM PUNCH (quantity) There are many versions of Rum Punch—to start with,

every rum-producing country has its own native variations. The following ecumenical—not economical—version combines the best features of them all. It's a bit of a production, but well worth the extra effort. Besides, the punch improves with standing a day or two, and it can be frozen if there's any left over (unlikely). This recipe serves ten to twenty persons, depending on their thirst and/or capacity.

1 fifth light rum (Puerto Rico, Virgin Islands), 1 pint dark rum (Jamaica), 1 fifth crème de banana—or blend 6 ripe bananas with the lime juice, 1 cup fresh lime juice, 1 quart pineapple juice—canned, or (better) freshly made, 1 quart orange juice—ditto 1 cup lemon juice—ditto ½ cup grapefruit juice (optional), 1 cup powdered sugar, 6 oz. club soda, 1 tsp. grated nutmeg, 1 tsp. cinnamon, ½ tsp. grated cloves

Dissolve the sugar and spices in the club soda. Pour *le tout ensemble* over a block of ice and decorate with slices of the fruits, plus (perhaps) a sprig or two of mint.

RUM SWIZZLE Here's a two-fisted, swashbuckling, classic rum drink, rarely called for in these days of lighter, more feminine (effeminate?) drinks. The Rum Swizzle has long been a favorite pastime in the British West Indies, especially around Barbados, where it is known as the Barbados Red Rum Swizzle. To be authentic, of course, it must be made with Barbados rum, no other.

Like most of the great classic cocktails, it's eminently simple:

> 2 oz. rum, preferably Barbados, juice of ½ lime, 1 tsp. powdered sugar, 2 dashes Angostura Bitters

Mix ingredients in a tall (Collins) glass filled with ice. Serve with a sizzle stick and allow the swizzler to swizzle his swizzle until it foams. A mint sprig makes a nice garnish.

The Gin Swizzle is precisely the same potion, substituting gin for rum.

RUSTY NAIL (COCKTAIL)

Not recommended for stepping on, but definitely for sipping on. The Rusty Nail is the only notable, or even noteworthy, mixed drink using Drambuie (or one of its imitations, such as Glen Mist or Glayva). A Rusty Nail is simply Scotch whisky and Drambuie (or substitute) on the rocks. The traditional proportion is 1:1, but you can cut the Drambuie as low as 1:3, if you prefer a drier drink. Add a twist of lemon peel to make it first class. If you like Scotch, you'll probably love a Rusty Nail, especially after dinner.

RYE WHISKEY An old ballad laments:

> Rye whiskey, rye whiskey,
> You've been my downfall . . .

Could well be. Or any other whiskey: Scotch, Irish, Australian. And truth to tell, rye whiskey is a taste-filled brew— even if you don't like the taste. It's even "tastier" than straight bourbon, the most taste-filled of American whiskeys. In fact rye whiskey is akin to bourbon, distilled at the same proof (below 160°), required to be aged the same: a minimum of 2 years in new charred oak barrels. It differs from bourbon only in that it is made from a minimum of 51% rye grains, not corn.

Rye whiskey is medium-priced and compares in cost with bourbons of similar quality. So if you like a heavy-flavored whiskey, the kind that stands up and talks back to you, or at least converses amicably with you, this may be your drink.

For some mysterious reason people of the Eastern U.S. often call a blended whiskey "rye." It's a total misnomer. Blends rarely, if ever, have any true rye whiskey in their lineage. Rye aficionados aver that rye makes the only perfect Manhattan.

Here are America's leading ryes listed by price per oz. of alcohol, best values first. Notice that rye whiskeys come in a mad jumble of varying proofs. Listing them by the price per oz. of alcohol is the only sane manner of ranking them.

Be advised: Unless you're a professional whiskey taster or an owner of one of the named distilleries, look for the best values—tasting them blindly, no mere mortal can distinguish between them.

RYE WHISKEYS

Old Quaker Straight Rye, 80°, $0.44/oz.

Rittenhouse Rye, 85°, $0.49/oz.

Rittenhouse Rye, 100°, $0.53/oz.

Hiram Walker Meadowbrook Straight Rye, 86°, $0.54/oz.

Old Quaker Straight Rye, 86°, $0.56/oz.

Jim Beam Rye, 86°, $0.56/oz.

Old Overholt Straight Rye, 86°, $0.56/oz.

Jim Beam Rye, 80°, $0.57/oz.

Overholt, "1810" Straight Rye, 93°, $0.63/oz.

Wild Turkey Rye, 101°, $0.81/oz.

S

SABRA LIQUEUR Sabra is usually referred to as a chocolate liqueur with a secondary orange flavoring. The producer, however, considers it an orange liqueur "with a hint of chocolate." Well, it's a pretty big broad large hint. The chocolate definitely predominates, and the color is a deep brown. The flavor of oranges does get through, however, making Sabra nicely balanced, not cloyingly chocolate-syrupy sweet.

Sabra is a new liqueur, made in Israel by Seagram. Sabra, in fact, means a native-born Israeli.

Sabra is 60° and comes in an interesting long-necked bottle fashioned after ancient biblical containers. It sells in the U.S. for about $12 (23 oz.).

Drink it straight up, or frappé, or on the rocks. It also goes well mixed with an equal amount of brandy, straight, or frappé. (Sip carefully!)

SABROSO The name in Spanish means "Tasty" or "Delicious," and it's not wholly a misnomer in this case, for this *is* a tasty coffee-flavored liqueur from Mexico. But the name is something of an exaggeration when Sabroso is placed alongside other coffee liqueurs, for a goodly number of them are tastier (see under **coffee liqueurs**).

Sabroso is an obvious imitation of Kahlúa, also of Mexican lineage, and it is very similar, except that it sells for less, $7 to $8 (23 oz.), compared with Kahlúa, around $10 (23 oz.). And Sabroso is not that much inferior.

ST. JAMES RUM It comes from the island of Martinique, one of the French West Indies, and it is the most popular *rhum* of France. Martinique rums are noted for their full-bodied lustiness, and St. James is a fine example of the breed. It is made by a unique process from the pure juice of sugar cane, concentrated under vacuum, and then fermented and distilled.

The name comes from the St. James sugar-cane plantations on the island, originally owned by the English. St. James Rum comes in a longish, squarish bottle, the traditional bottle of the early 18th century, the period in which the firm was founded.

St. James Rum is 94° and sells for around $9 (fifth).

SAMALENS ARMAGNAC Samalens is an old and respected name in Armagnac: The firm was founded 100 years ago, and Samalens is the only Armagnac firm that sells only *Bas* Armagnac, the highest type. *Bas*, ironically, means

"Lower," but the term is purely geographic, not qualitative. It refers to the preferred section of the Armagnac region. The label proudly proclaims: "Region du Bas-Armagnac, A.O.C." (Appellation d' Origine Controlée—meaning that the designation is strictly controlled by the French government).

Samalens possesses a vast collection of aged Armagnacs, some more than a century old. Samalens comes to the U.S. in a distinctive flagon-shaped bottle modeled after the goatskin flasks of the Basque shepherds. It is 80° and sells for $10 to $11 (fifth) in the U.S.—a good value.

SAMBUCA (or SAMBUCO, or SAMBUCCO) This is a latter-day Italian liqueur with a soft licorice flavor, akin to a host of anise-flavored liqueurs, but usually a more distinguished beverage. Sambuca does not get its flavor from aniseed, however, but from the *Sambuccus niger*, a kind of elderberry bush. Happily, some of the fresh elderberry flavor comes through in the beverage.

Sambuca has grown immensely in popularity over the past decade in the U.S. as well as in Europe, and today many American liqueur producers make a sambuca.

There are several neoclassical methods of enjoying your sambuca. One is to pour a small amount of sambuca on top of black coffee, set the sambuca on fire, drink the coffee—psst, after the flames have subsided. This is a very tasty cup of brew, but a bust as an alcoholic beverage, as all the alcohol's been consumed in the flames. A second method is

Sambuca con Mosca, "Sambuca with a Fly," especially popular in Rome. Here's how: float two or three "flies"—coffee beans—on top of the sambuca and set fire to the beverage (so that the sambuca will pick up some of the flavor of the "toasted" coffee beans). Even if you're not a pyromaniac, you can still enjoy your Sambuca con Mosca: Simply eat the piquant flies as you go—crunchingly—they're not too awful and the bitterness of the flies mixes nicely with the softness of the sambuca.

And if you can't abide nasty flies, you can simply buy your sambuca with a built-in coffee flavor. One such is the Italian Molinari Caffe Sambuca Extra, 80°, at around $10 (23 oz.).

There are some excellent sambucas being imported to the U.S. these days, but they vary widely in proof, and therefore also in price. They range from Botticelli Sambuca at only 40°, around $5, to some of the finest, at 84°, including these:

Sambuca Molinari Extra: $9 to $10 (23 oz.). A good value.

Sambuca di Galliano: $11 (23 oz.). Made by the same folks who make Liquore Galliano, and in the same giraffeneck bottle. This is good sambuca, but you're paying extra for a lot of advertising and a lot of bottle.

Sambuca di Trevi: Around $9 (24 oz.). A best buy!

Sambuca Romana: Around $11 (23 oz.). Fine beverage, but you're helping to pay for extensive advertising.

Stella d'Italia Sambuca: Around $11.50 (25.4 oz.). An elegant beverage.

Other proofs, other brands: Stock   Bora   Sambuca:

Around $7.50 (25.6 oz.); 78°. A reliable name, reliable beverage.

Sambuca Patrician: Good value at around $9 (25.6 oz.); 80°.

Leroux Sambuca: $8.50 (24 oz.); 80°.

SAM SYKES KENTUCKY STRAIGHT BOURBON WHISKEY

It's not widely available, and it's never advertised, but be informed that this is excellent bourbon whiskey, from the "Grande Champagne" area of bourbon-land, U.S.A., Nelson County, Kentucky. It's one of the best buys in bourbon anywhere, by any means, anyhow: about $4.50 (fifth), and, remember, this is 86° whiskey.

SANGRITA

Not to be confused with Sangaree, a fancy tropical drink, or with Sangria, a wine punch. Sangrita ("Little Blood") is a popular Mexican chaser, used with tequila. Its a kind of south-of-the-border Bloody Mary, only better. Here the alcohol is not added to the beverage, as with the Bloody Mary, but the Sangrita and the tequila are served separately. You can buy a commercial product, Sangrita de la Viuda, which is very good, but even better, make your own Sangrita, fresh.

For four servings, combine in a pitcher:

Juice of 6 oranges, juice of 1 lemon, juice of 2 limes, 1 small can tomato juice, 1 tsp. sugar, 3 tbsp. chili powder, 4 or 5 drops Tabasco, 1 small onion, finely grated (optional), salt to taste

Mix well and serve very cold—the tequila, ditto.

Note: If you want to be really authentic and make like a true *paisano*, delete the canned tomato juice and chili powder above and substitute as follows:

For the tomato juice, parboil 2½ pounds tomatoes; peel and grind them, drain off the juice, discarding the pulp. For the chili powder, grind 5 fresh seeded jalapeno peppers.

For each serving you will need two small glasses, 2 to 3 oz. Pour tequila in one, Sangrita in the other. Take a sip of tequila, followed quickly by a sip of Sangrita. If you have enough hands follow the Sangrita with a bite of a slice of lime.

SAUZA TEQUILA

Knowlegeable tequila fans (freaks?) are well aware that this is the brand of tequila most loved by the Mexicans themselves. And, in fact, Sauza is the world's best-selling tequila. It is not, however, America's most popular—Jose Cuervo is that.

Sauza—two syllables: *sow* (as in pig) *zah*—is fine tequila, as its popularity bears witness. It's pretty well promoted by its American distributor, National Distillers, but its price remains reasonable, though not bargain-basement. Sauza Silver, 86°, is around $6 (fifth) on the West Coast (add $1 in the East), and Gold, also 86°, perhaps a few cents more (again, West Coast; add $1 in the East).

There are more economical tequilas (see under tequila), and unless you're intent upon displaying labels, you'd be well advised to buy those less advertised brands, particularly if you're simply sloshing down your tequila in the form of Margaritas, Sours, and Sunrises.

Sauza also has a supertequila, Conmemorativo (not Commemorativo), 80°, at around $12 (fifth). It's wondrously smooth, and indeed it's John Wayne's drink (who else can afford it for Margaritas?), and small wonder that he always gets his man.

SAZERAC (COCKTAIL)

This is another one of those storied drinks, invented in the late 19th century, in New Orleans. In those days there were two bars in New Orleans called the Sazerac, and at least one of them created the drink of the same name. Here's how:

Into an old-fashioned glass (6 to 10 oz.), put:

2 to 3 oz. bourbon or blend
1 tsp. powdered sugar

Stir to dissolve sugar. Add:

1 or 2 ice cubes, twist lemon peel, dash Peychaud's Bitters, dash Pernod (or ojen, or abisante, or anesone, or any other *absinthe* substitute)

Stir briefly.

The Sazerac is an austere, dry, pungent kind of drink which will not be to everyone's taste.

SCHENLEY INDUSTRIES, INC.

Nothing is simple anymore. Once there was just Schenley Whiskey. Now there's Schenley Affiliated Brands Corporation, and Schenley Distillers Company, and Schenley Import Company, and Schenley Industries, Inc. It's hard to find the whiskey anymore.

The key word is diversification. Like almost all the major spirits and wine enterprises these days, Schenley is diversified and conglomerated and spread out from hell to breakfast. Besides its myriad holdings in spirits and wines, Schenley also markets distiller's grain (a by-product of distillation), pharmaceuticals, and dyes. And to muddy the waters still further, consider the fact that the giant Schenley parent company, at the top of all these affiliates and subsidiaries, is not itself self-sufficient, but is in turn owned by someone else: by Rapid American.

Schenley had its beginning around the turn of the century, in Pittsburgh, Pa. In those days the whiskey was called simply "Schenley." The company barely survived Prohibition by producing whiskey for "medicinal purposes"—tautology if you've ever encountered it, for by its very nature, all whiskey is medicinal!

Today Schenley is a worldwide network of distilleries, wineries, and distributorships. Exact facts and figures are difficult to come by, as Schenley is one of the most closemouthed operations this side of the KGB. Schenley seems reluctant to admit that they produce the brands labeled "Schenley"!

Here are some of the major brands of whiskeys belonging to the Schenley domain: **Ancient Age** Bourbon, Cream of Kentucky Bourbon, **J. W. Dant** whiskeys, Dawson Scotch whisky, **Dewar's** Scotch Whiskies, **George Dickel Tennessee Whiskey**, Grande Canadian Canadian Whisky, I. W. Harper Bourbon, MacNaughton Canadian Whisky, Old Charter Bourbon, Old Stagg Bourbon, Park & Tilford whiskeys, Power's Irish Whiskey, Schenley whiskeys, and Three Feathers Bourbon.

In "white" spirits, besides two gins and one vodka, Schenley markets Plymouth English Gin, Samovar Vodka, Olé Tequila, and Polmos Wodka Wyborowa, to mention a few of the more prominent names.

SCHENLEY RESERVE BLENDED AMERICAN WHISKEY

This has long been a popular American whiskey, routinely among the fifty best-selling brands of spirits in the U.S. And it's always been a good, smooth blend, and it has recently been even further improved. It was formerly 65% neutral grain spirits—that 65% is now light whiskey, which makes it, in a very true sense, an all-whiskey whiskey, in the same way that straights are 100% whiskeys. Schenley Reserve sells for about $5.50 (fifth).

SCHNAPPS

In Denmark, it's *Schnaps*, and in Sweden, *Snaps;* and in Germany and Holland, *Schnapps*—but in any language it's pretty much the same thing: any hard liquor. Sometimes the word is used more specifically, to mean Aquavit.

SCIARADA, 80°

It's an Italian liqueur and it comes in an elegant green bottle with an elongated Romanesque neck. It's pronounced *sha-RA-da*, which doesn't mean much of anything, and it has a very nice, clean, citrusy flavor, but at around $12 per 23 oz., it's definitely not a best buy. It is a kind of green version of golden-hued Grand Marnier, but it lacks the latter's wonderful complexity from its Cognac base.

SCORESBY RARE SCOTCH WHISKY

"If a body could just find oot the exac' proper proportion and quantity that ought to be drunk every day, and keep to that, I verily trow that he might leeve for ever, without dying at a', and that doctors and kirkyards would go oot o' fashion."

James Hogg (1770–1830), the Scottish poet, and friend of Scott, Byron, and Wordsworth, wrote those lines, and if Scoresby Scotch had been around at that time, one would judge that it might have been the Scotch whisky he had in mind.

Scoresby, however, is a comparatively recent invention—at least as Scotch whiskies go, for many of them date back 200 years and more.

Scoresby has long been hailed by knowledgeable Scotch fans as one of the best values in all the world of Scotch whisky. It sells for around $5 (fifth), and that is about as fundamental as Scotch prices get these days. Some Scoresby enthusiasts say that if you drink J&B, Cutty Sark, Johnnie Walker, or Chivas Regal, drink Scoresby instead and save $3 or more.

Scoresby Scotch can sell at a lowly $5 per fifth for two good reasons: First, it is never advertised, and in today's world this can be a multimillion-dollar saving. And secondly, it is bottled in the U.S. Shipping whisky from Scotland in bulk and bottling it in the U.S. represents considerable savings in both transportation and in taxes. As for transportation, the bottles weigh almost as much as the whisky; further, the whisky is shipped in "concentrated" form, at high proof, and then reduced in proof in the U.S. by the addition of distilled water. Bottling in the U.S. in no way affects the quality of the whisky. What difference if distilled water is added in Scotland or in the U.S.?

Scoresby is 86°, medium-bodied, full-flavored, yet smooth.

SCOTCH COOLER (COCK-TAIL)

This is a relatively new drink, but a good one, a needed one. It's the soul of simplicity:

Into an old-fashioned glass (or any squat type of glass, 9 oz. or more), put: 2 oz. Scotch, 1 tsp. white crème de menthe, and 3 or 4 ice cubes. Fill with club soda, stir once.

This is also called a Mint Cooler.

SCOTCH MILK PUNCH

For most people's tastes, Scotch and milk have a happy affinity. This tasty combination is simple, only mildly intoxicating, and healthful to boot. Put into a tall glass:

1 or 2 oz. Scotch, 1 tsp. sugar (preferably powdered), 6 oz. (more or less) milk.

Shake well, sprinkle a little nutmeg on top.

SCOTCH WHISKY

It's easy to define: Scotch whisky is whisky made in Scotland (and it's spelled "whisky," not "whiskey"). Even U.S. law, in a rare burst of internationalism, recognizes the fact. No whiskey in the U.S. can call itself Scotch. Scotch can, however, be shipped to the U.S. in bulk and bottled here. Lots of it is, and because of the vagaries of American tax law, such Scotch is always cheaper.

The Scotch claim that even apart from the law, Scotch whisky cannot be made anywhere except in Scotland. Many an avid American Scotch lover would readily agree. The Scotch say that it's the native grain, mainly barley, and the peat fuel, and especially the water. Even the very air is important, says the Scotsman.

Such exclusiveness is also claimed in favor of bourbon, for example—the real thing, it is said, can come only from Kentucky, and Tennessee whiskey, and Champagne and Burgundy wine all make similar exclusive claims.

As may be said of the statements of politicians: Sometimes it's true, sometimes it ain't. In the case of Scotch whisky, it ain't. In point of fact, "Scotch whisky" has been made commercially in the U.S., though it could not call itself that, and expert tasters, tasting blindly, could not detect it among other "true" made-in-Scotland Scotch whiskies. It was labeled "Scotch-type" and proceeded to fall flat on its "Made-in-America" face.

Scotch's most distinctive trait is its smokiness—those who don't like it call it medicinal. True Scotch lovers prize it; the more the better. Non-Scotch-lovers hate it; a little is too much. It comes from the smoke of peat fires—"peat reek" to the Scotsman—which dry the "green malt."

Hard-core, dyed-in-the-wool Scotch lovers disdain 99% of U.S.-imported Scotches as "mere watered-down" blends. Such hardy souls drink only "true" Scotch: 100% malt whisky. This requires virility—or something—for this is indeed a manly brew, admitting of no compromise, full-bodied, fit to set one's teeth on edge.

It is true that such pure malt whisky was once, only a century ago, considered the only true Scotch whisky. But in 1909, Scottish law, after four years of deliberation, hesitantly, with grave misgivings, declared that blended Scotch whiskies could also call themselves by that proud name.

Scotch whisky immediately proceeded to zoom in popularity, until today—incredibly—Americans consume as much of it as they do blended bourbon. Scotch whisky is one of the most popular whiskies in the world, selling something like 35 million gallons per year.

It is true that 99% of the Scotch imported to the U.S. is blended whisky: that is, pure, "original" malt whisky blended with grain (corn, rye, etc.) whiskies. But not with neutral grain spirits as our American blends are.

There will often be as many as thirty or forty different whiskies "married"—polygamously, for shame—in a single Scotch blend. That is why it is said that it is the blender who is the secret to the success of great Scotch whiskies.

Age is more important with Scotch than with bourbon. In fact, no Scotch less than 4 years of age can be brought into the U.S. unless its youthfulness is expressly stated on the label. Experts claim there is a distinct difference between an 8-year-old Scotch and the same whisky at 12 years of age. Perhaps a professional taster can detect such a difference, but it is far too subtle for 99% of American Scotch drinkers.

In recent years American tastes have run to lighter Scotches. Scotch distillers have been happy to accommodate; they have needed simply to increase the percentage of grain whiskies in their blends. This, of course, decreased the percentage of the strong, authoritative malt whiskies. Today most blends coming into the U.S. are around 60% light grain whisky and 40% heavy malt whiskey.

This lightness, however, has nothing to do with the color of the whisky, as is often supposed. The coloring of Scotch comes mainly from the aging barrels, preferably used sherry casks. When these are lacking, however, the color is readily supplied by the simple addition of caramel (burnt sugar).

Scotch whisky is unquestionably one of the world's great spirits. Its very popularity attests to that. Perhaps it takes a hardy Highlander to appreciate "true" Scotch—malt whisky—but millions of Americans, British, French, and people around the world will affirm that Scotch as we know it, blended, is among the world's greatest beverages. Says one Scotch lover: "It is refreshing, it is satisfying, and a dram or two doesn't make the drinker want to seize a cudgel and follow the skirling pipes on a raid against the Sassenach"—William E. Masse, *Wines and Spir-*

its (New York: McGraw-Hill, 1961), p. 306.

Because of its pervasive smoky flavor, Scotch makes a poor mixer. True-blue Scotch lovers allow it to be "adulterated" only with water, or soda, or finely cracked ice (Scotch mist). As a magnanimous concession you may be allowed to add a lemon twist, nothing more.

And the aficionados are mostly correct—there really are very few honorable Scotch mixed drinks. Three or four, at most: **Rob Roy, Rusty Nail,** Scotch Milk Punch.

Considered quasi-legitimate —which may be on a par with being quasi-pregnant—is the Scotch Old Fashioned, made exactly the same as the "straight" **Old Fashioned,** substituting Scotch for the bourbon. And if you're truly adventurous, there's the Scottish favorite, the Atholl Brose— don't pronounce it if you've been drinking. You may have to travel to the Hebrides to find a bartender who can concoct it, but he'll surely doff his tam to a fellow Scotch connoisseur when you order it. It's a combination of Scotch and oatmeal, plus sundry other strange ingredients. But don't remind the barman that Sam Johnson once defined oats as the favorite food of the Scotch people, but fed to livestock in the rest of the world.

There's an Americanized version which mercifully skips the oatmeal and substitutes whipping cream—talk about a giant leap forward! It's simplicity itself and it makes a heavenly little dessert:

Whip 1 pint heavy cream un-til it holds soft peaks; continue beating while slowly adding 3 or 4 oz. Scotch whisky and 4 tablespoons honey, until the cream holds stiff peaks. Serve the Atholl Brose on its own or, even better, over sponge cake or pound cake.

But the most important question of all remains to be answered: Among the vast array of some 4,000 different brands of Scotch whisky, about 200 of which are imported to the U.S., is there *really* any appreciable difference? Is there a significant difference between a $4 4-year-old Scotch and a $25 20-year-old one?

First, there are different *types* of Scotch, and these do taste different. Besides the robust pure malt mentioned above, there are three types: light-bodied, medium-bodied, heavy-bodied. Body is the "feel" or weight of the beverage in the mouth. These types are clearly distinguishable. Here are some typical Scotches of the various types:

LIGHT-BODIED SCOTCHES
Cutty Sark
MacKintosh
Scoresby
  MEDIUM-BODIED SCOTCHES
Ambassador
Ballantine's
Black & White
Chivas Regal
Haig
Usher's Green Stripe
White Horse
  HEAVY-BODIED SCOTCHES
Johnnie Walker Black Label
King George IV
Teacher's Highland Cream
Vat 69 ("Traditional")

It is for you, the consumer, to decide which of these types is to your taste. But within a type—now hear this!—there is a very scant difference between the various brands, no matter what the price, no matter what the age!

Now hear the shrill cries of outrage and protest from the Scotch purists of the world! Many will be prepared to lay down their lives in defense of their favorite brand. Especially if it's one of the more aged and expensive brands. So be it. But that's loyalty, not prudence or sagacity—much less, frugality. And know that expert tasters universally agree that the differences between brands of a given type of Scotch are so minute as to be negligible for the ordinary drinker of whiskies. You have only to taste a half-dozen brands blindly (labels hidden) to see—or rather, to taste—for yourself.

The only reasonable and responsible advice—unless money is of absolutely no concern whatever, and then you really do have problems—must be this: Within a given type of Scotch, *buy the most economical.*

SCREWDRIVER (COCKTAIL) It's said to have originated when American oil-rig workers in Iran (Saudi Arabia?), struggling to survive the desert heat, mixed vodka and orange juice, and lacking a proper barroom muddler, stirred their life-saving potion with a screwdriver. Another version says is was similarly invented, but by a couple of G.I.'s in France at the end of World War II.

It's one of the world's simplest drinks: vodka and orange juice. The usual proportion is about 1 jigger of vodka to about 4 oz. orange juice.

SEAGRAM COMPANY LIMITED This is the world's largest dealer in spirits and wines, the mammoth of all the conglomerate giants of the spirits industry. Nobody in the world distills as much spirits as does Seagram, nobody in the world markets as much alcoholic beverage as does Seagram.

The company today maintains distilleries and wineries in twenty-five countries around the world. In the U.S. alone there are plants in Kentucky, Indiana, Maryland, Pennsylvania, California, and Hawaii. In 1977, consolidated net sales, including those of its subsidiaries, reached more than $2.2 billion. (This figure includes income from oil and gas properties, through Seagram's wholly owned subsidiary, Texas Pacific Oil Co.) Total sales of liquor and wines alone now reach almost $1 billion a year (excluding excise taxes). This is an estimated 19% of the total U.S. wine and spirits market.

Here are some of the major brand names in spirits produced and/or marketed by Seagram:

Whiskeys: **Antique** Bourbon, **Calvert** whiskeys, Carstairs Scotch, **Chivas Regal Scotch, Four Roses** Whiskey, The **Glenlivet** Scotch, Henry McKenna Bourbon, **Jameson Irish Whiskey, Kessler** Blended Whiskey, Mattingly & Moore Bourbon, 100 Pipers Scotch, Passport Scotch, Paul Jones Whiskey, Seagram's whiskeys, and **White Horse Scotch.**

White spirits: Bolshoi Vodka, **Boodles Gin, Calvert Gin,**

Crown Russe Vodka, and El Charro Tequila.

Rums: Hudson's Bay Demerara, Myers's Palo Viejo, Polar Pure, Ron Añejo Cacique, Ron Llave, and Ron Montilla.

Liqueurs: **Cheri-Suisse, Leroux liqueurs, Lochan Ora, Sabra,** Sambuca Originale (see sambuca), **Tuaca,** and **Vandermint.**

To grasp the vastness of this huge enterprise, consider the fact that Joseph E. Seagram & Sons, Inc., of New York City, is just one of the subsidiaries, and it in turn includes these (and other) affiliated companies: Seagram Distillers Co., Four Roses Distillers Co., Browne Vintners Co., Calvert Distillers Co., Chateau & Estate Wines Co., General Wine & Spirits Co., and Gold Seal Wine Co.

Further, none of this is to mention Seagram's wine interests. In the U.S., Seagram owns Paul Masson, Christian Brothers, Gold Seal, and Henri Marchant. Abroad there is B&G, G. H. Mumm & Cie (Champagne), Heidsieck Monopole (Champagne), Brolio, and Julius Kayser, plus a galaxy of premier Bordeaux chateaux, including the foremost of them all, Chateau Lafite-Rothschild. And all of this is a mere skimming of the surface. There are hundreds more wines.

For the record: The Seagram Company Limited used to be Distillers Corporation—Seagram's Limited. The corporate name was changed in 1974.

The Seagram Company Limited must be doing something right, although bigness per se is neither good nor bad when it comes to the producing and marketing of alcoholic beverages. But the fact that Seagram has consistently produced and/or marketed some of the world's finest spirits, liqueurs, and wines is surely a commendation of some kind.

It is also clear that Seagram has usually been blessed with shrewd management at the top. A combination of perspicacity and great good fortune has resulted in wise and providential decisions at crucial times. (As a for-instance, see **Seagram's 7 Crown Blended Whiskey,** and note the wise decisions that led to its huge success.)

To Seagram's credit it should also be pointed out that the firm was the first major distiller to point out the inherent danger in the excessive use of alcohol. Seagram has consistently advocated moderation in its use.

That has all been the good news. The bad news is that somebody pays for all that Seagram advertising. Guess who. Seagram currently spends something like $53 million a year in advertising. That figure is almost double what was being spent just a few years ago. The increase has been largely dictated by sales slippage of some Seagram products, such as 7 Crown, Seagram's V.O., and Kessler.

And so, in sum, only one assessment is possible: Seagram, like all other human institutions—and all human beings—does some things well, some things ill. Cleave to the former, eschew the latter.

SEAGRAM'S CROWN ROYAL CANADIAN WHISKY

This is Seagram's *tête-de-cuvée,*

the cream of the vintage of all Seagram's many whiskeys. You can distinguish it from everything else in the world—not by tasting it blindly, but by the little purple velvet sack it comes in.

Crown Royal was created in 1939 to honor King George VI's visit to Canada. It is superbly smooth Canadian whisky—all Canadian whisky, almost by definition, is smooth. Whether its superiority amounts to $5 or $6 worth is another question. It is 80° and sells for around $12 (fifth).

SEAGRAM'S EXTRA DRY GIN

Some say this is America's finest gin. They're probably right. Experts have consistently praised this gin, and in blind tastings it has often been identified, incorrectly, as an import. It is America's third-best-selling gin—after **Gordon's** and **Gilbey's**. It is the No. 1 gin in at least fifteen states.

Seagram's Extra Dry is noted for its flavor and smoothness. It is 80° and sells for around $5.25 (fifth).

SEAGRAM'S 100 PIPERS SCOTCH WHISKY

This is a comparative newcomer to the Scottish scene—introduced only in 1968. And really not all that necessary. Seagram's already markets these Scotches, to name a few: **Chivas Regal, Carstairs,** Passport, **White Horse,** and The **Glenlivet.** Seagram's has heavily promoted 100 Pipers for a half-dozen years, another reason not to patronize it. You *know* who pays for all that promotion. 100 Pipers is 86° and is not bargain-basement: around $8 (fifth).

SEAGRAM'S 7 CROWN BLENDED WHISKEY

This is not only the biggest-selling whiskey in the U.S., by an impressive margin, but it is the biggest-selling brand of any spirit in the land. Some say that Seagram's 7 Crown accounts for an unbelievable 17% of the total blended-whiskey market. What is certain is that it sold something like 6.5 million cases in 1977. (The runner-up is another Seagram's product, Seagram's V.O. Canadian, with sales of almost 4 million cases). This is not a high-water mark for 7 Crown, however; in 1972 it sold 7.5 million cases.

Seagram's 7 Crown has been outselling other brands of whiskey for more than 30 years.

When first introduced in 1934, shortly after Repeal, 7 Crown had a sister whiskey at its side, 5 Crown. 5 Crown was a little lower in proof, and sold for a little less. Both whiskeys, of good quality, were instant successes in those thirsty days, when immature and raw spirits abounded.

Samuel Bronfman—Mr. Sam, head of Seagram—had made two bold gambles on his Crown whiskeys in the late 1920s, both of which paid off. Convinced that Prohibition would someday be repealed, Bronfman had amassed huge stocks of good mature whiskey in Canada. When Repeal came, Mr. Sam had the largest stock of fully aged rye and bourbon whiskeys in the world.

The second gamble was to market a blend, not a straight, as most American distillers were doing. The two Crowns became the first national brands of blended whiskey.

5 Crown was discontinued when World War II began. It was also about that time that 7 Crown moved from a clear square bottle to a round, amber-tinted one.

The name 7 Crown came from one of the daily tasting sessions at Seagram in 1934. Samples of blended whiskey were numbered consecutively. At one session, all tasters agreed on sample number 7. Mr. Sam added "Crown" to indicate that this whiskey was Seagram's *crowning* achievement. Well, at least that's the way the story's told.

Many believe that Seagram's 7 Crown is the finest of all blended whiskeys. Some claim that it is as good as any Canadian whisky. These are bold statements. It is true, of course, that American blends and Canadian whisky taste very much alike. In blind tastings they are often confused, as they are similarly mild and smooth.

The success of Seagram's 7 Crown has not been accidental. Right decisions came at the right times. Also, it is a superior whiskey, though it must be repeated that differences between blends are extremely slight. 7 Crown is a trustworthy name that several generations of Americans have grown up with—they're loyal, and they play it safe.

And if there is any superiority here, you're paying for it, for 7 Crown is one of the most expensive of American blends. In fact, it is the most expensive of the more common brands, as you can see in the listing of blends according to price, under **bourbon.** 7 Crown is 80° and sells today for about $5.50 (per fifth or 750 ml, which is 2 oz. less), about $1 more than the average blend.

SEAGRAM'S V.O. CANADIAN WHISKY It's V.O. for short, and calling for it so will bring you Seagram's V.O. Canadian Whisky in any respectable bar in the land. This is America's second-best-selling whiskey, after another Seagram product, **Seagram's 7 Crown** Blend. And it's the fourth-best-selling spirit in the U.S.: about 4 million cases in 1977, making it the best-selling imported whiskey from any land, at any price. **Canadian Club,** however, is yipping at its heels these days, and **Bacardi Rum** overtook it in total sales in 1976.

V.O. was created by that genius of the spirits industry, Samuel Bronfman. Yechiel Bronfman founded Seagram in Canada (where it is still headquartered) in the 1880s; he was succeeded by his son, Sam, whose business acumen raised Seagram to the lofty position of the world's largest dealer in spirits, where it still remains today (for more, see **Seagram Company Limited**).

V.O. is undoubtedly fine whisky, one of the world's smoothest. Canadian whisky, of course, is noted for its mildness and softness, and V.O. is an excellent example of the species. But here again, the differences from brand to brand are minute, and one would be sorely pressed to distinguish V.O. from other Canadian whiskies in a blind tasting. It sells for around $7.50 (fifth), a moderate price for an 86.8° Canadian (see listing under **Canadian Whisky**).

SEATTLE MIST People invent drinks daily—99% of them are wholly unmemorable. Seattle Mist is one of the remnant 1% that merits remembrance. It's brand new, surfacing only in mid-1977, in *Gourmet* magazine. And it's wholly different, wholly refreshing, utterly simple, and simply delicious:

In a chilled 12-oz. glass pour ¼ cup vodka over 3 or 4 ice cubes and stir in ½ cup each of unpasteurized apple cider and ginger ale. Makes one drink. (Note: Recipe from Michael Siskind, Seattle, Washington, in *Gourmet*, September, 1977.)

SETRAKIAN BRANDY This is a newcomer (1972) among American brandies, and a welcome one: a fine brandy, especially appreciated because of its modest price, about $5.50 (fifth).

Setrakian brandy is made by the California Growers Winery —Robert Setrakian is the president—which is also producing some credible, moderately priced wines under the Setrakian label.

Setrakian brandy has a marvelous flowery bouquet and a good smooth flavor. Good brandy, good value. Good enough to sip, not slurp.

SIDE CAR (COCKTAIL) This is one of the classic brandy cocktails, but you don't see it around much anymore. More the pity, for it is a simple, practical, tasty, healthful potion. And versatile besides: goes well before or after food.

The Side Car is said to have originated in Paris, and it was the "in" drink in American speakeasies during the sodden days of Prohibition. The Rx: 1 oz. brandy, 1 oz. Curaçao (triple sec or Cointreau), and 1 oz. lemon juice. Shake well with ice and strain into a chilled glass. You may vary the proportions, of course, according to taste.

SINGAPORE SLING (COCKTAIL) This historic gin drink was created at the Raffles Hotel in Singapore in the early 1900s; it became notorious along the West Coast of the U.S. in the 1950s. It's been simplified somewhat with the passing years, for it originally contained a wee bit of both Benedictine and brandy.

Today's version, to make one tall drink:
  1½ oz. gin, ½ oz. Cherry
  Heering (or cherry-flavored
  brandy), 1 oz. fresh lemon
  (lime) juice, several ice cubes
Fill the glass with water or soda and stir. And you might just try adding, as some mixologists still do, 1½ oz. brandy and ½ oz. benedictine.

SLING This term may have had a precise meaning once upon a time, but that time is long gone. It seems that "sling" originally referred to a mixed drink flavored with nutmeg, but it is now used for almost any mixed drink, usually one containing lemon and some liqueur.

SLIVOVITZ It can be spelled "slibovitz," "sliwowitz," "slivovice," "sljivovica," or any reasonable approximation, and it's as intriguing and foreign as the name sounds. It's a plum brandy—a true brandy, not a liqueur—from Central Europe, mostly Yugoslavia. In the U.S. there is nothing made which even remotely resembles slivovitz. We do make other fruit brandies in imitation of Europe's originals—kirsch, applejack—but here's one we don't even attempt.

Good slivovitz possesses the true fruit taste of the plums from which it is distilled, plus an edge of bitterness from the seeds, which are crushed along with the fruit.

Slivovitz, unlike most fruit brandies, is aged in wooden casks for at least 3 years. The wood gives it a slight golden tinge.

A surprising amount of slivovitz is imported to the U.S.—it is a favorite Jewish drink—including several kosher ones. The most important names are: Carmel, 100°; Navip, 100°; Slovin, 94°; and Polmos, 140°.

SLOE GIN It's not a gin, and according to many overenthusiastic consumers thereof, it's not slow. Aside from that, it's aptly named.

Sloe gin came to be called "gin" for the very good reason that it was originally made from gin. It was called "sloe" because it was made from sloe berries.

Today, however, it's rarely, if ever, made with a gin base, at least in this country, but with a high-proof neutral alcohol. The British, though, have a homemade version which still uses a gin base: 4 quarts sloe berries, 1 gallon gin, 2 pounds sugar, 1 oz. almonds. Put into a 2-gallon jar, shake twice a week for 3 months, then strain.

Sloe berries, of course, are still used—they're of the essence. They're not a berry, however, but a small wild plum, about ½ inch in diameter. (In England and Ireland the bush is called the blackthorn.)

Sloe gin originated in England but today it's more popular in the U.S. than in Britain. Every major American liqueur producer makes at least one sloe gin, most of them 60°, with a few as low as 42°. They're mostly priced from $5 to $6, and they are, one and all, absolutely identical. Buy the most economical. No British sloe gins are imported to these shores.

Some firms call their product "creamy" or "foamy" or some such descriptive nomenclature, referring to the fact that the beverage will produce a foamy head when shaken or stirred vigorously. Bravo, but it's the identical beverage.

Sloe gin is often associated with the stirrup cup, that old English tradition of a bracing draft of spirits before ascending to the stirrup for the fox hunt. In fact, it was such a good idea that the stirrup cup became a common gesture of hospitality to any departing guest. The British equivalent, one might say, of the modern, automobilized American "one for the road"—not always a divinely inspired idea, for it may happen that one who has had one for the road may end up with a cop for a chaser!

SMIRNOFF VODKA Every bottle of Smirnoff Vodka has the date 1818 boldly embossed front center. That was the year when the Smirnoff distillery was founded in Moscow. A century later (1914), Smirnoff Vodka was selling at the rate of 1 million bottles per day, and the Smirnoff family was said to be the richest in the world.

But then came the Russian Revolution (1917), and nothing remained. In exile in Paris, Vladimir Smirnoff, a fourth-generation descendant of the founder, Peter Smirnoff, set up a small distillery. In 1934 he gave another Russian exile, Rudolph Kunett, the American franchise for Smirnoff Vodka. Kunett (originally Kunettchansky) built a small distillery in Bethel, Conn. This was the first vodka distillery in the U.S. But sales went nowhere: The name Smirnoff had been tremendously important in Russia, but it meant nothing in the U.S.A. Smirnoff Vodka barely survived, selling a mere 6,000 cases per year. Vodka was strictly freakish in those days. Not even Russians living in America drank vodka—they drank American whiskey!

Enter (1934) John G. Martin, president of **Heublein, Inc.,** of Hartford, Conn. Martin gambled. For a mere $14,000 (plus some royalties) he bought the Smirnoff name and formula. Production was moved to Hartford, Conn.

Success came in a most strange manner. Some Smirnoff Vodka had gone to a distributor in South Carolina with cork stoppers that said "Smirnoff Whiskey." The distributor began proclaiming "Smirnoff's White Whiskey . . . no taste, no smell." Somehow it caught on, and Smirnoff Vodka was on its way.

Production of Smirnoff Vodka ceased during World War II. After the war, vodka sales began to climb slowly but steadily, mostly due to such new drinks as the **Screwdriver** and the **Bloody Mary.** The Moscow Mule, invented before the war, under the guiding talent of the same John G. Martin, was also a factor in the rising sales.

By 1961, vodka production had reached almost 20 million gallons annually, a twenty-fold increase in the space of 10 years, and Smirnoff led the pack.

Today it's more of the same. Smirnoff Vodka is far and away the best-selling vodka in the U.S.: almost 6 million cases per year, vs. its nearest rival, another Heublein product, **Popov,** at less than 2 million cases. It is the second-best-selling spirit in the land, outdistanced only by **Seagram's 7 Crown Blended Whiskey.** Incredibly, Smirnoff Vodka accounts for almost one-third of America's total consumption of vodka. It is said to be the free world's single most popular brand of liquor. Today, Smirnoff is produced in thirty-three other countries, besides the U.S.

For more than 160 years consumers have attested to the superiority of Smirnoff Vodka. It has always been made with painstaking care and solicitude. Smirnoff Vodka is always redistilled, and it is intensely filtered through a special, secret combination of different charcoals. It is premium vodka. But the fact still remains that vodka, by definition, is virtually pure neutral grain spirits, and the differences between different brands of vodka are necessarily miniscule. One has

only to taste a number of vodkas blindly to corroborate that
simple truth.

Smirnoff Vodka may be a
premium beverage, but it has
a price tag to match; it is one
of the most expensive of all
vodkas (see listing under
vodka). The "regular" Smirnoff
comes in both 80° and 100°,
the 80° selling for about $5.50
(fifth) and the 100° for about
$1 more. Then there is
Smirnoff Silver Label, 90.4°,
specially designed for Martini
fanciers, selling for around
$6.50 (fifth). It's your money.

**SOUTH AMERICA—BRAN-
DY** South America, of all
places, produces one of the
world's most renowned—or notorious—brandies: Pisco. Pisco is made from Muscat and
Mission grapes, but not from
the free-flowing juice thereof—from the pomace, the
vile gook that remains after the
juice has been extracted. Pomace brandies—grappa is another—are not noted for their
suavity and grace. They have a
tendency—some would say
more than a mere tendency—
to be rather woody and rough.

Pisco is a zestful beverage, a
bit fiery, at least by *gringo*
standards, certainly distinctive,
and possessing a certain "foreign" charm. It is different, but
does not qualify as an abomination, as some would have us
believe. Let Pisco not be con-
demned simply *because* it is
different.

As shipped to the U.S., Pisco
is only 80° or 90°, but it is
noted for its insidious ways, especially when mixed. *Con
mucho cuidado!* Pisco is briefly
aged in beeswax amphorae and
great care is taken to make

sure it retains some of the odor
and taste of the beeswax.

Pisco brandy is used in two
notable drinks, Pisco Punch
(see below) and the Pisco
Sour. Pisco Punch has a romantic, almost lurid past. It
was popular along San Francisco's notorious Barbary Coast
in the Gold Rush days and it
became the specialty of one
particular saloon, the Exchange
Bank, one of the city's most
elegant establishments of the
day. Mark Twain was a fre-
quent visitor.

At the Exchange Bank,
Pisco Punch became an institution and a ceremony. Each order was individually prepared,
in utter secrecy, behind locked
doors, in another part of the
building. Only one person
knew the formula, the proprie-
tor, Duncan Nicol, a dour and
taciturn Scot, who took his
secret with him to the grave.

The Exchange Bank survived
the 1906 earthquake and fire
by a whisker, but succumbed to
the near approach of the Igno-
ble Experiment, Prohibition.

But today the Exchange
Bank Saloon stands again. And
Pisco Punch is slurped once
more. On almost the selfsame
spot where it originally stood,
an exact replica of the original
saloon, complete with long ma-
hogany bar and ancient engrav-
ings, is encompassed within the
huge Transamerica "Pyramid"
in downtown San Francisco.
And the featured drink—you
guessed it—is Pisco Punch. It's
not precisely the same mysterious concoction of Duncan Nicol, with gum arabic syrup and
such, but it's certainly a reasonable facsimile. The modernized
formula is the result of patient

research and joyous experimentation.

LATTER-DAY PISCO PUNCH,
(AFTER DUNCAN NICOL AND THE
EXCHANGE BANK SALOON)

2 ice cubes, 1 tsp. pineapple juice, 1 tsp. lime (or lemon) juice, 2 cubes pineapple, 1 jigger Pisco brandy

Combine all in a wine glass, about 8 oz., fill the glass with ice water, stir.

SOUTHERN COMFORT This is the best-known and the best of the few indigenous American liqueurs. (There are just three other classic, invented-in-America liqueurs: Forbidden Fruit, rock & rye, and herbsaint.)

There are sundry tales as to Southern Comfort's origin. One says that it was invented by a bartender by the name of Louis Herron, in St. Louis, Mo., around 1875. Another more romantic legend says that it all began with the famous pirate Jean Lafitte (died about 1826), who commandeered a British vessel with two casks of the stuff aboard. The only certain historical fact is that the Southern Comfort Corporation came into existence in 1934, with the end of Prohibition. If Southern Comfort hadn't been "invented" before that, it was at least invented then.

The "Southern" part of the title comes from the fact that it was in the New Orleans area that Southern Comfort first became known and appreciated. Today it is made in St. Louis, Mo.

Southern Comfort is made from a base of fine aged bourbon, and flavored primarily with peaches, but also with oranges and various herbs. The exact formula—like the formula for every other liqueur in the entire world—is, of course, a trade secret. But the Southern Comfort Corporation is the most closemouthed of all the world's secretive producers of liqueurs. They won't even admit that their liqueur has a bourbon base—they might not even admit that it's a Comfort!

Southern Comfort is normally a stout 100°, although an 80° is also marketed now in some areas, and it is often used simply as a substitute for bourbon: When a cocktail calls for bourbon, simply use Southern Comfort. This adds flavor and complexity to virtually any bourbon cocktail. It may also add slightly to the cost of the drink, as Southern Comfort is somewhat more expensive, *mutatis mutandis*, than a comparable bourbon.

Southern Comfort 100° sells for $7 to $8 (fifth). It is often overlooked as an after-dinner liqueur. Its high proof makes for careful, deliberate sipping—either straight up or on the rocks. It has lots of peachy-citrusy-bourbonish flavor.

Janis Joplin, the late, prematurely departed rock star, probably did more for the promotion of Southern Comfort, especially among the young, than all the firm's advertising executives. Joplin used to appear on stage brandishing her bottle of Southern Comfort, and periodically drawing 100° Comfort therefrom. In 1977 almost 1.5 million cases of Southern Comfort were sold.

SPAIN—BRANDY A lot of Hemingway characters drink a

a lot of Spanish brandy, and *bravo* for them, for it's a wholesome and tasty beverage. It used to be made almost wholly from sherry grapes, and even today it generally possesses a certain "sherriness," either from the grapes themselves, or from being aged in sherry barrels.

Spanish brandy is distinctly earthy—like Hemingway characters. It's full-flavored and decidedly sweeter than French brandy.

The important brands imported to the U.S. are these:

Cardenal Mendoza Gran Reserva: 90°; frightfully good and frightfully expensive, about $22 (fifth).

Felipe II: Made by Hijos de Augustin Blazquez ("Sons of Blazquez"), Cadiz. Sells for around $8 (fifth), a reliable brandy.

Gonzalez Byass: The Sobrano is their stock-in-trade; retails around $7 (fifth). The Lepanto, smooth and mature, is top of the line, 82°, goes for around $19 (fifth)—ouch.

Osborne Veterano: 84°; highly regarded; about $8 (fifth).

Pedro Domecq: Biggest U.S. importer. Several different labels can be found—somewhere—in the U.S.: Three Vines, 80°; sells around $6.50 (fifth) (this is Domecq's best buy, by far); Fundador, 80°, around $8 (fifth), and not worth it—harsh and heavy; and Carlos I, a fine 12-year-old brandy—and well it should be fine, at about $20 per fifth (good, but not that good); and Carlos III, more reasonably priced, at around $10 (fifth), but who can drink it wondering

whatever happened to Carlos II?

Sandeman Capa Negra: 80°; good quality, good flavor. Not as sweet as most Spanish brandies. Good value at $6 (fifth) or even less.

Terry: Another producer of sherries; offers three brandies in the U.S.: Three Star, 84°, around $6.40 (fifth); Centenario, sweet, flavorful, about $7 (fifth); and Terry I, tasty and complex, about $11 (fifth).

SPIRITS In today's usage the word means simply "distilled alcoholic beverages." The name comes from the fact that distillation is a process whereby vapors—spirits—rise up like ghosts—spirits—from the fermented mash when heat is applied.

There are thousands of spirits made around the world, and all the more important ones—more than 1,000—are mentioned in this book.

The principal types of distilled spirits are: **brandy, cognac, gin, liqueurs** (or cordials; they're synonymous), **rum, vodka,** and **whiskey.**

STINGER Lucius Beebe, the famous bon vivant and gastronome, was once asked what he would do if stranded by a blizzard in the Alps. Without a moment's hesitation he replied that he'd pray for two St. Bernards, one laden with brandy, the other with crème de menthe, so that he could assemble some life-preserving Stingers.

The Stinger is one of the few classic brandy mixed drinks. (The others are the **Brandy Alexander** and **Sidecar.**) Like most good cocktails it's simplicity itself: 1 jigger brandy, 1 jigger white crème de menthe; shake well with cracked ice and strain into a chilled cocktail glass.

The Stinger serves equally well before or after dinner, and if you want a less sweet drink, simply halve the crème de menthe.

STOCK This is a brand name of Italian brandies and liqueurs. Stock is a huge enterprise, with eight plants in Italy alone; headquarters are in Trieste. Stock also makes vodka, vermouths, and marsalas. Stock spirits are exported to some 120 countries around the world.

The firm began back in 1884, with brandy, and that's what it still does best. Stock Brandy is the world's best-selling. It comes in several versions:

Stock 84: it's 80°, sells for around $6.40 (fifth). It is by far Stock's most popular product. It is smooth and tasty, with just a touch of sweetness.

Stock Royal Italian: It's 10 years old, 86.8°, sells for around $6.75 (fifth), a good value at just a fraction more than Stock 84.

Stock Grappa Brandy: 80°; sells for around $7.75 (fifth).

Stock also makes a full line of liqueurs, and they're among the most economical of all imported liqueurs, most of them going for around $7 (fifth) or less. They are good.

STREGA The name, *STRAY-gah,* means 'Witch" in Italian, and the story is that two beautiful maidens, disguised as witches, created this wonderful golden-hued liqueur for the city of Benevento, in southern Italy, where it is still made today. The tradition says that if two persons share the witches' Strega they will remain united in love for all eternity.

Liquore Strega—to give it its full name—is at least 100 years old. The recipe may date back even further, but it was first made—after the witches gave him the recipe—by one Guiseppe Alberti, and it is still made by Guiseppe's descendants.

Some compare Strega to yellow Chartreuse, and it does have a definite herbal, almost medicinal character, but it is more forceful and robust than Chartreuse and evidently has a tinge of citrus in its lineage. It lacks Chartreuse's delicacy and finesse.

Strega is said to use more than seventy herbs, spices, barks, and fruits in its production. It's most important flavor ingredient is angelica. Strega can be found around the world; it is as popular abroad as it is at home.

There are a number of cocktails made with Strega, ranging from the Frigid Witch (Strega, lime juice, crushed ice) to the Red Sea (Strega, dry vermouth, rye whiskey, and Elixir China), none of them very noteworthy. The best way to appreciate Liquore Strega is straight up (perhaps somewhat chilled) or over vanilla ice cream.

Strega sells in the U.S. for $11 to $12 (23 oz.) for both the 80° and the 85°. (If you have a choice, buy the 85°: more liqueur, less distilled water for your money).

SUNDOWNER (COCKTAIL) This is a relatively new drink,

but a delightful, different, and delicious one. It's appropriate either preprandially or post-.

Into a cocktail glass, put:
1 oz. Benedictine (or Van der Hum), 1 oz. vodka, 4 oz. orange juice (approx.), ½ oz. lemon juice, ice cubes
Stir. Enjoy.

SUNNY BROOK KENTUCKY STRAIGHT BOURBON WHISKEY and KENTUCKY BLENDED WHISKEY
This brand name, Sunny Brook, goes back to 1801, to Minneapolis, Minn., of all places, where it was used by Rosenfield Bros. & Co., who were in the whiskey business there. It is considered to be the first whiskey brand name advertised on a nationwide basis.

Like many another American whiskey, Sunny Brook has suffered some slippage in sales over the past five years, though it is still among the fifty top-selling brands of spirits in the U.S. National Distillers acquired Sunny Brook in 1929.

Both the straight and the blend are standard, good 80° whiskeys. They have always been well priced, at around $4.50 (fifth) for both the blend and the straight. Sunny Brook is an excellent value.

SUNTORY LTD.
If asked, "What is the world's best-selling whisky?" how many Americans would even pick the right continent—much less the right type of whisky or brand? The answer, incredibly, is Japan's Suntory "Old" Whisky, with 1977 sales of 10 million cases! Its closest rival is Seagram's 7 Crown, at about 6.5 million cases for the same year.

Suntory Limited is now the third largest distiller in the world, with annual sales over $2 billion. Its whisky alone comes in 14 different brands with a staggering—in several senses—total annual production of more than 20 million cases. Suntory's Hakashu Distillery, built in 1972, has 24 pot stills, and is the largest malt whisky distillery in the world.

Notice that Suntory spells it whisky, not whiskey, evidently because their Suntory whiskies are Scotch-type whiskies, and in Scotland they spell it "whisky," without an "e."

Suntory also produces wines (at last count there were about 20 different brands), brandies (7, at least, all Suntory brand), beer (available throughout the Orient and Hawaii), a line of liqueurs and pre-mixed cocktails (Hermes is one of the major brand names), rum, vodka, gin, even tequila (all under the Suntory label), nonalcoholic beverages (from a bottled squash drink to a canned ice coffee), and a wide range of imports (from Robert Mondavi California wines, to Stolichnaya Russian Vodka to Southern Comfort to Martell Cognacs). Suntory's total number of potable products is now more than 200—and growing. Suntory was founded in 1899 by Shinjiro Torii, a 20-year-old vintner, who began by producing some sweet wines which he labeled Akadama. (Akadama means red ball—still on the label—symbolizing the rising sun.) The entire line of Akadama wines is now available in the U.S. With his wine profits Torii took a daring, unprecedented gamble: he set out to make Scotch whisky in Japan! Of course he realized that it could never be called Scotch, for Scotch, by international agreement, can be made only in Scotland. It took Torii six years, 1923 to 1929, to produce his whisky, and another ten years to get it accepted. Today Suntory whisky is the mainstay of the Suntory empire.

Suntory whisky is Scotch whisky in everything but name. Suntory, of course, says that their whisky is not Scotch; neither is it Bourbon, or Canadian, or anything else—it's simply Japanese whisky. But even the company concedes that Suntory whisky is "slightly east of Scotch." Suntory whisky is made from the selfsame ingredients as Scotch, by the selfsame process; it is aged in the same white oak barrels that Scotch is. Even the water is said to be the same: pure mountain water, fresh from a babbling brook, or so the commercials say. Scotch whisky makers have always maintained that Scotch whisky can only be made in Scotland, not merely legally, which, indeed is the case, but practically: there is *something* in Scotland, they say, be it in the water, the peat, the barley, or the "mountain dews and damps," a certain quintessential Scotch *something* that cannot be duplicated anywhere else in the world. (For more on the subject, see Scotch Whisky.) This untruth, or at best, half-truth, or quarter-truth, has been endlessly repeated until even mere Scotch-consumers believe it. Suntory is Exhibit A to the contrary. More than one tale is told of blind tastings in which professional tasters or Scotch

connoisseurs selected Suntory as a born-and-bred-in-Scotland Scotch, even a superior one. (For one such incident, see *Gentleman's Quarterly*, Winter 1977–1978, p. 134.) These are the Suntory whiskies presently being imported to the U.S.:

Suntory "Old," 86.8°, $8.50 (fifth). The word "Old" is nowhere on the label; it is "Old" in the sense that it is the first, the original Suntory whisky; this is the world's best-selling whisky, far and away.

Suntory "Royal," 86.8°, $10.50 (fifth). The company's premium whisky and standard-bearer abroad.

Suntory Signature, 86.8°, $59 (fifth). The highest-priced whisky in the U.S. It comes from the private stock of Keizo Saji, president of Suntory Limited. It is blended from stocks with an average age of 25 years, is served at parties and official functions of the Emperor of Japan. Suntory even makes a Bourbon-type whiskey called "Rawhide," presumably without a taste to match. It has a covered-wagon on the label; it is not imported to the U.S.

Suntory imports three liqueurs to the U.S., and whatever else may or may not be said of them, they are different:

Midori Melon Liqueur, 46°, $12 (750 ml.)

Suntory Cherry Blossom Liqueur, 44°, $10 (24 oz.)

Suntory Green Tea Liqueur, 50°, $11 (24 oz.)

SWEDISH PUNCH (or PUNCH) It's also called Caloric Punch—for no good reason. It's not a mixed drink à *l'Americaine*, but a liqueur, usually bottled, made with **Batavia arak,** a robust, pungent rum from Indonesia; hence its third name: Arak Punsch. It's spiced with assorted aromatic flavorings and is the national liqueur of Scandinavia, a potent, spicy, heart-warming beverage. It may be taken neat or diluted with hot water, whereupon it turns milky.

T

TANQUERAY SPECIAL DRY GIN Though it was virtually unknown in this country a scant 20 years ago, Tanqueray Gin is America's second-best-selling imported gin today (after Beefeater). It's in.

Tanqueray Gin has a long, even noble history. The family fought in the Crusades under Richard I. Note the crossed pikes on the label. notice also the noble "T" crest on the bottle. And for no known reason, the bottle is in the shape of an English fireplug. Tanqueray was already making good gin in the early 1700s, England's "Gin Age." In those days anything went, as long as it didn't corrode glass and wouldn't explode when exposed to air.

Tanqueray Gin is still made only in England. As an import it's more expensive, of course, than domestic gins, selling for around $7.50 (fifth). Imported gins are *au courant* these days—which is to say, they're more popular, not necessarily better. (For more, see comments on domestic vs. imported gins, under gins.) Tanqueray Gin, however, is a slightly superior product: It is a trifle tastier, a tiny fraction more aromatic. It's 94.6°. Whether these wee, wee differences are worth an additional $2.50 per fifth over most domestic gins is a matter of privy decision.

TEACHER'S SCOTCH WHISKY William Teacher, a proper Scotsman, of Glasgow, went into the whisky business in 1830, at the age of 19. That was the year he opened his first "dramshop" in Glasgow. He did a spirited business, and was soon blending his own whisky. His most successful blend he dubbed "Teacher's Highland Cream."

William Teacher & Son built its first distillery in 1891, at Ardmore in Aberdeenshire. (Up to that time the company had been buying its malt and grain whiskies.) In 1960, Teacher's purchased the Glendronach Distillery, one of the oldest distilleries in Scotland. The Glendronach Single Malt Whisky—the label says "Teacher's Glendronach"—can be found in the U.S. (about $13 a fifth), but most of the output goes into Teacher's blends.

Teacher's was one of the last independent brands of Scotch whisky, but in 1976 it too succumbed to conglomeration, and joined the Allied Breweries Group.

Teacher's Highland Cream (about $8 a fifth) is a full-bodied Scotch, 86°, with rich, full aroma and taste. It's a "Scotchy" Scotch, and this probably accounts for its pronounced drop in sales in recent years in the U.S. Teacher's top-of-the-line is its Royal

Highland, 12 years old, selling at around $12 (fifth).

TEN HIGH STRAIGHT BOURBON WHISKEY
This ever popular bourbon whiskey is a product of Hiram Walker, Inc. It's declined slightly in sales in recent years, but virtually every whiskey has done that.

Ten High is a good, reliable bourbon—it deserves its popularity. It must be added, of course, that it does not differ notably from most other comparably priced straights, nor, for the matter of that, from the more expensive straights. It is comparatively heavy-bodied. The 80° sells for around $5 (fifth); there is also an 86°.

TENNESSEE WHISKEY
In everything except name, Tennessee whiskey is nothing more nor less than bourbon—but don't tell that to a Tennessean or a whiskey-drinking, pistol-packin' resident of Bourbon County, Kentucky. Tennessee whiskey is made by the selfsame process as bourbon, from the identical ingredients. In fact, it could call itself bourbon, if it so chose. But it don't so choose. Never has, never will. It's made in Tennessee, of course, and natives of that state will tell you that they can detect the difference between their home product and Kentucky bourbon. With the labels visible, yes.

Many Tennessee whiskeys boast of the fact that they're charcoal-filtered. Many whiskeys are charcoal-filtered, including some bourbons, and even a few blends. Most Tennessee whiskeys also proclaim the fact that they're "sour mash," but this is neither a plus nor a minus. (For details on sour mash, see under bourbon.)

None of this is to say that Tennessee whiskey is not good whiskey. On the contrary, it is among the best. But note that it is priced accordingly: Tennessee whiskeys, as a group, are America's most expensive whiskeys, and ordinarily, they do not constitute good values. Here are America's leading Tennessee whiskeys, listed according to price per oz. of alcohol:

> **Jack Daniel's** No. 7 Green Label Sour Mash, 90°, $0.59/oz.
>
> **George Dickel** Old #8 Sour Mash, 86°, $0.60/oz.
>
> **George Dickel** Old #8 Sour Mash, 86.8°, $0.67/oz.
>
> **George Dickel** Old #12 Sour Mash, 90°, $0.67/oz.
>
> **Jack Daniel's** Old No. 7 Sour Mash Black Label, 90°, $0.70/oz.

To see how these Tennessee whiskeys compare in price with bourbons of equal quality—not well—see the listing of straight bourbons, under bourbon.

TEQUILA
One of the most unlikely, implausible beverages in the world certainly has to be this distilled Mexican spirit. It's literally distilled cactus juice. (If you want to be very technical, tequila is made from the agave or century plant, which is strictly not a cactus—but it looks like one and tastes like one!) And it tastes like no other potion on all of God's green earth.

None of this is to say that tequila tastes bad—it tastes different. And some *gringos* are apparently coming to appreciate the difference. Tequila is the fastest-growing liquor in the U.S., with sales of more than 5 million gallons in 1975. Incredibly there are more than 250 brands available in the U.S. today, most of them only a few years old.

This tequila boom started, as have so many fads, both spirituous and spiritual, with California's young people, who were looking for an economical spirit their parents didn't drink. Tequila filled the bill exactly.

Americans used to talk with distinct condescension about fiery, rotgut, hangover-laden Mexican tequila. Commercial tequila has never deserved any of those modifiers. It has its own distinctive taste, but what spirit has a more distinctive taste than bourbon? It is not highly alcoholic—almost all tequila comes at 80°. As for hangovers, tequila, consumed in the same amount, over the same period of time, under the same circumstances, will cause neither more nor less hangover than any other alcoholic beverage of the same potency. (For more on this distressing but necessary subject, see **hangovers.**)

Tequila is distilled at an unusually low proof, around 104°, compared to vodka, for example, "brought over" at 190° or more. This explains why tequila is such a tasteful beverage, vodka so tasteless. Most tequila comes to the U.S. unaged. Some, however, is aged in wooden casks a year or more. This maturing process makes a mellower brew and gives the tequila a slight amber tinge. This is called "Gold" and sells for a little more.

Coloring can be added, however, by artificial means. And usually is.

Some tequila bottles bear the word "Añejo" on the label. It means "The Aged One," but age, of course, is wholly relative. In this case "The Aged One" has a fullness of years in the amount of at least one.

Ascending to the very tequilan heights, there is Tequila Centenario or Conmemorativo, made only once every six years, to commemorate the inauguration of a new president. At least two of these are imported to the U.S.: Sauza Conmemorativo, 80°, $11.85 (fifth); and Jose Cuervo 1800, 80°, $11.20 (fifth).

In buying tequila, especially south of the border, look for the Mexican government's seal of authenticity on the label: D.G.N. (Direccion General de Normas). To qualify for the seal, a tequila must be at least 51% from the blue agave, essential to the production of good tequila. The more blue agave—all other things being equal—the better the tequila. And that is why good tequila can never be really cheap: The blue agave takes at least 10 years to come to maturity, it can be grown within a very limited area, and once it's been harvested, it has to be replanted.

Mexicans have a delightful ritual for drinking tequila. The props are three: tequila, salt, lime. (Notice that in Mexico some brands of tequila come with a little bag of salt tied around the neck of the bottle—in case of emergency.) The most common form of this noble tradition is to take a lick of the salt, throw back a shot of straight ice-cold tequila, and follow it quickly with a healthy squeeze of lime directly in the mouth. *Olé!* Actually the three ingredients may be, and are, taken in any order at all, except that the tequila is never taken first. Well, almost never. After several of these historic Mexican exercises, any order is legit.

To make sure your tequila is at the right temperature for straight consumption, simply stick it in the freezer—better, keep it there perpetually.

Tequila has skyrocketed in popularity in the U.S., not as a straight drink, but as the base of that great international favorite, the **Margarita** cocktail. Other inspired and inspiring tequila cocktails are these: **Sangrita, Tequila Sour,** and **Tequila Sunrise.** There is also—so help me!—a **Freddie Fudpucker,** of questionable heritage and very recent vintage.

Tequila does not vary as widely in price as do other spirits, and with good reason, for it's all basically the same beverage: made in exactly the same way, from the same single ingredient. Unless you're a true tequila aficionado and can appreciate Jose Cuervo's 1800 at $11.20 (fifth), or Herradura Añejo at $14 (fifth), be advised to buy the most economical tequila you can find.

Here are the best buys available in the U.S., based on price per oz. of alcohol:

BEST BUYS IN TEQUILA

Vuelo Gold, 80°, $0.47/oz.
Corrida White, 80°, $0.48/oz.
Gavilan, 80°, $0.48/oz.
Corrida Gold, 80°, $0.48/oz.
Papagayo White, 80°, $0.48/ oz.

Papagayo Gold, 80°, $0.48/ oz.
Newport Rosita White and Gold, 80°, $0.49/oz.
White Tavern Fonda Blanca, 80°, $0.49/oz.
White Tavern Gold, 80°, $0.49/oz.
Pedro Domecq White, 80°, $0.49/oz.
Jose Gaspar White, 80°, $0.50/oz.
Jose Gaspar Gold, 80°, $0.50/oz.
La Prima, 80°, $0.50/oz.
Tequila Terana, 80°, $0.50/ oz.
Pancho Villa White, 80°, $0.51/oz.
Pepe Lopez White, 80°, $0.51/oz.
Beamero Silver, 80°, $0.51/ oz.
Pancho Villa Gold, 80°, $0.52/oz.
Arandas White, 80°, $0.53/ oz.
La Capa, 80°, $0.54/oz.
Montezuma White, 80°, $0.54/oz.
Old Mr. Boston, 80°, $0.54/ oz.
Olé White and Gold, 100°, $0.54/oz.
Pedro Domecq de Oro, 80°, $0.54/oz.
Beamero Gold, 80°, $0.54/oz.
Pepe Lopez De Oro, 80°, $0.55/oz.
Amigo, 80°, $0.55/oz.
Matador White, 80°, $0.55/ oz.
San Matias White and Gold, 80°, $0.55/oz.
Jose Cortez White and Gold, 80°, $0.56/oz.
Arandas Oro, 80°, $0.56/oz.
Montezuma Gold, 80°, $0.57/ oz.
Fleischmann Numero Uno, 80°, $0.57/oz.

Olé White and Gold, 80°, $0.58/oz.

Pedro Domecq, 86°, $0.58/oz.

Matador Gold, 80°, $0.59/oz.

Don Emilio White and Gold, 80°, $0.59/oz.

Acapulco Gold, 80°, $0.60/oz.

El Charro Silver, 80°, $0.61/oz.

Two Fingers White, 80°, $0.63/oz.

Olmeca Silver, 80°, $0.63/oz.

El Charro Gold, 80°, $0.63/oz.

Gavilan Especial, 86°, $0.64/oz.

Gavilan, 86°, $0.65/oz.

Bullfighter, 80°, $0.66/oz.

Jose Cuervo White, 80°, $0.66/oz.

El Toro, 80°, $0.67/oz.

Olmeca Gold, 80°, $0.67/oz.

Sauza Silver, 80°, $0.67/oz.

Two Fingers Gold, 80°, $0.67/oz.

Jose Cuervo Gold, 86°, $0.72/oz.

Sauza Extra Gold, 80°, $0.72/oz.

Jose Cuervo Gold, 80°, $0.72/oz.

Herradura Silver, 92°, $0.81/oz.

Herradura Reposado, 92°, $0.91/oz.

TEQUILA SOUR (COCK-TAIL) It's not as popular in these latter days as the **Margarita** or the **Tequila Sunrise**, but if you like sours (one of the world's most felicitous types of mixed drinks), you'll like a Tequila Sour. Here's all you need:

Juice of ½ lemon, 1 tsp. powdered sugar, 1 jigger tequila, couple of ice cubes

Shake all that stuff together, and then drain it into a sour glass (Delmonico glass, about 6 oz.), and fill with club soda. Garnish with half a slice of lemon or orange and a maraschino cherry.

TEQUILA SUNRISE (COCK-TAIL) It not only looks like a sunrise, it tastes like one. It's a brand-new drink, wholly "in," the latter-day successor to that other inspired tequila drink, the **Margarita**. You won't find it in any bartender's guide more than 5 years old—they didn't even know what tequila was in those olden days. The Sunrise is a judicious blend of sweet and sour and refreshingly simple:

1 glass (4 to 6 oz.) orange juice, a few ice cubes, 1 jigger or so tequila, a few dashes of grenadine

Mix tequila and orange juice. Add grenadine slowly, allowing it to settle. Let your Sunrise consumer stir the drink himself, so that when (s)he does so, he or she may behold the sun rise in the Sunrise. *Olé* and *salud!*

TIA MARIA It means "Aunt Mary" and it's a coffee liqueur from Jamaica—and a fine one. It's often compared with its Mexican counterpart (and predecessor), Kahlúa. Tia Maria is lighter and drier, more suitable than Kahlúa for straight-up sipping. It's a wholly admirable beverage, no matter how consumed. (For how it compares with others, see under **coffee liqueur.**) It sells in the U.S. for around $10 (23 oz.), almost exactly the same price as Kahlúa.

TOM COLLINS (COCKTAIL) If there is anything more delightfully refreshing than a long tall Tom Collins on a blistering, merciless summer's day, it's never been publicly disclosed. Tinkling with solid ice, sweating profusely, gaily garnished, it can resuscitate the wilted, even the moribund.

The Tom Collins was probably named after Old Tom Gin, a sweetened form of gin popular in England a century ago.

You can, of course, buy commercial Tom Collins mixes, and they are quite satisfactory, but for a *real* Tom Collins, proceed as follows:

Into a tall glass—preferably 12 or 14 oz., for a short Tom Collins is a contradiction in terms—put:

1 jigger (1½ oz.) gin—even 2 jiggers, as this is a long drink, 1 oz. fresh lemon juice, 2 tsp. powdered sugar, ice cubes

Fill with club soda and stir. Optional garnish: Lemon slice, maraschino cherry, orange slice.

TRAPPISTINE Presumably it might have been as famous as **Benedictine**, but somehow Trappistine never quite made it. It's similar to Benedictine, and quite as good, with a marvelous herby flavor. Like Benedictine, it is of ancient origin—though it does not go quite so far back—and it is also of monkish origin. It was created in France at the Abbaye de la Grace de Dieu, by the Trappist monks, and hence its name. Trappistine uses true Armagnac as its base—a wonderful way to start any liqueur! Unfortunately, it is not normally imported to the U.S.

Many of the world's finest liqueurs had a monastic origin—**Chartreuse** and Benedictine, to name only the two best-

known—but there are many others less celebrated. Besides Trappistine there are Carmeline (named after the Carmelite monks), Monastique (a German liqueur, in imitation of Benedictine), and Claristine, which was originally a generic name, but is now a registered proprietary name owned by **Leroux**. Like Trappistine it is an imitation Benedictine, and a vaguely authentic one at that, and at about half the price. Leroux claims that its Claristine was originated by the "Clarise" nuns—another name for the Poor Clares—in Belgium some 150 years ago, and the formula purchased by the Leroux family. (This may be an apocryphal tale, however, as the Poor Clares are an exceedingly strict contemplative order of Franciscan nuns, not normally given to such frivolities as the making of spirituous liqueurs!)

TRIPLE SEC The name means "thrice dry," and this orange-flavored liqueur once was something of the sort: three times as dry as its sister spirit, the normally sweet **Curaçao**. Today the name is almost a total misnomer, for today's triple secs are often sweeter than Curaçao.

For all practical purposes, the only difference between triple secs and Curaçaos today is that triple sec is colorless. It's often defined simply as "white Curaçao."

Generally speaking, American-made triple secs are as good as their European counterparts. (The reverse is usually the case—joyous exception!—most European liqueurs are superior to their American imitations.) Most American triple secs are 60° (**De Kuyper** offers both a 60° and an 80°) and sell for $5 to $6 (24 oz.) in New York State, somewhat less in the Western U.S..

European triple secs are usually higher-proof than American ones. **Bols** is 78° (25 oz.); **Cusenier**, 70° (24 oz.); **Garnier**, 80° (24 oz.); **Marie Brizard**, 78° (23.6 oz.). And most of them are considerably more expensive, hovering around $10, and Bols is a whopping $20 or more per quart.

The most famous of all triple secs is that made by the firm of **Cointreau**. In fact, its triple sec became so popular that when competitors began producing their own triple secs, Cointreau simply dropped "Triple Sec" from the label and called it by the family name, "Cointreau."

Cointreau is one of the largest-selling liqueurs in the world—some say *the* largest-selling. Today's Cointreau is still made according to the same secret formula that Edouard Cointreau Jr. devised more than a century ago. Five different oranges—or orange peels, to be exact—are used, from everywhere from the West Indies to Israel.

In the U.S., Cointreau used to produce a complete line of liqueurs under the Cointreau label, but the company now produces them under its Regnier label. Cointreau Liqueur (Triple Sec) is, however, still their big seller.

Recently introduced in the U.S. is Cointreau and Brandy, 80°, drier than the straight Cointreau, and a harmonious blend; it sells for around $10 (fifth).

Cointreau is unquestionably one of the world's finest orange liqueurs. It is often compared to **Grand Marnier;** Cointreau is the lighter, sharper, drier, of the two, and it lacks Grand Marnier's many-splendored complexity. It is 80° and sells for $10 to $11 (24 oz.). It's best appreciated straight or on the rocks.

TUACA It sounds vaguely Mexican or Spanish, but it's *puro Italiano*, dating back, it is said, to the days of Lorenzo the Magnificent (d. 1492), who cherished it. In fact, the Medici coat of arms—Lorenzo was one of the clan—surmounts the classic Tuaca label. Americans are just 500 years late in discovering the magnificent liqueur of the Magnificent Lorenzo.

Some say Tuaca tastes of oranges and coconuts—others say of almonds and vanilla—others of citrus fruits and brandy. The truth of the matter is that it tastes of all these things, for Tuaca is a delightfully complex beverage, with a many-splendored taste. You can't define or describe the taste—you only know it's delicious.

The label calls Tuaca "demi-sec," which is precisely what it is: semi-dry. The relatively high proof, 84°, is assurance that it is not overly sweet.

Already a few Tuaca-based cocktails have begun to circulate, none of which are very notable, and the worst of which must surely be T 'n T, Tuaca and Tequila! But the best way to enjoy your Tuaca—or even somebody else's—is to sip it daintily, remembering that it's a hefty

84°, straight up or on the rocks, with a lemon twist or a squeeze of lime.

TULLAMORE DEW IRISH WHISKEY It used to come from the town of Tullamore in the dead center of Ireland. Today it's one of seven brands made by the giant Midleton Distillery in County Cork—the others: Jameson, Power's Gold Label, Paddy's, Murphy's, and Dunphy's. For some reason Tullamore is not highly esteemed by the Irish themselves—Paddy's is their favorite—but it's good standard Irish whiskey, no better than the others, but no worse either. It is 86° and has a pleasant softness.

There is also a 12-year-old Tullamore Dew in a crock, selling for around $11.50 (fifth). It is highly regarded.

TVARSCKI VODKA It might sound as Russian as Leonid Brezhnev, but it's as American as Jimmy Carter. In fact, it's made by the American Distilling Company of Pekin, Ill., and is any place on earth more American than Pekin, Ill.?

Tvarscki Vodka is American Distilling's single best-selling product: in 1977 more than 500,000 cases. Tvarski is good, standard American vodka. It is moderately priced, the 80° selling for about $4 per 750ml (2 oz. less than a fifth) in California. It's available in 90° and 100° too.

And speaking of Jimmy Carter, American Distilling believes they have the solution to the President's 3-Martini luncheon dilemma. In April 1978 the company launched Double Tvarscki Vodka, a

jolting, mind-numbing 160°! No need now for three Martinis at lunchtime—a single one made with Double Tvarscki will incapacitate one for the rest of the afternoon. Says the company: "It will make the Screwdriver, screwier, and the Bloody Mary, Bloodier"—and Mary-er. The company cautions potential consumers to use twice as much mix with this double-barreled stuff, or half as much vodka per drink. That's the theory. But will they? Or will they simply make their drinks twice as strong?

Double Tvarscki is touted as a money-saving innovation. It's true, it does not sell for twice as much as regular Tvarscki; Double sells for around $7.50 (fifth). But again it will constitute a saving only if it reaches twice as far.

Tvarscki also comes in an array of flavors: cherry, apple, lemon, lime, orange, mint, grape, strawberry, blackberry, peppermint. These sell for just pennies more than the regular vodka. Clearly, if vodka is your bag, Tvarscki has something to suit your every mood and fancy: four different proofs of vodka, plus ten different flavors.

TWO FINGERS TEQUILA Almost all tequila brands—except for Jose Cuervo and Sauza—are new on the American scene; virtually all arrived within the past decade. But Two Fingers is one of the latest comers of all; it's been around only a couple of years. But thanks to careful merchandising and an ocean of promotion, it's already a big seller, in both the Eastern and Western U.S.

The name does not refer to

the amount of tequila one is supposed to pour, as the Germans say, "Zwei Finger," but to a shadowy, perhaps apocryphal, figure who used to cross the Mexico–U.S. border in the '30s to peddle his celebrated tequila. He had only two fingers on one hand and so was he known. No one ever knew his real name, and he disappeared as mysteriously and completely as he had appeared. At least that's the way the back label of Two Fingers Tequila tells it. And, apocryphal or no, it's a good story— and a good tequila.

Two Fingers Tequila comes in a black crock-type bottle. It's in the medium-price range: around $6 (fifth) in California (both White and Gold versions), and about 50¢ more on the East Coast. Like practically all the other 250-odd brands of tequila shipped from Mexico to the U.S. these days, Two Fingers is good, trustworthy tequila. For practical purposes, it is no better and no worse than any of the others. (For a complete listing, by cost, see under **tequila**.)

U

UNITED STATES—BRANDY

Not many years ago people sniffed at American brandy—today they sniff it, appreciatively and delightedly, in tulip-shaped glasses. American brandy has truly come of age. This is not to say that it has replaced, or that it will ever replace, the finest of French brandies (notably **Cognac** and **Armagnac**). But it is to say that American brandy is an excellent beverage in its own right.

American brandy is a very different beverage from all the other great brandies of the world, and in recent decades it has achieved its own notable success. It is a good, not great, drink: smooth, clean, fruity and grapy, with distinct sweetness. Don't look for the finesse, power, complexity of a gracious old Cognac. They're not there.

Almost all American brandy comes from California, and that state today produces more brandy—almost 50 million gallons—than all of France.

Technically, American brandy may be made from any grape in the world—and sometimes has been. But almost all American brandy today is made from two respectable grapes (although rather colorless from a wine man's point of view): the Thompson Seedless and the Flame Tokay.

It is aged in American oak, usually for around 4 years, although only 2 years is required by law.

The use of a small amount (2½% by volume) of "rectifying agents" is allowed: mainly sugar, caramel (for color), sherry, port, and fruit extracts. These are not "adulterants"—they are "mellowers."

Most California brandy finds its way into mixed drinks—notably the **Stinger, Side Car, Brandy Alexander,** and in the Yuletide, **Eggnog**—but more and more Americans are learning to sip their California brandy, neatly, as the British put it, or on the rocks, as the Americans put it, or with a splash of water or soda.

One newly-invented Brandy drink deserves special mention, so tasty and toewarming is it: the Brandy Life. It's an invention of the ski-people, and is highly recommended after a morning on the slopes. The Rx:

1 oz. California Brandy
½ oz. Rum
1 level tablespoon honey
Apple wedge with peel
4 oz. hot water
Lemon slice stuck with cloves

Pour Brandy and Rum into an 8 oz. heated mug or cup. Stir in honey. Add apple and lemon. Fill with water. Stir well. Drink deeply. (Note: Recipe courtesy Emanuel Greenberg. Originally published in *Playboy* magazine.

Copyright © 1975 by Playboy.)

Tastes differ, of course, for brandy, and perhaps more so than with any other spirit. Some prefer a powerful, hearty spirit—others, a soft and mellow and sweetish one. Even among California brandies there is a considerable range of types and styles.

On the other hand it needs to be said that there is a general consensus as to which are California's finest brandies. They are listed below in descending order of excellence. These rankings represent a cross-section of opinion but are still only an approximation. It is impossible to give a strictly numerical order of excellence. After all, one man's elixir is often another man's poison. But the list does give an overview of California's brandies, from most respected to least appreciated.

CALIFORNIA'S BEST BRANDIES, IN VAGUELY DESCENDING ORDER OF EXCELLENCE

Christian Brothers X.O. Rare Reserve
Guild Blue Ribbon 12-year-old
A. R. Morrow 100°
Korbel
Cresta Blanca St. Emilion
E & J
Cresta Blanca Vintage
Ceremony 5-year-old and 8-year-old
Conti Royale
Setrakian
Almadén Centennial
Paul Masson
Leroux 5-Star
Guild Blue Ribbon ("Regular")

Christian Brothers ("Regular")
Coronet V.S.Q.
Royal Host Blended
Old San Francisco
Leroux Deluxe
A. R. Morrow 80°
Lejon
Cribari
Jacques Bonet
Royal Host 6-year-old
Franzia
Hartley

USHER'S GREEN STRIPE SCOTCH WHISKY This is one of the few truly historic whiskies of the world. It was Andrew Usher, a wily Scotsman, who made the first commercial *blended* Scotch whisky, in 1853. Up to that time "Scotch" meant only the severe single-malt whiskies, beloved in Scotland, but scarcely known anywhere else. Today, more than 90% of the Scotch so joyously consumed around the world is blended Scotch whisky. In effect, Usher's Green Stripe was the world's first blended Scotch.

Usher's today is the property of J. & G. Stewart Ltd., which in turn is a part of the giant Distillers Company Limited, and it is marketed in the U.S. by sprawling Brown-Forman of Louisville, Ky. And you ask whatever happened to the corner grocery store? The world's conglomerated!

Usher's is good, wholesome, Scotch whisky, medium-bodied, medium-priced, is 80° and 86° and sells for around $6 (750ml, 2 oz. less than a fifth) for the 86°.

V

VAN der HUM Whatever else is said about it, this tangerine-flavored liqueur from South Africa has the most original and intriguing name in all the world of liqueurs; Van der Hum means "What's His Name," so called because nobody could remember the name of the inventor.

Van der Hum dates back to the 17th century and is the only indigenous South African liqueur. It has brandy as its base—this gives it a certain lustiness—and is flavored with the peels of Seville oranges and native tangerines (*naartjie*). Spices include nutmeg, cloves, cinnamon, and cardamom.

Van der Hum is a most commendable beverage, aromatic and citrusy in flavor, with hardy brandy undertones. It comes to the U.S. at 60°, sells for $10 to $11 (24 oz.).

VANDERMINT It's a chocolate-mint liqueur from Holland, and it comes in an eye-catching blue-and-white crock-type bottle which seems to epitomize Holland. But the container is more noteworthy than the contained. Vandermint, despite a fancy price tag, is standard chocolate-mint liqueur. It is virtually indistinguishable from American-made chocolate-mint liqueurs selling at less than half the price. **Hiram Walker** Chocolate-Mint goes for around $6 (¾ quart), Vandermint for $12 (23 oz.). And note that ¾ quart is 24 oz. of the Hiram Walker against only 23 oz. of the Vandermint.

VAT 69 SCOTCH WHISKY An ancient jest says it's the Pope's phone number, but it's not nearly that complicated. It's exactly what the name says: the whisky from Vat 69. William Sanderson, "British Wine & Cordial Manufacturer," began blending Scotch whisky in 1863. His first commercial concoction was called simply "Mixture Whisky." But Sanderson wanted the best mixture possible. He put his various blends in numbered little casks or "vats," and brought in some skilled blenders and friends. There were almost a hundred vats in all, but it was unanimous—at least so does Wm. Sanderson & Sons Ltd. spin the yarn—the whisky from Vat 69 was clearly the best!

Sanderson's of Leith, Scotland, joined **Booth's** Distilleries in 1935, and it was about this time that the firm ceased the production of its liqueurs, and other Scotch blends, to concentrate on Vat 69. In 1939 both Booth's and Sanderson's joined the **Distillers Company Limited.**

Vat 69 is excellent Scotch whisky, and has consistently ranked well in blind tastings. It now comes in two styles: Tra-

217

ditional and Gold. The Traditional is the old black label—the word "Traditional," of course, is nowhere on the label. It is a true Scotch lover's kind of blend: peaty, smoky, lusty. The Gold is a new, lighter blend, designed especially for the American market, to meet the American demand for lighter whiskies—indeed, its full name is Gold Light. It has been generally well received, but some experts have found it "rough." The Traditional, 86.8°, sells for around $8.50 (fifth), and the Gold, 86°, for about $6.50 (fifth).

VIRGIN ISLANDS—RUMS

Along with Puerto Rican rums, these are Americans' favorite rums. They're similar to the Puerto Rican variety in both appearance and taste; most of them are light in color and body. Unlike Puerto Rico rums, they're unaged and come to the U.S. in bulk and are bottled here in the U.S. The best-known of them are from the island of St. Croix, and they are called Cruzan rums. The name is usually on the label. Practically all Virgin Island rums are 80° and they all sell for about the same price: $4 to $4.50 per fifth (somewhat higher in the Eastern U.S.). Here are the most popular brands in the U.S. in ascending order of price; all 80°:

Pirate Rum VI, White or Gold, 80°, $4.37
Carnaval, White or Gold, 80°, $4.49
Brugal, White or Gold, 80°, $4.54
Old Mr. Boston, Light or Dark, 80°, $4.65
Marimba Special Reserve,
White or Gold, 80°, $4.67
Old Croix, Light Dry or Dark, 80°, $4.91
Cruzan "Clipper," White or Gold, 80°, $5.45

VODKA

The name means "little water," but it behaves little like water. Behaves more like pure alcohol—which it virtually is, with a little water.

Vodka, even by the definition of U.S. regulations, is "without distinctive character, aroma, taste, or color." It is a spiritless spirit, the most tasteless of all the world's great spirits, for it is essentially pure neutral grain spirits with distilled water added. No flavoring whatever is used—in fact, vodka is often purified of all extraneous taste by being filtered through charcoal. The more careful the process, the purer and better the vodka.

This is American vodka we're talking about. Imported vodkas are a slightly different breed, purposely made with just a wee tot of some kind of flavor. One Polish brand, Polmos Zubrowka (or Zubrovka) is flavored with buffalo grass, and even has a blade of the stuff in the bottle. You may like it, if your tastes run to buffalo grass —the buffalos' do—but otherwise Zubrowka, is strictly an acquired taste.

Also being imported into the U.S. these days are vodkas from England, Russia, Austria, Finland, Holland, Denmark, and even kosher vodka from Israel. All of these are more expensive than our domestic vodkas, and that's precisely why some people buy them!

Foreign vodkas come in a wide assortment of flavors, including sweet versions, and in a variety of colors: yellow (from saffron), blue, brown (walnut shells), even lavender. At least in their native land they come so, and a few of these weirdies (not weirdos) are now being brought to the U.S. Here are some:

Starka: It's specially aged, has an amber tinge; it's older, if not better.

Okhotnichya: "Hunter's Vodka"; recommended when hunting polar bears on Finnish fjords.

Pertsovka: Pepper-flavored, from Russia—not recommended unless you enjoy the sensation of smoke coming out of your ears.

The only way to drink imported vodkas, of course, is straight, icy-cold, or as a concession to ice-happy Americans, on the rocks. To do it right, à la Russe, accompany the vodka with caviar or smoked salmon. Nazdarovie!

In Russia and Poland a bottle of vodka is often encased in ice for festive occasions—this keeps it at exactly the right temperature for drinking straight. If you want to impress your left-leaning friends, you can make your own vodka-encasing ice block. Put your chic imported bottle of vodka in a goodly-sized pot, fill the pot with water, put the whole business into the freezer. When the water is frozen, put the pot in hot water, and presto, the pot falls away like a discarded hunk of space hardware, and there you have your ice block encompassing your genuine imported vodka.

Eastern Europeans prize their vodka most dearly; it really is their national drink. The story is told of the Russian Army recruit being interrogated by induction officials. "Do you smoke?" "Yes." "You must stop." "Do you like women?" "Yes." "That must stop." "Do you drink vodka?" "Yes." "That must stop." "Will you give your life for your country?" "Sure—what's left to live for?"

Considering the costliness of imported vodkas, it is sheer profligacy to use them in any type of mixed drink. The vodka is totally submerged in a Bloody Mary, Screwdriver, or Moscow Mule. Conserve money: Use only economical domestic vodkas for mixes. Save that Russian vodka for some visiting cosmonaut or commissar.

A mere 25 years ago nobody, but nobody, drank vodka. Even had you known of its existence, you would scarcely have been able to find any. Nobody sold vodka because nobody drank vodka. Vodka, as every red-blooded, bourbon-drinking American could have told you, was a vile potion made from Polish potatoes, drunk by Russian Cossacks before they played Russian roulette.

Eu, tempora mutantur et nos mutamur in illis! Egad, how indeed have the times changed and we with them! Today, heresy of all abominable heresies, vodka outsells bourbon in these United States of America! Joe McCarthy was right: The Russians and Communists are everywhere!

And is it really made from potatoes? Used to be, can be, still is, but not much. Today vodka is made principally from grains—mostly corn and sorghum in the U.S. It is distilled at high proof, 190° and more, which leaves it virtually tasteless.

And this, of course, is precisely the reason for vodka's phenomenal rise in popularity over the past few years: Its neutrality makes it the ideal mixer; it's even more nonpartisan than gin.

Vodka can be substituted for gin in any mixed drink where gin is the traditional base: The Tom Collins becomes a Vodka Collins; Gin and Tonic, Vodka and Tonic. Even the Vodka Martini, considered an unspeakable abomination just a few years ago. And so on, down the interminable list.

The most popular vodka drinks are these: **Black Russian, Bloody Mary, Bullshot, Grasshopper, Harvey Wallbanger, Moscow Mule, Russian Bear, Screwdriver,** and **Seattle Mist.**

Remember that when you buy vodka, especially the American variety, you're simply buying alcohol, period. So if you have a particle of sense and frugality about you, buy the most economical. Even if there are subtle, infinitesimal differences between brands— and sometimes there are—is it sensible to pay $2.75 more per fifth when your modish $7.75 brand is going to be absolutely and totally lost beneath tomato sauce, ginger beer, beef bouillon, and Worcestershire sauce?

Expert tasters tasting blindly have been consistently unable to distinguish the most expensive American vodkas from the least expensive. Even some ultra-chic imported vodkas, when reduced to the same proof as their American counterparts, could not be distinguished.

Many large liquor stores

have their own private brand of most spirits. These are almost always excellent values, and probably nowhere more so than in the case of vodka, which by definition is simply water-diluted beverage alcohol.

Here are your best buys in American vodkas, listed according to price per oz. of alcohol, best buys first.

BEST BUYS IN AMERICAN VODKAS

Allenka, 110°, $0.33/oz.
Nickolai, 100°, $0.36/oz.
Nuyens, 80°, $0.36/oz.
Regal Club, 80°, $0.36/oz.
Cossack, 100°, $0.37/oz.
Nuyens, 100°, $0.37/oz.
Skol, 100°, $0.37/oz.
Hankey Bannister, 80°, $0.38/oz.
Park & Tilford, 80°, $0.38/oz.
White Crown, 80°, $0.38/oz.
Berov, 80°, $0.39/oz.
Boord's, 80°, $0.39/oz.
Georgi, 80°, $0.39/oz.
Glenmore, 80°, $0.39/oz.
Kazak, 100°, $0.39/oz.
Lance, 80°, $0.39/oz.
Personal Choice, 80°, $0.39/oz.
Rare Export, 80°, $0.39/oz.
Relska, 80°, $0.39/oz.
Romanoff, 80°, $0.39/oz.
Smolka, 80°, $0.39/oz.
White Tavern, 80°, $0.39/oz.
Zarkow, 80°, $0.39/oz.
Alexi, 80°, $0.40/oz.
Cossack, 80°, $0.40/oz.
Custom House, 80°, $0.40/oz.
Duggan's, 90.4°, $0.40/oz.
Fleischmann's Royal, 100°, $0.40/oz.
Jacquin, 100°, $0.40/oz.
Mayflower, 80°, $0.40/oz.
Nickolai, 80°, $0.40/oz.
Nikoff, 80°, $0.40/oz.
Skol, 80°, $0.40/oz.
Crown Russe, 100°, $0.41/oz.

Danski, 80°, $0.41/oz.

Fleischmann's Royal, 80°, $0.41/oz.

Jacquin, 90°, $0.41/oz.

Popov, 80°, $0.41/oz.

Popov, 100°, $0.41/oz.

Romanoff, 80°, $0.41/oz.

Stitzel Weller's Canada Dry, 80°, $0.41/oz.

Tvarski, 80°, $0.41/oz.

Canada Dry, 80°, $0.42/oz.

Gordon's, 80°, $0.42/oz.

Hiram Walker Crystal, 80°, $0.42/oz.

Hiram Walker, 100°, $0.42/oz.

Kamchatka, 80°, $0.42/oz.

Majorska, 80°, $0.42/oz.

Old Mr. Boston, 80°, $0.42/oz.

Stonehouse, 80°, $0.42/oz.

Tamirov, 90°, $0.42/oz.

Wolfschmidt, 100°, $0.42/oz.

Gilbey's, 80°, $0.43/oz.

Gordon's, 100°, $0.43/oz.

Jacquin, 80°, $0.43/oz.

Majorska, 100°, $0.43/oz.

Schenley, 80°, $0.43/oz.

Booth's High Ninety, 90°, $0.44/oz.

Gilbey's, 100°, $0.44/oz.

Haller's, 80°, $0.44/oz.

Old Mr. Boston, 100°, $0.44/oz.

Vicker's, 80°, $0.45/oz.

Wolfschmidt, 80°, $0.45/oz.

Crown Russe, 80°, $0.46/oz.

Relska, 100°, $0.46/oz.

Samovar, 86.8°, $0.48/oz.

Smirnoff, 100°, $0.50/oz.

Samovar, 80°, $0.51/oz.

Samovar, 100°, $0.52/oz.

Smirnoff, 80°, $0.52/oz.

Smirnoff Silver Label, 90.4°, $0.53/oz.

W

WASSAIL It's a toast, it's a festival, it's a song and a bowl, it's even a verb—but most of all it's a hale and hearty festive drink. Wassail—pronounced *WAH-sl*—is an old old custom dating back to Anglo-Saxon Britain. It began as *Wes hael,* "Be hale." And Wassail has remained an integral part of Christmas, lo these many centuries.

Wassail can have and has had all manner of ingredients: red wine, white wine, mead, sundry spirits, Madeira, sherry, not to mention all manner of fruits afloat therein. Today it's usually made with sherry and/or beer (ale): a happy combination, despite your initial misgivings! Apples have become the accepted fruit, but one is still allowed unbridled license in combining the beverages.

Here followeth a most godly, salubrious and hallowed Wassail bowl, fit for prince or pauper. Let it inaugurate your holiday season, serving it first on Thanksgiving, and as often as possible thereafter, fully until the Twelfth Night, the Feast of the Epiphany, January 6! *Wes hael!*

WASSAIL FOR THE LIKES OF 20 OR 30 STOUT YEOMEN
12 small apples, cored and baked. 4 cups sugar, 1 can (12 oz.) beer, 1 tbsp. powdered nutmeg—or better yet, two whole nutmegs, cracked, 2 tsp. ginger—or even better, a small stick of fresh ginger, 6 cloves, ½ tsp. mace, 6 allspice berries, 1 stick cinnamon

Dissolve the sugar in the beer, adding all the spices.

Add two bottles of dry or medium sherry (or Madeira, yummm) and four (12 oz.) cans of beer or ale. Bring to a simmer over medium heat, but don't boil.

Separate a dozen eggs. Beat the yolks until lemon-colored, and the whites until stiff. Fold them together and place the mixture in your punch bowl. Add the heated wine, slowly at first, beating briskly with a wire whisk.

You may add a cup or two of brandy or Cognac at this point, but this is already a very tasty beverage, and a rather stout one at that.

Now add the apples, perhaps quartered if they were large (to make for easier consumption).

Stir carefully and lovingly, and ladle the Wassail into heated mugs or cups. Provide small spoons to convey the apples mouthward.

WHISKEY Whether spelled "whiskey" or simply "whisky," it is one of the longest words in all the world of spirits. There are some forty different types made around the world, and eight principle kinds of whiskey are found on American shelves: **bourbon, Canadian, corn, Irish, malt, rye, Scotch** and **Tennessee.**

Two other terms appear on American labels: "American whiskey" and "light whiskey." American whiskey is simply blended whiskey, and is treated under **bourbon.** Light whiskey is also a type of **bourbon.**

Two minor whiskies are also worthy of mention: **Australian** and **Japanese.** There is even a Chinese whiskey, but it's best left to those with a taste for birds' nests (cooked, presumably) and 1,000-year-old eggs (scrambled, surely).

The very name "whiskey" is outlandish—just listen to the sound of the word! Wild, woolly. And it's properly named, for whiskey is a wild potion, tamed only by sparing, judicious, and careful consumption. It means "water of life." It can be that, should be that. Whiskey's wild. Domesticated, it's good fun.

As for the spelling, the usual rule is that Scottish and Canadian makers favor the forms "whisky/whiskies" and American, Irish, and most other makers favor "whiskey/whiskeys." But it's not quite that simple. Brown-Forman (Old Forester, Early Times, etc.) uses "whisky." The Old Bushmills label reads "Irish Whiskey—A Blend—100% Irish Whiskies," thus casting a vote in each camp. Yet the rule is observed by most manufacturers; for example, the various Calvert blends are "whiskey," except for Lord Calvert Canadian, which is "whisky." In this book, "whiskey" is used except when the subject is Canadian

or Scotch (or a Scotch-type product such as Suntory).

WHISKEY SOUR (COCKTAIL) This is one of the few drinks that is so good that a special glass was created for it. The Whiskey Sour glass, also called the Delmonico, is a slender, tulip-shaped glass, 4 to 7 oz.

Beyond question, the Whiskey Sour is one of the best of the swarms of before-dinner drinks: It's short, it's concentrated, it's nonfilling.

Combine these ingredients in a cocktail shaker:

2 to 3 oz. blended whiskey (or bourbon), juice of ½ lemon (2 tbsp.), 1 tsp. powdered sugar, 3 or 4 ice cubes

Shake vigorously, and strain into a sour glass (or wine glass, under duress). Garnish: maraschino cherry and/or slice of orange.

You can also make a good, frothy Whiskey Sour in an electric blender, but in this case use only 1 or 2 ice cubes, so as not to unduly dilute the potion.

This is simply the basic recipe for a sour, and any kind of sour can be made using this formula, and changing the spirit: Rum Sour, Brandy Sour, Scotch Sour, Applejack Sour, etc.

WHITE HORSE SCOTCH WHISKY White Horse Whisky got its name from the famous White Horse Inn in Edinburgh, Scotland, which, in turn, got its name from a beautiful white horse that Mary Queen of Scots was accustomed to ride down the "Royal Mile," in the area where the inn later stood.

In the mid-18th century all Edinburgh knew the White Horse Cellar as the starting place for the London stage coach, which departed at 5:00 A.M., Mondays and Fridays. Today the White Horse back label still shows a picture of the original inn, with a four-in-hand stagecoach leaving for London. Below the picture is the complete text of an advertisement of 1754: "All that are desirous to pass from EDINBURGH to LONDON, or any other place on their road, let them repair to the 'WHITE HORSE CELLAR,' in Edinburgh, at which place they may be received in a STAGE COACH every MONDAY and FRIDAY, which performs the whole journey in eight days (if God permits), and sets forth at five in the morning. Allowing each passenger 14 pounds weight, and all above, 6 pence per pound. February, 1754."

The White Horse front label says, "Estab. 1742," and that's correct—in a way. "White Horse" Whisky didn't come into existence officially until 1891 (when the name was registered), but 150 years before that, in 1742, there existed a group of "bothies," illegal distilleries, at Lagavulin, on the island of Islay. This illicit operation went on for more than 50 years, and it wasn't until the early 1800s that the operation became "legit." The whisky made at Lagavulin, like all whisky of that time, was unnamed and unlabeled, but it was what would later be known as Lagavulin Pure Islay Malt Scotch Whisky, a well-esteemed, strongly flavored Islay malt whisky.

It was Peter Jeffrey Mackie, known as "Restless Peter" in his day, due to his incessant activity, who bought the Lagavulin Distillery around 1890, and it was he who chose the name "White Horse" for the blended whisky which the Mackies had been producing on Mackie Street in Edinburgh. It had been called simply "Mackie's Whisky." Peter Mackie wanted the full-flavored Lagavulin malt as the base for his newly named White Horse blend.

Lagavulin Single (from a single distillery) Islay Malt Whisky, 12 year old, 75°, is not normally available in the U.S. But that may be just as well, as it is strictly for the stout of heart and palate—for true-blue Scotch lovers. It is *very Scotch*.

Peter Mackie—after 1920, Sir Peter Mackie, for that was when he was made a baronet —was said to be "one-third genius, one-third megalomaniac, and one-third eccentric." He was the true founder of White Horse Scotch, and it was he who assured its international success. Peter insisted on the importance of aging good whisky. He preached: "Most of the riotous and obstreperous conduct of drunks comes from the young and fiery spirit which is sold, while men who may over-indulge in old, matured whisky become sleepy and stupid but not in a fighting mood." Sir Peter died in 1924. In 1927, White Horse became a part of the giant Distillers Company Limited.

White Horse's most prodigious historical feat was accomplished when the Duke of Windsor, living in self-imposed exile in Vienna, after having abdicated the throne of Britain the previous year (1936), sent a wire for his "magnificent white horse which he had used as King." The reference was not for a four-footed cream-colored hayburner, but to a certain Scotch whisky of the same name.

Today's White Horse is a blend of some forty different whiskies, both malts and grain whiskies. Lagavulin, of course, is basic to the blend. Two other important malts, both owned by White Horse (but not sold under their own names), are Craigellachie and Glen Elgin.

White Horse Distillers Ltd. markets one other Scotch whisky (beside Lagavulin and White Horse itself): Laird o' Logan, sometimes referred to as "Logan De Luxe," its top-of-the-line.

White Horse is an excellent medium-bodied Scotch. The company's slogan, "I can tell it blindfolded," is not a *total* untruth. It depends on who the "I" is. A professional taster, blindfolded, could perhaps detect White Horse. Casual Scotch drinkers, never. This is only to say that good medium-bodied Scotches are remarkably alike!

White Horse 86° sells in the U.S. for about $8.50 (fifth).

WILD TURKEY KENTUCKY STRAIGHT BOURBON

The name is derived from what this whiskey does to you: makes you *wild*, you *turkey!* And that is not pure fiction, for this bourbon is often noted, not for its quality or honored history, but simply for its potency. People apparently buy Wild Turkey simply because it is 101°, one of the highest proof whiskeys in the land. (The highest proof whiskey commonly sold in the U.S. seems to be W. L. Weller's Special Reserve Blend, at 107°. See under **Old Fitzgerald**.) Wild Turkey actually comes in an 86.8° version, but the 101° model far outsells the tamer one. Does this say something about Americans'—or mankind's—penchant for the bizarre, the different?

Wild Turkey comes as both a bourbon and a rye, and both are prestige beverages—with prestige pricetags.

These are the wild ones: Wild Turkey Kentucky Straight Bourbon, 8 years, 101°, $11 (fifth); Wild Turkey Kentucky straight Bourbon, 7 years, 86.8°, $9 (fifth); Wild Turkey Straight Rye, 8 years, 101°, $10.50 (fifth). Wild Turkey Bourbon 101° also comes in several different ceramic decanters, $20 to $40 (fifths), strictly for the stout of heart and ample of means.

Another Wild Turkey recently hatched is Wild Turkey Liqueur. At a formidable 80°, it's a bird of like feather: tasty, potent, smooth. Indeed, at $14 (fifth) it has a serious duty to be all of those things.

WINDSOR SUPREME CANADIAN WHISKY

In recent years Canadian whiskies have gained great acceptance in the U.S., and Windsor is one of the front-runners. In fact it is now in ninth place among all spirits sold in the U.S.A.

A lot of people agree that Windsor's eminence is deserved, that Windsor is, indeed, a superior spirit. It is the property of the National Distillers

Corporation, which claims that Windsor's excellence is due to its being produced in the Canadian Rockies, and its flavor comes from the mountain water and the locally grown grain. Windsor is 80° and sells for about $5.75 (fifth).

Y

YELLOWSTONE KEN-TUCKY STRAIGHT BOUR-BON WHISKEY This is one of America's oldest whiskeys: It traces its ancestry back to 1836, when it was first made on a small scale for private consumption. Its fame spread rapidly, and in 1872 it was named, for no good reason, after the newly created Yellowstone National Park in Wyoming.

Yellowstone Bourbon is unique in several respects. First, it is distilled in taller than normal stills; this is said to produce a lighter, more delicate whiskey. Second, the oak barrels in which it is aged are also different. The staves are wider—this is said to affect the aging process—and the wood is more deeply charred than is customary. This is said to give the whiskey its slightly reddish cast.

Yellowstone has always been highly regarded by bourbon lovers. It is fine whiskey. The 86° sells for under $6 (fifth); the bonded 100° for around $7 (fifth); the 7-year-old 90° for just over $6 (fifth).

YUKON JACK This is a recent arrival on America's liqueur scene, imported from Canada, distributed by Heublein. It's made from good, smooth, blended Canadian whiskies; it's on the dry side (for a liqueur), and comes in both 80° and 100° versions. Yukon Jack is light and well balanced, but it lacks depth of flavor. It sells in the U.S. for around $7.50 (fifth) for the 100° and $7 (fifth) for the 80°, surely reasonable prices, but they don't compensate for Jack's lack of character.

Index

A

Abisante, 1
Abricotine, 9
Absinthe, 1, 7, 163, 175
Advocaat (advokaat), 2
Almadén Centennial Brandy, 2
Almonds, Crème de, 152
Amaretto, 3–4, 5
  list of, 3–4
Ambassador Scotch Whisky, 4
Amer Picon, 5
American Distilling Company, 4, 22, 33, 73, 124, 213
  list of brands, 4–5
Amorita Amaretto, 5
Ancestor, Dewar's Scotch Whisky, 5–6, 68
Ancient Age Kentucky Straight Bourbon Whisky, 6
Angostura Bitters, 6
Anise and anisette liqueurs, 1, 6–8, 141, 161, 175
Antique Kentucky Straight Bourbon Whisky, 8
Applejack, 8, 38, 79
Appleton Rum, 8–9
Apricot liqueurs and brandies, 9
Apry, 9
Aquavit, 9–10, 126
Arak (Arrack), 10–11
  Batavia, 10, 18, 205
  Punsch, 205
Arandas Tequila, 10
Aristocrat Brandy, 11, 147
Armagnac, 11, 34, 77, 116–117

Larressingle Reserve, 128
Samalens, 11, 184–185
Asbach Uralt, 11–12, 83
Atholl Brose, 191
Aurum, 12
Australian whisky, 12, 223

B

B & B (Benedictine and Brandy), 13, 21
Bacardi Rum, 13–15, 195
Bahia, 15
Bailey's Original Irish Cream, 15
Ballentine's Scotch Whisky, 15–16, 111
Banana Liqueur, 16–17
Barbados rums, 17
Barbancourt Rum, 99
Bartender's Guide, 149
Barton Brands, Ltd., 17, 123
Barton Reserve Blended Whiskey, 17
Barton's Q.T. Premium Light Whiskey, 17–18
Batavia Arak, 10, 18, 205
Beam (James B.) Distilling Co., 18–20
  decorative bottles, 19
  list of brands, 18
Beam's Choice Kentucky Straight Bourbon Whiskey, 19–20
Beaulieu Brandy, 20
Beefeater Gin, 19–20

C

H

ABOUT THE AUTHOR

E. Frank Henriques is an Episcopal priest, Pastor of the Trinity Church, Sutter Creek, in the heart of the Mother Lode, in the Sierra foothills of California. He is also the author of *The Signet Encyclopedia of Wine* (New American Library), published in 1975. He is presently working on an updating of that book, to appear in late 1979. He is married, the father of five children.

Father Henriques was born in San Francisco and educated principally in Santa Barbara, California. He served in the Roman Catholic ministry for more than fifteen years, and in the ministry of the Episcopal Church in Texas for eleven years. He has a bachelor's degree in Liberal Arts, and two degrees in Theology. His expertise in the field of wines and spirits comes, he says, not from extensive "lab work," but from probing study, diligent note-keeping, and "a fond regard" for his subject-matter. He believes that he may well have the most extensive notes on current wines and spirits of anybody in the world. He is also at work on a book on the Bible— "something," he says, "which has never been done, despite the thousands of books already written on the Bible."

Ⓢ

SIGNET Cookbooks

☐ **COOKING WITH WINE by Morrison Wood.** The best of the world's most famous foods can now be prepared in your own kitchen. An expert shows how available ingredients are transformed into exotic fare by the creative use of American wines and liqueurs. (#W7950—$1.50)

☐ **EVERYDAY FRENCH COOKING by Henri-Paul Pellaprat.** A former Cordon Bleu professor has written an easy-to-use, complete French cookbook. (#E6016—$1.75)

☐ **THE JOY OF COOKING, Volume I by Irma S. Rombauer and Marion Rombauer Becker.** America's all-time best-selling cookbook is now being published in two convenient-to-use volumes. Volume I of this revised and enlarged edition contains main course recipes that will turn all your meals into delicious dining. (#E8625—$2.50)

☐ **THE JOY OF COOKING, Volume II by Irma S. Rombauer and Marion Rombauer Becker.** This volume of America's all-time bestselling cookbook contains recipes for appetizers, desserts and baked goods that will put the finishing touch on any meal you plan. (#E8691—$2.50)

☐ **THE LOS ANGELES TIMES NATURAL FOODS COOKBOOK by Jeanne Voltz, Food Editor, Woman's Day Magazine.** Discover the joys of cooking and eating naturally with this book of over 600 savory, simple-to-follow recipes. Whether you are concerned with taste or nutrition, these delicious and healthy recipes—high in fiber content—will delight everyone from the gourmet chef to the dedicated dieter. (#E7710—$2.50)

☐ **BAKE YOUR OWN BREAD And Be Healthier by Floss and Stan Dworkin.** This illustrated, step-by-step guide will take you through each stage of preparation for making and storing a whole breadbasket full of old favorites and new variations. (#W7318—$1.50)

To order these titles, please

use coupon on next page.

SIGNET Books for Your Reference Shelf